Framing Truths
Parodic Structures in Contemporary English-Canadian Historical Novels

Martin Kuester analyses the role of parody in the historical novels of three contemporary Canadian writers: Timothy Findley, George Bowering, and Margaret Atwood. He defines parody in its etymological sense of 'singing alongside,' used here to refer to the adoption of preceding literary structures with ironic, but not necessarily humorous, intent.

Kuester maintains that Canadian novels as far back as *Wacousta* have relied on methods of parody, albeit rather crudely; contemporary historical novels, especially the metahistorical parodies of Findley, Bowering, and Atwood, are more self-confident and sophisticated. Findley strives in his novels for the underlying coherence of a modernist work by integrating material from the Bible, novels of the Great War, and modernist poetry into the pacifist manifesto of *The Wars* and the anti-fascist one of *Famous Last Words*. Bowering, after philosophizing about the writing of historical novels in *A Short Sad Book*, integrates literary and non-fictional texts into his own parodic universe of *Burning Water*. More overtly political than this male version of postmodernism, Atwood bases her parodies on such genres as travel and fashion magazine writing in *Bodily Harm* and on dystopian novels in *The Handmaid's Tale*. The latter work, with its various narrative frames and levels, serves as a complex summary of the possibilities of structuring historical novels by means of parodic principles.

Kuester's analysis concludes by placing these works in a larger international framework of parodically structured novels.

MARTIN KUESTER is Wissenschaftlicher Mitarbeiter, Universität Augsburg.

THEORY/CULTURE

General editors:
Linda Hutcheon and Paul Perron

Martin Kuester

FRAMING TRUTHS

Parodic Structures in Contemporary English-Canadian Historical Novels

UNIVERSITY OF TORONTO PRESS

Toronto London Buffalo

© University of Toronto Press Incorporated 1992
Toronto Buffalo London
Printed in Canada

ISBN 0-8020-2818-7 (cloth)
ISBN 0-8020-7690-4 (paper)

Printed on acid-free paper

Theory/Culture Series 12

Canadian Cataloguing in Publication Data

Kuester, Martin
  Framing truths

  (Theory/culture ; 12)
  Includes bibliographical references and index.
  ISBN 0-8020-2818-7 (bound) ISBN 0-8020-7690-4 (pbk.)

  1. Parody.   2. Canadian fiction (English) – 20th
  century – History and criticism.*   3. Novelists,
  Canadian – 20th century – Criticism and interpretation.
  I. Title.   II. Series.

  PS8191.P3K84 1992   C813'.08109054   C92-093951-1
  PR9192.6.P3K84 1992
                          76662

This book has been published with the help of a grant
from the Canadian Federation for the Humanities,
using funds provided by the Social Sciences and
Humanities Research Council of Canada.

Contents

Acknowledgments

I would like to thank all institutions, colleagues, and friends who gave me the personal and financial support enabling me to write this study: the World University Service of Canada; the Department of English, University of Manitoba; the University of Manitoba Alumni Association; and the Canadian Federation for the Humanities. I would like to extend personal thanks to Robert Kroetsch, who as a teacher and friend would always listen to new ideas about parody and to new parodies of ideas. David Williams provided invaluable support through his teaching and his willingness to discuss what incorporating parody really means. He and his family generously provided the travelling Canadianist from Germany with a home in Winnipeg during longish research visits to Canada. I would also like to thank the other readers of the dissertation that forms the backbone of this book, Professors Linda Hutcheon and Gerald Friesen, for encouragement and insightful comments. My thanks are also due to the editorial staff of University of Toronto Press, especially Gerald Hallowell and Ken Lewis, for their expert help.

Thanks are equally due to other friends and colleagues in Canada and Germany for their hospitality and support. John O'Connor and his family provided generous hospitality during my research visits to Toronto; Amanda Pounder did the same in Ottawa. At Augsburg, Professor Walter Pache and my colleagues in the English Department and the Institute for Canadian Studies provided a stimulating environment in which to continue the work begun on the Prairies. Dr Geoffrey Davis of Aachen University of Technology was kind enough to include an earlier version of part of chapter 4 in *Crisis and Creativity in the New Literatures in English: Canada* (Amsterdam: Rodopi 1990), the proceedings of the Eleventh Annual Conference on Commonwealth Literature in German-Speaking Countries.

My family has supported me through long years of studies and has always backed my interest in Canadian literature, even if that meant year-long absences. Finally I thank my wife, Hildegard, to whom I would like to dedicate this book, for her interest in my work and her support in preparing the final draft.

FRAMING TRUTHS

1 Introduction: New Versions of an Old Concept

> I imagined Loulou sitting on the other side of Flaubert's desk and staring back at him like some taunting reflection from a funfair mirror. No wonder three weeks of its parodic presence caused irritation. Is the writer much more than a sophisticated parrot? *Julian Barnes*[1]

Judging by the subtitle of this study, 'Parodic Structures in Contemporary English-Canadian Historical Novels,' a reader might well expect a treatment of humour in Canadian literature from Paul Hiebert to Paul Quarrington. Such an enterprise, however, is not the intention of this book. The term *parody*, which may give rise to such expectations, is here used in a structural sense in which humour is a possible quality of parodies but not a necessary prerequisite.

In order to justify the use of such a structural model of parody, one has to abstract from the usual connotations that the term has gathered during the last two or three centuries. Instead, one must go back to the concept as it was used by eighteenth-century critics and theorists such as Samuel Johnson, and as it has been reintroduced by contemporary theorists. According to Johnson, parody is a 'kind of writing, in which the words of an author or his thoughts are taken, and by a slight change adapted to some new purpose.'[2] Johnson does not specify what the intended effect of the change is to be, and thus in this definition the stress is primarily on the structural relationship between parodied and parodying text. The present study focuses on the kind of narrative structures that Canadian novelists take over from their predecessors – whether they be Canadian, American, or European – and it asks how they adapt their models to the present Canadian literary and social environment. After a brief theoretical overview of the development of the concept of parody (chapter 1), the structural model of parody will be applied to three Canadian historical novels of 'classical' status (chapter 2) and then to six contemporary historical novels published (to some acclaim) in the 1970s and 1980s.

The meaning of the term *parody*, more than that of many other literary notions, depends very much on the historical situation in which it is used. In her recent book on the subject, Linda Hutcheon even suggests that its dependence on the respective historical context is so strong 'that there are probably no transhistorical definitions of parody possible.'[3] Within the present study, references to a structural, formalist definition start out from the underlying structural relationship between texts that applies to all parodies, whatever their historically determined connotations may be. Especially for the six contemporary texts in the centre of the book, these connotations and their influence on the parodic act will then be analysed.

During the last two centuries, the term *parody* has been narrowed down from what it meant in Johnson's time and has come to be applied to a genre that is regarded not only as secondary but also as a degraded version of the parodied text. However, as will be shown, this somewhat derogatory meaning of *parody*, so current today, is not necessarily allied with the classical usage of the word. Still, this restricted use of the term has had the consequence that in contemporary literary criticism *parody* is most often used in connection with the concept of satire, although the hierarchical relationship between the two concepts differs from one critic to the next, so that some see parody as a genre related to – or a sub-genre of – satire, whereas for others it is only a satiric strategy.[4] Even though several of the texts on which this study will focus are highly satirical, this satirical character does not necessarily reflect on their parodic structure, which should of course be taken for granted.

In a recent overview of research on the topic, Clive R. Thomson shows that in contemporary criticism there are two, or rather three, major approaches to the phenomenon of parody. The first approach that he identifies is the semantic/pragmatic one taken by theorists who see parody 'more as a modality or mode than as a *genre*,' and whose aim is 'to elaborate a flexible typology, using the methodology of pragmatics, which would allow us to classify texts possessing seemingly similar yet different meanings.' Theorists belonging to this group have the ambition 'to work out what parody, in essence, *means*,' and they wonder if it is 'a mocking, disdainful, respectful or playful modality.' Their approach 'is based in the work of Northrop Frye (and, if one goes further back, in the Aristotelian tradition in which ideas pre-exist their being put into words), who holds that satire is social, and that parody is formal.' The second approach is the structuralist (or, in Thomson's words, 'syntactic/linguistic') one of theorists such as Geneviève

Idt and Michael Riffaterre, who are mostly interested in the purely formal relationship between parodied and parodying text. Besides these two 'puristic' approaches to the concept of parody, there exists a combination of the two, represented by Mikhail Bakhtin's work, 'one of the most detailed, however unsystematic, discussions of parody that has been written in modern times.'[5]

While this study stresses parody's character as a modality or mechanism rather than as a genre, and thus is more or less part of Thomson's first category, it is primarily interested in the formal and structural relationships between texts. It will then relate these structural findings back to the pragmatic situation and semantic context in and for which parodic texts are written.[6]

The theoretical overview in the following pages will sketch the development of the concept of parody from ancient Greece to postmodern Europe and North America. Without even trying to give a complete history of the term, it will attempt to characterize parody as a progressive literary modality that becomes useful and effective in the self-definition of a 'new' literature that is situated between the influential poles of the European and the American traditions. In this sense, a text which is parodic becomes a serious re-working of literary models and is much more than just a 'parodisitic'[7] copy of some imperial master narrative. It should also become clear in the course of the overview why an approach such as the present one is needed in order to complement related ones based on the concept of intertextuality.

Unfortunately, the origins of the term *parody* in ancient Greece (etymologically, the prefix *para* plus the verb *aidein* meaning 'to sing') are somewhat hazy. Greek literary theorists do not seem to agree, any more than do their modern interpreters, on a clear-cut definition. Aristotle does not give a definition of parody but only claims – in his discussion of the modes of imitation – that Hegemon in his parodies describes people as worse than they are in real life, whereas poets such as Homer or Cleophon describe them as better than or exactly as they are. Judging from the context, one may conclude that the author of the *Poetics* thus shares the view of parody as a genre, and as a 'negative' one at that. Gérard Genette tries to locate parody in Aristotle's system of genres and differentiates between two types of action – high and low – and between two modes of representation – narrative and dramatic:

> La croisée de ces deux oppositions détermine une grille à quatre
> termes qui constitue à proprement parler le système aristotélicien des

genres poétiques: action haute en mode dramatique, la tragédie; action haute en mode narratif, l'épopée; action basse en mode dramatique, la comédie; quant à l'action basse en mode narratif, elle n'est illustrée que par référence allusive à des œuvres plus ou moins directement désignées sous le terme de *parôdia*.[8]

This *generic* and *negative* definition, which would at first sight restrict parody to 'low' subject matter, tending towards what is generally referred to as *burlesque*, is not the only one, however, that can be derived from ancient Greek sources: Fred W. Householder shows, for example, that the prefix *para* does not necessarily imply confrontation and negativity; it also has the meaning ' "like, resembling, changing slightly, imitating, replacing, spurious." ' He concludes that 'our basic sense, then, would seem to have been "singing in imitation, singing with a slight change [e.g., of subject matter]," ' so that the stress in *parody* lies on the structural (and maybe even semantic) effect of doubling and completion. David Kiremidjian also works with the form/content dichotomy in parody; for him, the Greek rhapsodists' 'improvisations were in the same manner and style as the originals, but treated local quotidian reality rather than heroic exploits. Our own most general and fundamental notion of parody rests on the early practices of the rhapsodists: Parody is a literary mimicry which retains the form but alters the content of the original.'[9]

Other theorists such as the Germans Wido Hempel, Theodor Verweyen, and Gunther Witting have it the other way round. They point out that parodies are first used at a time when poetry and music have not yet become art forms independent of each other. For them, *parodia* means an innovation in the technique of recitation of epic poetry: the poem is no longer recited in a singing fashion but in the normal tone of an actor speaking dialogue. Whether we agree with Householder and Kiremidjian that in parody the contents change while the form is kept, or whether we agree with Hempel and Verweyen/Witting that the form changes while the contents remain stable (i.e., what other critics separate from parody as travesty), it has become obvious that parody originally signifies a structural relationship between two texts.[10]

The important structural elements of parody are already in existence here: an imitated (parodied) text and an imitating (parodying) one, which follows either the content or the form of the original while changing the other element. The recitation of an older text in a new medium or the framing of a new one in an old medium will of course change the reception of these texts by the audience. This change does

not, however, automatically imply negative connotations of degrada-
tion that are nowadays quite regularly associated with the concept of
parody. What we have here is a new form for an old message (or an
old form for a new message), which (1) draws attention to its own
form and (2) helps to renew interest in the message itself by severing
the message from its expected traditional (or envisaged new) form.
Parody – at least the first type – can here function as a structural
mechanism of literary change but also as a means of semantic commentary on the content of the parodied text. In Kiremidjian's words,
'a parody forces us to be aware of form as an artifice or as an artificial
discipline which is brought into relation with a radically different phenomenon, that of natural experience itself.'[11]

One must always keep in mind, of course, that the division of the
text into content and form undertaken here is a simplification insofar
as these two elements – especially in parodies – influence each other
and are interdependent.[12] Although one cannot really define parody
as either an old message in a new form or a new message in an old
form, the important aspects of a parodic text lie in the incongruity
between these two elements. We should note again that the fact that
there is a semantic element accompanying the structural changes does
not imply that these changes have to be in the direction of humorous
or comic effect.[13]

Parodic treatment can, on the one hand, reject the changes it invokes,
or it can, on the other, encourage or at least accept them. Thus we can
differentiate between conservative and progressive parody. Generally
speaking, it is the progressive type of parody on which this study
concentrates, even though some of the early examples of Canadian
parodies will not seem to be very 'progressive' to all readers.[14]

Already, and especially in this context, one should point out that
Aristotle's definition of parody as a genre is not very useful if we are
looking for parody's contribution to literary evolution; that is, if we
are interested in progressive parody. To analyse this progressive aspect,
parody is best defined as a mechanism or a modality that can be applied
to any genre (or, of course, as the text resulting from this treatment).
If we redefine parody in this way, we avoid the difficulties that critics
such as Kiremidjian have in seeing it as a sub-genre of satire or 'only
one but one of the most important' of its mechanisms. Kiremidjian
himself is only one step away from severing the connection between
satire and parody: 'Satire has its own forms and thus articulates its
"content" or "objects" in terms of that form. Like tragedy or comedy,
satire will "hold the mirror up to nature," even though the satiric mirror

has its own particularly grotesque curvature. Parody, on the other hand, has no form, structure, or mechanism of its own, but must adopt, by its very nature, the form of the original to which it refers and to which it owes its existence.'[15]

The Greek theories of parody thus fall into two classes, one seeing parody as a genre – the Aristotelian strain – and the other, and in our case more interesting, one – going back to ancient theories of art and music – interpreting it as a mode, or a special type of imitation (an imitation of literary models rather than Aristotelian *mimesis* of reality). This latter concept of parody as imitation exists also in Roman literary theory. One can, for example, detect a similar principle ·in Horace's concept of imitation as 're-creation, not repetition.' Later theorists of literature such as Quintilian also claim 'that [parody's] real function lies not in the reproduction of earlier methods of expression but in conducing to the discovery of new effects and to the development of style in general.'[16] The practice of classical Latin authors such as Virgil and Ovid can also be explained by reference to parodic principles in the original sense. Instead of anachronistically approaching the problem of writing an epic 'by a Greek route,' Virgil takes the Homeric story and re-works it by integrating it into the Roman world-view of the *Aeneid*. His epic 'was to be a thing which would outvie the Greeks, be the Roman equivalent of the *Iliad* and *Odyssey*.' Later on, Ovid erects his own parody: 'Against the antique mythology of Homer and against also the modern, Augustan use of it by Virgil, – he set his own peculiar blend of iconoclasm and human sympathy.'[17] Fittingly, Erwin Rotermund sums up his overview of parody in antiquity by claiming that at least some 'ancient rhetoricians used the term [of parody] with reference to the technique of integrating foreign literary elements into their own discourse and of conjoining the two to form a new unit.'[18]

In the Renaissance, the Italian Julius Caesar Scaliger repeats Greek theories of the origin of parody in his *Poetics*. He sees a humorous element inherent in it:

> Quemadmodum Satyra ex Tragoedia, Mimus e Comoedia: sic Parodia de Rhapsodia nata est. Quum enim Rhapsodi intermitterent recitationem, lusus gratia prodibant qui ad animi remissionem omnia illa priora inuerterent. Hos iccirco [parodous] nominarunt: quia praeter rem seriam propositam alia ridicula subinferrent. Est igitur Parodia Rhapsodia inuersa mutatis vocibus ad ridicula sensum retrahens.[19]

In the same way that satire developed out of tragedy, and mime out of comedy, parody stems from rhapsody. Whenever the rhapsodists interrupted their recitation, those entered the stage who jokingly, for the mind's relaxation, inverted everything that had previously been performed. For this reason they were called parodists, as they undermined the serious message by means of another, ridiculous one. Parody is thus an inverted rhapsody that is drawn towards a ridiculous meaning through a change in voices. (My translation)

Following Aristotle, Scaliger thus still sees parody as a genre: the relationship between rhapsody (epic) and parody resembles those between satire and tragedy or mime and comedy. But Scaliger also refers to a kind of parody *in honore*, more or less admitting that for him the meaning of parody is not necessarily an adversative one. Here – and in a way similar to some of the classical theories – the function of parody already goes beyond that of a pure genre, and one may wonder whether it would not be preferable to interpret it as a mechanism or a modality of literary change already at this stage. Critics such as Rotermund point out that the sixteenth century knew *parodiae morales* and that treatises on poetics in the seventeenth and eighteenth centuries use the term as meaning formal imitation without insisting on the resulting discrepancy. In England, John Florio defines *parodia* in his *A Worlde of Wordes* (1598) as 'a turning of a verse by altering some wordes.' This definition, while going back to the ancient models, also points forward to eighteenth-century theories such as Samuel Johnson's.[20]

From Scaliger onwards, parody again develops in two directions. On the one hand, theorists see it as a humorous genre of secondary value; on the other, it is interpreted as one of the modes underlying literary evolution.[21] Samuel Johnson's view has already been mentioned. According to Therese Fischer-Seidel, Johnson distinguishes between parody as a modality (*Darstellungsverfahren*) and the function that it can fulfil, and thus avoids equating – as most other definitions do – parody with only one of its possible functions. The practice of the eighteenth-century novelists proves Johnson right, even if he himself has problems with mock-heroic burlesque, in which he criticizes 'a disproportion between style and sentiments' which turns into 'an element of corruption, since all disproportion is unnatural.' In the same way that the first novel, Cervantes' *Don Quixote*, was a parody, early English novels such as Fielding's *Joseph Andrews* are parodic. In fact, the Aristotelian system of genres established by Genette runs parallel to Henry Fielding's. The French structuralist calls *parody* what the eighteenth-century novelist had called 'a comic epic poem in prose' in his preface to *Joseph Andrews*: 'The EPIC, as well as the DRAMA, is divided into tragedy and comedy. HOMER, who was the father of this species of poetry, gave us a pattern of both of these, though that of the latter kind is entirely lost; which Aristotle tells us, bore the same relation to comedy which his *Iliad* bears to tragedy.'[22] Jane Austen, too, is 'a novelist who began with parody' in *Northanger Abbey* before she 'left parody in the strict sense behind.' Her work, the forerunner of the realist nineteenth-century novel, is a clear-cut example of the progressive rather than secondary function of parody.[23]

In English literature, the evolutionary impulse that had been behind parody in the eighteenth century is lost in the nineteenth, and here parody – although quite popular and widespread as an entertainment – loses its evolutionary force in literary development. While little happens on the English scene, there are, however, important new French and German theorists who stress the progressive function of textual re-working or re-contextualization in parody, and their theories continue from where their English predecessors left off in the eighteenth century. Claude Abastado claims that, starting at the end of the nineteenth century, some writers – stressing the creative possibilities inherent in parody – see more in it than just a minor genre or an addition to existing successful genres: 'L'accent est mis non plus sur l'imitation mais sur le changement qu'implique la parodie.'[24] In Germany, as Sander L. Gilman shows in his work on Nietzschean parody, even within 'humorous' parody the artist can choose between two different models: while the Hobbesian strain of interpretation is based on laughter arising from tension between the social polarities and infringement of conventions, Kantian parody favours a dissolution of this tension. While Schiller follows Hobbes's model, Goethe is also interested in non-derogatory parody, and he 'turns to the Kantian view that pleasure can be produced by the advent of laughter through the resolution of tension.' According to Goethe's Kantian approach, 'the poet as parodist can create works of art within the parodic mode which are independent of their models and which stand as great works of art, ennobling the low.'

Nietzsche first follows in Goethe's footsteps: in his juvenilia, he starts from a position favouring a type of parody which does not demean the original while it is still clearly related to it: 'Parody is, for Nietzsche, primarily an artistic mode of expression, the creative mode par excellence.' This position implies that every artistic act is a parodic one reacting to earlier models, but also an active one insofar as the parodist re-functions the past models he parodies. This Nietzschean version of parodic re-functioning underlies much of twentieth-century philosophy and literature and becomes especially important in the contemporary styles of postmodern writing.[25]

Towards Modernism: Early Twentieth-Century Theories, Russian Formalism, and Structuralism

At the beginning of this century, theorists and practicians of parody mainly continue the more traditional work of their nineteenth-century predecessors, without responding to the Nietzschean innovations. Most of the time, they see parody as a modality in which critical characteristics are clearly secondary to entertaining qualities. There are, however, exceptions: in his 1931 history of parody, George Kitchin presents 'burlesque as a serious art, a long-established mode of criticism, which is often far more incisive, and certainly more economical than the heavy review to which the public has been accustomed since the days of Dryden.' For Kitchin, though, since the seventeenth century parody has always come down on the side of conservative respectability, reinforcing the establishment. Concerning modern prose parody, however, he adds that from Jane Austen to Bret Harte parodies have also had a positive effect, if not for the parodied author, then at least for the parodists learning the tricks of the trade by emulating their forebears: 'they attach themselves mollusc-like to work of their predecessors, which they proceed to demolish by means of parody.' Later critics such as Harry Levin also see parody in a wider sense as an active structural principle underlying the works of Joyce and Eliot.[26]

Claude Abastado claims that only the structuralists of the 1960s began to do serious research regarding the formal relationships in parody between imitated and imitating text. They drew parallels between parody and related phenomena, such as citation, cliché, and stereotype, in the context of studies of dialogism and intertextuality.[27] Such a statement may have been true enough for French structuralism, but other, earlier 'structuralists' such as the Russian Formalists had already worked with the concepts of stylization and parody since the 1920s. And seemingly independent of Continental structuralist theories, Anglo-Saxon scholars such as David Kiremidjian had already analysed parody as a means of literary development. Kiremidjian, for example, claims in 1964 that

during the past decades criticism has become acutely aware of the importance of parody in the general development of literary forms, principally those of the novel, in the first half of this century. The simple passing of time has given us perspective on that general achievement, and the view that parody is merely another means of devaluating the objects of imitation, or of expressing the ironies of past and present, can no longer be maintained. The widespread presence of parody suggests a greater importance in the very ways in which the modern imagination and the modern sensibility have been formed, and also suggests the organic function it has had in the development of the primary modes of expression for perhaps the past one hundred years.[28]

David Baguley has shown that even earlier texts, which we would normally see as the precursors of those mentioned by Abastado and Kiremidjian, are affected by parodic tendencies. They are not at all cut off from 'the process of generic development for which parody, in some form or other, as the Russian Formalists have shown, provides an important motive force, whether as a factor consolidating tradition ... or as an agent of change that violates literary norms and exposes stereotyped procedures and themes.'[29]

Among the Russian Formalists, Viktor Shklovsky and Jurij Tynjanov – following the example of such mechanistic theories of literature as Bergson's – are those most concerned with questions of parody. Discussing *Tristram Shandy* in his *Teorija prozy*, Shklovsky declares this parodic novel to be 'the most typical novel in world literature.' Parody for him is a timeless mechanism that, in Peter Hodgson's words, 'effect[s] the changes in a given tradition by dismantling and recycling prominent literary models.'[30]

While Shklovsky views parody as a merely destructive mechanism, Tynjanov points to its constructive features. He is the first to see the transforming mechanisms of parody and stylization as important elements in generic change and literary evolution. One of his best-known examples of a parodic relationship between a writer and his or her successor is given in his essay 'Dostoevsky and Gogol,' which studies the relationship between Dostoevsky's *The Manor of Stepanchikovo* and Gogol's *Correspondence with Friends*.[31] Tynjanov later expands his findings about parody into 'the best result that research in parody has so far produced,' a theory of literary history and evolution. For him, literature is a system composed of three classes of series – literary, extraliterary, and social. Parody, as one of the literary series, is influenced by its relations to other literary elements as well as by its relations to the two other classes of series. Among the most important formal aspects of parodies, Tynjanov counts the incongruity between their elements and the mechanization of narrative processes.[32]

The ideas of the Russian Formalists are criticized and further developed by the Russian scholar Mikhail Bakhtin in his theories of dialogism. Whereas ancient genres such as the epic (but also other, more traditional narratives told from a single point of view) had been dominated by a single unifying perspective, modern societies can no longer produce such a coherent world-view or corresponding literary works of art. The monological style is typical of societies and eras in which one point of view or ideology is clearly dominant. One way of reacting against the coherent perspective and world-view of traditional monological texts is to parody them. Among such multi-voiced texts parodying older ones which have become stylized and stilted there were, in Roman times, satire and, later on, Menippean satire. Bakhtin also mentions the rich parodic literature of the Middle Ages which appropriated religious texts for secular purposes, and – extending his research on the function of parody and stylization in generic change – he arrives at *the* dialogic genre *par excellence*, the novel. It goes beyond the univocal, monological style of writing that dominated older genres such as the epic: 'The novel parodies other genres (precisely in their role as genres); it exposes the conventionality of their forms and their language; it squeezes out some genres and incorporates others into its own peculiar structure, reformulating and re-accentuating them.'[33] Bakhtin sees the language of the novel as 'a *system* of languages that mutually and ideologically interanimate each other,' and within this system parody is a method of introducing and quoting earlier texts, of in fact starting a dialogue with older or foreign ways of seeing things. In Bakhtin's words, 'the author may ... make use of someone else's discourse for his own purposes, by inserting a new semantic intention into a discourse which already has, and which retains, an intention of its own ... Parodying discourse is of this type, as are stylization and stylized *skaz*.'[34]

It is important to note the differentiation between imitative stylization with its 'unidirectional aspirations' and more controversial parody whose 'aspirations pull in different directions.' Bakhtin introduces the distinction in his book on Dostoevsky: in both, 'the author ... speaks in someone else's discourse, but in contrast to stylization parody introduces into that discourse a semantic intention that is directly opposed to the original one.' Parodistic discourse 'becomes an arena of battle between two voices.' Although he sees parody as a genre, Bakhtin also looks beyond his definition: '... parodistic discourse itself may be used in various ways by the author: the parody may be an end in itself (for example, literary parody as a genre), but it may also serve to further other positive goals (Ariosto's parodic style, for example, or Pushkin's).'[35]

Bakhtin's theory of dialogism here takes up and recycles the older theories of parody and makes them useful in the context of studies of the novel. He qualifies his point of view, however, as far as modern parodies are concerned. What was true for medieval parodies no longer applies to contemporary parodic practice: '... one must not transfer contemporary concepts of parodic discourse onto medieval parody (as one also must not do with ancient parody). In modern times the functions of parody are narrow and unproductive. Parody has grown sickly, its place in modern literature is insignificant.'[36] As this study intends to show, parody has in fact recovered – if it ever had to – from its narrowness and unproductiveness, and it plays an important and invigorating role in modern and postmodern novels.[37]

Bakhtinian parody in the extreme sense develops into carnival, an 'authorized transgression of norms,'[38] a 'temporary liberation from the prevailing truth,' and 'the feast of becoming, change, and renewal': 'A second life, a second world of folk culture is thus constructed; it is to a certain extent a parody of the extracarnival life, a "world inside out." We must stress, however, that the carnival is far distant from the negative and formal parody of modern times. Folk humor denies, but it revives and renews at the same time. Bare negation is completely alien to folk culture.'[39] Such a transgression of norms may also be seen as a step towards the expansion of literary possibilities, as an element of literary evolution, but its very temporariness leaves it open to Roland Barthes's criticism of being nothing but 'une parole *classique*,' a type of discourse that has forever renounced its hope of being able to contribute to the further development of literature and/or society. Bakhtin's mention of the principle of carnival, of authorized transgression, thus has become one of the cruxes of Bakhtinian interpretations: 'the paradox of parody.' Even though the Russian stresses its positive aspects, carnival as authorized but temporary transgression can be interpreted as a conservative as well as a progressive method, and it shows the two faces of parody in a clear light: 'The presupposition of both a law and its transgression bifurcates the impulse of parody: it can be normative and conservative, or it can be provocative and revolutionary.'[40]

Parody in the Age of Postmodernism and Post-Structuralism

The affinity of parody and postmodernism lies in their common
strategy of revision, a rereading of the authorised texts which turns
all texts into pretexts. *David Roberts*[41]

Bakhtin's works on parodic novelistic discourse were written during
the 1920s and grew out of the ideas of Russian Formalism. When,
much later, they were received by Western literary theorists through
the mediation of Eastern Europeans such as Tzvetan Todorov and Julia
Kristeva, the epistemologies underlying literary criticism had changed,
and thus these ideas were integrated into theories of French structuralism and post-structuralism. It was Julia Kristeva who introduced the
term *intertextuality* in her 1966 essay 'Le mot, le dialogue et le roman'
in order to translate the ideas of Bakhtinian dialogism. In a recent
interview, she states that the concept of intertextuality, while on the
one hand remaining faithful to Bakhtin's ideas, 'demonstrates, on the
other, my attempts to elaborate and enlarge upon them.'[42] According
to Leon S. Roudiez, this term 'has nothing to do with matters of influence by one writer upon another, or with the sources of a literary
work; it does, on the other hand, involve the components of a *textual
system* such as the novel, for instance.' Still, Kristeva argues that 'any
text is constructed as a mosaic of quotations; any text is the absorption
and transformation of another. The notion of *intertextuality* replaces
that of intersubjectivity, and poetic language is read as at least *double*.'
In Kristeva's view, 'Bakhtin considers writing as a reading of the an-
terior literary corpus and the text as an absorption of and a reply to
another text.' In the same way that Bakhtin saw parody – especially
in its modern form – as a somewhat marginal strategy of dialogism,
because the second perspective is subjected to the narrator's point of
view, Kristeva does not value it very highly. She obviously does not
think much of 'the pseudo-transgression evident in a certain modern
"erotic" and parodic literature.' Still, her successors who further developed the concept of intertextuality almost always see parody as one
of the intertextual modes. Most of them would agree with Laurent
Jenny's statement: 'Mais, si la parodie est toujours intertextuelle, l'in-
tertextualité ne se réduit pas à la parodie.'[43]

Post-structuralist and intertextual methods of interpretation are of
course applicable to any kind of literature, but they do lend themselves
especially to the interpretation of contemporary and postmodernist
literature. Postmodern novels frequently use techniques of foreground-

ing the process of writing that Linda Hutcheon and others have called 'narcissistic narrative' or metafiction. In describing the mirroring effect in modern literature, David Kiremidjian concludes that 'art, precisely when it produces its finest and subtlest effects ... will do so on the basis of its own literal being.'[44] Parody certainly is such a metafictional technique of textual self-mimesis; by definition, it is always metafictional or at least 'meta-linguistic' in the sense that parody – whatever its purpose – is based on a primary text rather than (or in addition to being based) on 'real life.' In fact, as I will argue later, even non-fictional texts rely on such textual and textualized material. Especially when we deal with events in the past, 'real life' is accessible only through texts.

Margaret Rose has dedicated a whole book to this metafictional type of parody, but parody has of course many more aspects than just that of metafiction, and it can have many functions that go much further. Rose shows, for example, that metafictional parody has, among others, the 'heuristic function' of changing the reader's horizon of expectation 'while also serving the author in the task of freeing himself from earlier models.' The ultimate example of such a parodic metafiction would be a kind of parody which leads reader and text into an aporia, a *mise en abyme aporistique* or *antithétique* and a dead end. There are critics of postmodern literature who go so far as to see a new mode of parody – destructive parody – in such works as Beckett's *The Unnamable*, where all literary conventions are dismantled. Parodies as understood in the context of this study, however, must be able to be more productive and to support generic change.[45]

Linda Badley has a similar view of the function of postmodern parody when she suggests that 'parody has ceased to be a sub-genre of satire and become something else.' As we have seen, to define the role of parody as that of a genre or a sub-genre is already an overly strong restriction of a more general technique, whereas parody has always been what Badley takes postmodern parody to be: 'a mode in its own right, one that now merges with and often – in "metafiction" – transcends and subsumes the genre of which it was once subordinate.'[46]

Parody: A Working Definition for Contemporary Texts

As has become obvious in the course of this historical overview of the development of the concept of parody, the older definitions of the term have been restructured by recent theorists and put to new uses in their discussions of contemporary literature. As Wolfgang Karrer shows impressively in his work on parody, travesty, and pastiche, the premises upon which the differentiations among these three are based have been extremely unstable in literary history and from one critic to the next; parody, travesty, and pastiche might be more reliably viewed as specialized cases of a more general, global term of parody. Parody in its turn is now generally seen as one of the types of intertextuality, which in itself has become one of the main concepts dominating contemporary literary theory. Many theorists of intertextuality have redefined the notion of the personal authorship of a text. They see a text as the confluence of many different textual influences, and they no longer accept the concept of authorial intention, an idea that is material, however, for a fruitful discussion of parody, at least at the stage of the (re)creation of parody. Intentionality – of whatever kind – on the part of the speaker is a basic element of the parodic situation.[47]

In this context, Karlheinz Stierle makes a helpful distinction between two types of intertextuality: *produktionsästhetische Intertextualität* deals with intertextual aspects in the process of literary production (focusing on the parodist), whereas the term *rezeptionsästhetische Intertextualität* is applied to intertextual aspects of the reading process. Stierle rightfully insists on the importance of intention in the former type.[48] Without a writer's intention to take a text and rewrite it, no secondary text can be created, and without his or her intention to make a text do different things, or the same things differently, than its predecessors, the secondary text will not have an existence of its own. As Gary Saul Morson puts it, 'the fact that it is intended by its author to have higher semantic authority than the original must be clear.'[49]

It is another question whether the reader recognizes a parody as such or not. Michel Deguy, for example, claims that a parody cannot work unless the imitated model is recognized by its addressees. As indicated earlier, the interest in this study is in progressive rather than conservative parody, that is, in new modes of writing. Such a new mode can only be born out of parody, however, when and if the readers are no longer aware of the text's parodic existence; at least, they should see more in it than just another version of a primary text. Hans Kuhn, for example, argues convincingly that over the years parodies gradually change their character in the eyes of their readers. His example is that of Don Quixote, who to us is no longer just comic but rather touching and dignified. Tynjanov, too, asks, 'What happens if the second level [i.e., that of the parodied text] exists, perhaps even in the form of a definite text, but has not penetrated into [the reader's] literary consciousness, was not recognized or just forgotten?' Furthermore, to complicate things, in addition to readers' not being aware of the parodic quality of a text, some works are read as parodic although they were never intended that way. Such cases are certainly not that rare in new literatures, when authors in colonies such as nineteenth-century Canada imitate the literature of the cultural centres. Here the intention at the outset is not a parodic one – in fact the original intention is that of pure imitation or emulation – and for this reason, interpretations of this type of inadvertent parody will not form a major part of this study.[50]

Recent approaches to parody seem to agree that, as Jean-Jacques Hamm writes in his introduction to a special issue of *Etudes littéraires*, parodic intention has given way to 'des stratégies textuelles et à des pratiques de lecture s'appuyant sur un corpus critique contemporain dont le lecteur informé reconnaîtra les figures.'[51] But unless one wants to define the author of a text as a complete product of outside influences (in Russian Formalism: series), it seems that – even if a written text is nothing but a writer's reaction to so many pre-texts – there exists a writing and re-forming subject somewhere in the process of the production of a parody.

It is true that if we recognize a parody, this has an effect on our reading of the original: we will never be able to return to the parodied text and read it in the same 'naïve' way in which we read it when we did not know the parody. Anthony Wall calls this effect parodic glue or *colle parodique*. He shows that parody is not a transparent mechanism: 'elle implique plutôt un processus sémiotique qui a comme conséquence l'impossibilité de retourner naïvement en arrière à la recherche d'une origine perdue. Car la parodie, telle que nous la voyons, n'est pas le résultat d'un processus annulable.'[52] This effect of a revaluation of literary tradition, of seeing older (or hypo-)texts in a new way because the new or (hyper-)text has changed our perspective, is true also for texts that we do not normally see any longer in a parodic context, and one may for example construe a line of 'progressive' parodies from Homer through Virgil, Ovid, Boccaccio, Chaucer, and Spenser to Shakespeare, or another one from Hesiod through Homer and Ovid to Milton. David Lodge's character Persse McGarrigle in *Small World* may after all not have been so wrong in pretending to have written a thesis on T.S. Eliot's influence on Shakespeare.[53] Margaret Rose in her pragmatic approach to parody sees this revisionary aspect as an expression of what she calls the 'parodistic episteme': 'In focusing on problems specifically associated with the interpretation of texts, and on the role of the reader outside the text, as well as on the role of the parodist as reader of the text parodied, the parodist raises questions about the role of the reception of literary texts played in both the formation of the author's expectations of the reader and of theirs for his work.'[54]

The perspectives of reception and production aesthetics link the theory of parody also with Harold Bloom's concept of creative misprision and misreading, especially with the technique that he calls *clinamen* and which 'appears as a corrective movement in [a poet's] own poem, which implies that the precursor poem went accurately up to a certain point, but then should have swerved, precisely in the direction that the new poem moves.' When Bloom mentions Milton's capability of ingesting his precursors, this is just another perspective on the parodic line culminating in Milton's work.[55]

While studies such as Wall's and Rose's clearly show that the mechanism of parody is far too complicated and complex to remain transparent or reversible, this does not mean that it is not a mechanism. In opposition to Wall's claim that 'dans la conception mécaniste de la parodie, la vérité est toujours la main-mise de l'hypotexte,' I would say that the important feature is rather the parodic process itself, the change that the parodied text undergoes in becoming the parody (which, of course, can often be judged only from the perspective of the latter). During this process, as Wolfgang Karrer points out, not only the elements that are substituted for others are responsible for the new semantic aspect of the parody, but also the elements that are held over from the original text change their function and meaning.[56]

A definition like the following one by Erwin Rotermund seems useful in the context of the above discussion, if one disregards the restriction to humorous texts, which Rotermund does not hold to be mandatory either:

> A parody is a work of literature that takes over formal and stylistic elements, and often even its subject matter, from another work of any genre, and then partially modifies the borrowed elements in such a way that a clear and often comical discrepancy arises between the single layers of its textual structure.[57]

Verweyen and Witting's definition comes even closer to the view of parody as a strategy:

> A definition of the parodic way of writing as a specific method of textual modification that by principle refers back to a pre-text in a non-affirmative manner but is not *a priori* definable as either innovative –

let alone emancipatory – or clearly destructive in its function seems to describe the role of parody in literary evolution more adequately than the explanations of Russian Formalism and other theories inspired by it.[58]

Margaret Rose's definition is quite concise and stresses the integrative function of parody – 'the critical refunctioning of preformed literary material with comic effect' – although she insists on the humorous character of parody. She explains that

by incorporating parts of the target text into the parody in a way which preserves the balance of dependence and independence between the texts, the parodist can both ensure the closeness to his target necessary for an accurate firing of his arrows of satire, and preserve the essential features of the target which will make the parody outlive the demise of the target's readership.[59]

Following along the same lines as Rose, the Canadian Linda Hutcheon has developed her pragmatic theory of parody that combines structuralist influences with the Russian Formalists' ideas of parody as a means of literary evolution and the pragmatic aspects of the tamer versions of intertextuality. She surpasses Rose's approach in going beyond metafictional parody, which she had already dealt with in the context of her *Narcissistic Narrative*, to view parody as a pervasive element in most twentieth-century art forms. Furthermore, as the title of an earlier essay – 'Parody without Ridicule' – indicates, she does not restrict her definition of parody to humorous contexts. In its most general formulation, Hutcheon's definition of parody is 'imitation characterized by ironic inversion' or, in other words, 'repetition with critical difference': 'Parodic art both deviates from an aesthetic norm and includes that norm within itself as backgrounded material.' What Margaret Rose called re-functioning is now referred to as trans-contextualization. As Hutcheon points out, parody's precursor in literary history was Renaissance imitation, whose similarity to parodic strategies has already been shown.

One of the drawbacks of Hutcheon's theory of parody as a genre is her reliance on purely semantic and pragmatic relationships between two texts, so that, except for a rather vague reference to the ironic character of these relationships, 'there will be no systematic analysis of techniques of parody.'[60] It is true that such systematic analyses can become very tedious without providing much insight, but on the other hand a closer look at the parodied text, the basic techniques involved in the parodic process of textual transformation, and the parodic text which is the product of this process might be useful.

While this study centres on the structural relationship between parodied and parodying texts, it restricts its corpus to works from one country, Canada, in fact to works from only one of this country's two literatures. It has to take into account the pragmatic aspects affecting literary production and reception in this country and also, of course, the special aspects of parodic activities. There are different ways of approaching what Hutcheon calls parody's 'ideological or even social implications.'[61] Margaret Rose, for example, points out that one can distinguish between ironic parody, which reacts against earlier literary conventions, and satiric parody, which attacks persons or ideas. While the distinction as such between the two types of parody is sensible, the naming of the types is not, for certainly irony is an integral part of both, even though satire itself, of course, 'need not be restricted, to the imitation, distortion, or quotation of other literary texts.'[62] Reflecting the distinction Tynjanov made between literary and extra-literary series, Rose's distinction picks up the traditional one made by critics such as John A. Yunck between stylistic and exemplary parody:

> Both Stylistic and Exemplary Parody, then, imitate, usually humorously or ironically, the style, manner, and sometimes the ideas of an established text or author. The difference between them is this: Stylistic Parody, by applying this style and manner to a trivial or absurd subject, thereby mocks the author of the original text. Exemplary Parody, imitating a respected or authoritative text in applying its style to a degraded or disreputable subject, mocks the subject in the light of the ideals of the parodied text.[63]

Linda Hutcheon stresses the fact that a parody's 'target' text is always another work of art, and that social and moral criticism is the realm of satire. For her, parody uses irony on a structural level, whereas satire uses it on a pragmatic one. Hutcheon is certainly right when she states that both satire and parody make use of irony as a 'rhetorical strategy,' a fact that might be lost in Rose's distinction. However, as indicated earlier on, parody as I see it is a rhetorical strategy in its own right – albeit a sub-strategy of irony – rather than a genre. After all, this view of parody as a modality or trope goes only a little bit further than Hutcheon's own, since she herself states that '... irony can be seen to operate on a microcosmic (semantic) level in the same way that parody does on a macrocosmic (textual) level, because parody too is a marking of difference, also by means of superimposition (this time, of textual rather than of semantic contexts). Both trope [i.e., irony] and genre [i.e., parody], therefore, combine difference and synthesis, otherness and incorporation.'[64] One might wonder, then, whether it is really necessary to have two terms for similar structural relationships on two different levels of discourse. Would it make sense to see both relationships as ironic? In her more recent works, such as *Splitting Images: Contemporary Canadian Ironies*, Hutcheon herself seems to be placing parody within the greater field of irony as 'the ironic use of intertextual references.'[65] I would thus suggest to 're-functionalize' the distinction that Hutcheon had made above between parody and satire: irony is, generally speaking, a structural relationship between two statements, and parody imbeds such an ironical structural relationship in an intertextual (and thus literary) context.

Progressive parody (or, more precisely, the parodic process), to conclude, is a mechanism of literary reception and adaptation of traditional texts used by writers who feel themselves to be in a situation in which the old text cannot or should not be seen – at least not exclusively – in the generally accepted way any longer. The parodist includes the old text in a new context or frame that incorporates it (and the narrative 'energy' that the old form brings with it) in a new perspective. The parodied text is in a way 'taken hostage' by the parodist and is only allowed to return to freedom (i.e., the reading public) if it contributes to the parodist's objectives. Still, this incorporation of the older text into the new one often leaves its traces in the new product. A parody is hardly ever a Bakhtinian stylization, in which the new text is completely under the new narrator's control. More often than not, the dialogue continues within the dialogic text, so that one may say that, in general, parody means a distancing process from the original directedness of the parodied text: a sense of difference in repetition.

Such a parodic difference in repetition is – as this study will show – of special importance in the context of the new literatures in English that have to define their own stances in opposition to a strong literary tradition stemming from the British Isles. The Canadian case offers a fascinating example of the revising and incorporating parodic strategies employed in a new literature which is situated, as T.D. MacLulich formulates it in his book of the same title, 'between Europe and America,' and is thus influenced by, not just one, but two strong national literatures – English and American – as well as many pervasive international movements. These influences, which are often accompanied by extra-literary and extra-cultural – political and economic – pressures have to be adapted to the new, Canadian environment. Literary models may be imitated or emulated, and experiences may be repeated in a new country and a new literature defining their independence; but they have to be repeated with a difference, if not with a vengeance.

2 Parodies of History

Parody in the Context of Canadian Literary History

As the preceding chapter has shown, parody may be defined as a literary mode that younger writers can use in order to define their own position in opposition to accepted tradition. 'Young' literatures such as the English-Canadian one ideally illustrate such literary dependencies and parodic counter-reactions as they may be explained by a theory based on the Russian Formalists' interpretation of literature as an evolutionary series. This model, in which parody plays a major role, has come in for criticism by theorists who forget that the Formalist system includes other – extra-literary and social – series than just the literary one, and that all these series influence each other within the literary system. Critics – and this of course applies also to those studying Canadian literature in English – should always take all these different classes of series into account. The problem with Canadian literary criticism up to the 1970s, though, has been that it has relied too much on the other – non-literary – series and not enough on the one feature of writing in which the Formalists were primarily interested: its literariness.

The focus of this study on parodic structures in Canadian literature is thus justified by Canada's cultural situation as a young country that shares the language of many other countries, but especially that of historically dominant England. In the realms of politics and commerce (as well as in the publishing market), England's former position as the centre of an empire has now been taken over by an overwhelmingly strong United States. Canadian literature can thus be grouped with the 'new literatures in English' of other Commonwealth countries struggling for their own cultural and political sovereignty. A similar situation with regard to French-language literature exists between Quebec and

France. Research into the somewhat comparable situation (with respect to Germany) of Austria has shown that parody is a means of counteracting a feeling of almost total dependence on an overpowering neighbour. The important role of parody in 'marginal' – for example, Latin American – literatures has been pointed out by critics such as Severo Sarduy and Jean Franco. The latter focuses on the element of parody and self-parody and 'examines the way Latin American novels redeploy materials from the European bourgeois tradition in what she calls a carnivalesque way, that is, in a way that transforms or inverts value, hierarchy, and significance.' Mary Louise Pratt claims that these tendencies, inherent in Latin American literature, have their parodic counterparts in Canada, and she refers to examples such as Marian Engel's *Bear* and Margaret Atwood's *Lady Oracle*.[1] Lorna Irvine, too, insists that 'for Canadians, this "experience of both participating in and standing outside" the language of their own country which, in its turn, dramatically reflects colonial positions toward dominating countries like England, France, and the United States, influences, in idiosyncratic ways, the metaphors and structures of their literature.'[2]

In this context, one should not necessarily restrict one's analysis of parodic structures in Canadian literature in the same way that Linda Hutcheon does in her more general work on parody. There, at least, she is not interested in 'how the social and psychological interact with the established intention, attitude, and competence of either actual addresser or receiver.' Instead, 'it is only the encoded intention, as inferred by the receiver as decoder, that will be dealt with ...'[3] If there are distinct ways in which Canadian novels parody their models, then I would insist the social and psychological background of the encoder will have to be taken into account, even though the role of such a background will not be as important as it has been in other studies of a more thematic kind.

Parody and the Historical Novel

In Canadian literature, as in any other literature that is not cut off from international cultural life, the possibilities of literary imitation and literary parody are of course unlimited; indeed, as the reception of Latin American models by such Canadian novelists as Robert Kroetsch, Jack Hodgins, and others has shown, new trends are taken up wherever they may come from.

In order to narrow down the range of texts under consideration here, I will concentrate on works belonging to a genre which – *pace* George

Woodcock's point of view that 'the historical novelist ... is in any case a rather rare Canadian species' – has been called an 'important tradition of Canadian fiction' by critics such as Tom Marshall and Linda Hutcheon: the historical novel. Historical writing in Canada, even what we would nowadays normally refer to as non-fiction, was – as the Canadian historian Carl Berger has shown – 'generally regarded as an especially instructive branch of literature.' Helen Tiffin has identified the use of history as an important aspect of all the postcolonial literatures, and she underlines its 'unique role as literary *genesis*.' In Canada this field has been covered by critics such as Ronald Hatch, Tom Marshall, and Dennis Duffy. As Hutcheon and Duffy have pointed out, there has been 'a rebirth of the historical novel in Canada' in recent years, and the authors often mentioned in this context are Rudy Wiebe, Chris Scott, Timothy Findley, Graeme Gibson, and others. But as none of the Canadian critics – with the exception of Hutcheon in *A Poetics of Postmodernism* – have clearly defined what the term *historical novel* means for them, we have to go to foreign scholars in order to arrive at a working definition, even though the problem of defining historical novels as such is not at the centre of interest here.[4]

While the existence of such a genre as the historical novel is too obvious to be denied, it is not always easy to give a clear-cut definition of this literary phenomenon. Scott's Waverley novels have always been generally accepted as *the* models of the genre, and in the nineteenth century historical romances emulating this type were very popular. In fact, many Canadian texts from the last century belong to this category. While the historical romance is still one of the most successful genres on the literary scene as far as its popularity is concerned, it is nowadays overshadowed by other types of historical fiction. As well, more and more critics agree that Georg Lukács's concept of the realist historical novel, as put forth in his *The Historical Novel*, is too narrowly based on Sir Walter Scott's writings. It is hardly any longer useful in the context of twentieth-century literature, but comprehensive and generally accepted theories of historical fiction are scarce. Most of the general books and overviews on the subject deal with rather traditional nineteenth-century examples and stop short of the contemporary novel.[5] This is unfortunate because, as David Cowart points out, there is an 'increasing prominence of historical themes in current fiction': 'Produced by writers sensitive to the lateness of the historical hour and capable of exploiting technical innovations in the novel, this new historical fiction seems to differ from that of calmer times. A sense of urgency – sometimes even an air of desperation – pervades the historical novel since mid-century, for its author probes the past to account for a present that grows increasingly chaotic.'[6] Even a recent volume such as Barbara Foley's *Telling the Truth*, although it delivers, as the subtitle indicates, a comprehensive overview of the theory and practice of documentary fiction, can be criticized for not treating the whole gamut of experiments taking place in that realm of historical fiction that she rightly qualifies as the 'metahistorical novel,' and part of which she saw, in an earlier publication, to be moving in an 'increasingly "apocalyptic" direction.'[7]

As far as the content and function of historical novels are concerned, some of the 'postulates' about novels and historical novels that Murray Baumgarten lists in a 1975 essay may be helpful in our context. He states that novels are conditioned by history and that 'individually as well as collectively, they also function as one of the conditions that makes it possible to comprehend history.' He claims that they 'raise the question of consciousness and value at the intersection of public and private realms in a unique way because they explore the possible unities of a discourse hinged upon temporal experience.'[8] A definition based on these postulates would also accept those novels as historical that deal with historically conditioned problems in the contemporary world, so that here one of the basic ingredients of a historical novel, the distance in time, might be replaced by social or geographical distance, as long as the social or geographical differences imply that we deal with societies or groups at different stages of their historical development. This definition would be similar to the pragmatic one given by David Cowart:

> I myself prefer to define historical fiction simply and broadly as fiction in which the past figures with some prominence. Such fiction does not require historical personages or events ... nor does it have to be set at some specified remove in time. Thus I count as historical fiction any novel in which a historical consciousness manifests itself strongly in either the characters or the action.[9]

Combining elements of Baumgarten's and Cowart's definitions, I would suggest that historical novels in the context of this study are works of fiction that deal with questions of historical consciousness in a historically conditioned situation on the levels of author, narrator, characters, or action.

For a long time, critics based their conception of the historical novel on a commonsense model of history and historiography, relying on the assumption that it was possible to represent historical events exactly as they happened. In the wake of Croce's and Collingwood's theories, however, it has become a generally accepted notion that the historian – at least the historian who still intends to write a narrative history – uses some of the subjective methods of historical reconstruction (in Collingwood's terms, 'the re-enactment of past thought') that were long thought to be admissible only in the novelist's realm. As Avrom Fleishman puts it, 'Both the novelist and the historian are trying to find meaning in otherwise meaningless data, to rethink and complete the rationale of covert and often duplicitous behavior, to reconstruct the nexus of past actions.' Leon Braudy focuses on narrative form in history and fiction in his study of the eighteenth-century writers and historians Hume, Fielding, and Gibbon.[10] Such an approach to historical works is based on what Bernard Bergonzi says was once a generally accepted notion and what Berger had also stated about the writing of Canadian history, namely, that 'historiography was a form of literature.' The parallels between history and fiction and the development of theories of history and historiography up to 'l'entrecroisement de l'histoire et de la fiction,' with its fictionalization of history and its historicization of fiction, are magisterially discussed in Paul Ricoeur's *Temps et récit*, especially in the section entitled 'L'Histoire et le récit.'[11]

Although Ricoeur does not fully agree with him, I would see the American Hayden White as one of the most important contemporary theorists in this field of narrative historiography, especially as far as the parodic or intertextual aspects dealt with in this study are concerned. White's concept of metahistory picks up an earlier distinction made by Northrop Frye in his essay 'New Directions from Old,' when the Canadian scholar distinguishes in an Aristotelian manner between the tasks of the historian, whose work refers to an external model and 'is judged by the adequacy with which ... words reproduce that model,' and of the poet, who 'has no external model for ... imitation' and whose work is judged 'by the integrity or consistency of ... verbal structure.' Frye admits, as White does more forcefully later on, that in both cases – history and literature – we are dealing with a text on the page, and he also admits that there are close affinities between the styles of historical and fictional writing: 'We notice that when a historian's scheme gets to a certain point of comprehensiveness it becomes mythical in shape, and so approaches the poetic in its structure.'[12]

In his own writings on the writing of history (i.e., in his metahistory), Hayden White goes much further than Frye. Referring distinctly to the Canadian as his predecessor, he emphasizes the importance of the

textual character of both historical and fictional writing. In his controversial theories on historiography, it is his method 'to consider historical narratives as what they most manifestly are – verbal fictions,
the contents of which are as much invented as found and the forms
of which have more in common with their counterparts in literature
than they have with those in the sciences.'[13] Linda Hutcheon clearly
indicates that such a reference to historical facts as verbal fictions does
not mean that these facts never existed. In her essay 'History and/as
Intertext,' she also points out that in contemporary metafictional historiographic novels the interplay between fiction and history is of central importance and that 'the questions raised by historiographic
metafiction regarding reference in language (fictive or ordinary) are
similar to those raised by theoretical discourse today.' And she concludes 'that historiographic metafiction's complex referential situation
does not seem to be covered by any of the theories of reference offered
in today's theoretical discourse.'[14]

Our situation is, however, that 'we cannot know the past except
through its texts: its documents, its evidence, even its eye-witness accounts are *texts*.' This is not the place to go further into the episte-
mological and philosophical questions of reference that arise when
'data drawn from presumably extratextual sources enter the text primarily to corroborate the text's thematic design and are incorporated
into a fictive totality,'[15] into questions, that is, of the relationship between words and things, of historiographical text and historical fact.
As this study is interested in the relationship between texts, namely,
historical novels and their underlying subtexts, and not so much in the
relationship between these subtexts and the reality they pretend to
represent, questions concerning the philosophy of history do not enter
its realm.

Although they are based on historical facts, historiographic texts
follow the same 'literary' rules as other kinds of writing and are formed
according to strategies of what White calls *emplotment*. Such strategies
include, for example, the *suppression, subordination*, or *highlighting* of
various elements: 'The events are made into a story by the suppression
or subordination of certain of them and the highlighting of others, by
characterization, motific repetition, variation of tone and point of view,
alternative descriptive strategies, and the like – in short, all of the
techniques that we would normally expect to find in the emplotment
of a novel or a play.'[16] White generally differentiates between four
modes which the emplotment can follow: romance, comedy, tragedy,
and satire. In his later writings, he points out that the form of 'nar-

rativization' chosen by a historiographer implies a 'conceptual or pseudoconceptual "content" which, when used to represent real events, endows them with an illusory coherence and charges them with the kinds of meanings more characteristic of oneiric than of waking thought.'[17]

We clearly see that in historical literature, as in any other kind of historical writing or – as indicated in the earlier sections of this study – in almost any kind of writing in general, there is a certain amount of rewriting of older texts going on, a certain amount of what I have called parody. Based on the work of other structuralist theorists such as Michel Foucault, Margaret Rose develops a similar model, in which she sees parody as a positive mode of thinking and views the historian as a parodist: 'While literature has ironically found a new authority for itself as history ... the historian as parodist – as, that is, a self-critical archeologist of his own text – has today also taken on new authority and fame in the world of literary texts and structuralist historiography ... To the historian aware of his or her role as parodist the texts of history must moreover take on the form of prefigured literary or fictional texts to be deconstructed as such.'[18] Dominick LaCapra arrives at a similar position when he criticizes the traditional historian's approach in his rhetorical or dialogical theory of historiography, which is clearly inspired by Bakhtinian theory. The traditional, restricted view that he rejects 'underplays the way the "voice" of the historian may be internally "dialogized" when it undergoes the appeal of different interpretations, employs self-critical reflection about its own protocols of inquiry, and makes use of modes such as irony, parody, self-parody, and humor, that is, double- or multiple-voiced uses of language.'[19]

T.D. MacLulich is the first critic to apply Hayden White's theories of historiography to Canadian literature and especially to early exploration reports, which – as he shows – can be interpreted as the Canadian counterpart of early European historiography. In his essay 'Hearne, Cook, and the Exploration Narrative,' he stresses to what extent the early exploration narratives form a genre of their own and – as in the case of Hearne's report – are 'shaped by hitherto unrecognized literary influences.' As he feels that exploration accounts rarely fall into White's modes of comedy and satire, and that the American's other terms, romance and tragedy, are not suitable either, MacLulich redistributes the literary territory covered by the latter terms so that exploration narratives 'are emplotted in one of three ways, either as *quests*, as *odysseys*, or as *ordeals*.'[20] Quests are crowned by a happy ending, while an ordeal ends in disaster; in odysseys, the narrative concentrates more

on the explorer's environment and personality than on the actual outcome of the expedition.

In Canada even 'scientific' historical texts often seem to have an
especially strong slant towards the literary realm. This is true of the
type of popular histories written by Pierre Berton, but also of some of
the writings of an eminent historian such as Donald Creighton, who
is certainly the Canadian historian most strongly influenced by literary
models.[21] George Woodcock states, for example, that some historians
'remember that, for the ancients, history like poetry had its muse, and
writers like Creighton recognized the extent to which they were ser-
vants of Clio, not merely by cultivating the art of writing so that the
best of their books could rank as literary masterwork, but also by
shaping their accounts to draw a grand pattern, a myth, out of the
mass of heterogeneous facts.'[22]

In the same way that medieval historians had to 'emplot' the facts,
highlighting some and suppressing others, when they wanted to go
beyond the writing of mere chronicles listing events, the Canadian
explorers had to rewrite their exploration reports if they wanted to
present them as reading material and coherent narratives to a general
public. And in a similar manner the different schools of Canadian
historiography had to 'emplot' facts in order to make them fit general
theses of metropolis and hinterland, of progressive or conservative, or
of the Laurentian or continental schools of Canadian history.[23]

Among writers of fiction such as Hugh Hood, Rudy Wiebe, Matt
Cohen, Graeme Gibson, Timothy Findley, and Heather Robertson, it
is, in Tom Marshall's words, 'perhaps indicative of the present stage
of our evolving literary culture that these writers and others have been
engaged in what may be termed the "re-visioning" of Canadian history
and character – that is, each attempts to reveal to Canadians a new or
more "true" fictional version of our collective past.'[24] This process of
re-visioning is an expression of the general phenomenon among the
literatures in former colonies that Helen Tiffin calls postcolonial counter-
discourse: 'Post-colonial cultures are inevitably hybridised, involving
a dialectical relationship between European ontology and epistemology
and the impulse to create or recreate independent local identity.' In
this context, 'the rereading and rewriting of the European historical
and fictional record are vital and inescapable tasks.'[25]

The main part of this study deals with the range of strategies of
historical re-visioning, the kinds of parodic 'frames'[26] through which
history is viewed that can be ascertained in contemporary English-
Canadian novels. The authors chosen represent three different schools

of writing: Timothy Findley stands for the modernist or modernistically influenced; George Bowering represents the playfully postmodern; and Margaret Atwood, the feminist.

Although the main focus of this study is not on taxonomic questions regarding the historical novel, it is interesting to see that the novels selected (two per author) not only represent different schools of writing, but also cover almost the whole spectrum of the historical novel that David Cowart projects 'with an eye to the mythic quaternities of Blake, Jung, and Northrop Frye.' His four rubrics are 'The Way It Was,' 'The Way It Will Be,' 'The Turning Point,' and 'The Distant Mirror.' Two of the novels chosen here are included by Cowart himself in his typology: Atwood's *The Handmaid's Tale* is interpreted as a major example in the second rubric of 'fictions whose authors reverse history to contemplate the future'; and Timothy Findley's *Famous Last Words* is included among the turning-point fictions 'whose authors seek to pinpoint the precise historical moment when the modern age or some prominent feature of it came into existence.' A novel such as Bowering's *Burning Water* straddles the line between the first and fourth rubrics: although it does not really belong to the 'fictions whose authors aspire purely or largely to historical verisimilitude,' it is only partly one of the 'fictions whose authors project the present into the past.'[27]

The rest of this chapter will concentrate on some of the forerunners of contemporary historical novels, showing that parodic structures have always existed in Canadian writing.

Wacousta: From Factor to Syndrome

As judged by the standards of European or American historical novels such as Scott's Waverley novels or Cooper's Leatherstocking tales, Major John Richardson's *Wacousta* is not necessarily a good book. Still, it is in the company of such works that critic J.D. Logan places it at the beginning of this century, and doubtless Richardson would have thought this to be appropriate, as he himself claimed to be 'the first and only writer of historical fiction the country has yet produced.' At least the title *Wacousta* has reached mythical status in Canadian studies: not only did Robin Mathews coin the term *Wacousta factor* in an essay on Canadian literature; recently, Gaile McGregor based a whole book of Canadian cultural criticism, of 'explorations in the Canadian langscape,' on a pattern derived from the novel: the *Wacousta syndrome*. As this novel is an early native product, its dependence on European and American models, more precisely its reaction to foreign narrative patterns, is at the centre of my interest. The obvious models to which it reacts (and features of which it integrates into the 'Canadian' frame) are British historical romances such as Scott's – the 'matrix from which the authors could develop a New World form of romance'[28] – and their American counterparts such as Cooper's *The Last of the Mohicans*. Another strain of influence goes back to American Gothic novels such as Charles Brockden Brown's *Edgar Huntly*.

If we are to believe Walter Scott in his preface to *Waverley*, another – and even earlier – historical novel set in Canada might have been written by his younger brother Thomas, who thus 'would have made himself distinguished in that striking field, in which, since that period, Mr. Cooper has achieved so many triumphs.' Even though this Scottian historical romance never materialized, *Wacousta* fills this gap, and many of its features are reminiscent of Scott and his romantic Highland retreats. According to Winnifred Bogaards, this is not surprising: 'Anyone, whether historian or novelist, who wished to write about any time in Canada's past, was automatically provided with the "classic Scott situation" of two nations, two cultures in conflict.'[29]

Indeed, the prehistory of *Wacousta*, the story of Reginald Morton's thwarted love for a young lady hidden away in a Scottish *locus amoenus*, is a motif that might have come straight from *Waverley*; it is 'stock material of Scottish romance in the age of Sir Walter Scott.' *Waverley* dealt with the events leading up to and following the battle of Culloden, and in *Wacousta*, Clara Beverley, the girl mentioned above, is the daughter of a 'fugitive Jacobite father' who has withdrawn from active life after the defeat.[30] Carole Gerson claims that 'Richardson's recourse to Scotland for the primary impetus of a novel about the Pontiac conspiracy demonstrates that in 1832 even a native-born Canadian found it impossible to divorce the romantic novel from its connection with Sir Walter Scott.'[31]

The method in which the Scottish background is integrated into the Canadian narrative is a simple one of narrative framing, one of the three ways in which – according to Jay Macpherson – 'the romantic novel can conveniently bring in other time ranges':[32] Reginald Morton (alias Wacousta), the disappointed lover turned vengeful Indian, tells the Scottish prehistory of the novel's main action as a first-person narrative within the general third-person narrative of the novel. The effect is that a European story is integrated into a Canadian one, that it lives on not only in a foreign environment but also in an unusual narrative contrast to the savage brutalities committed by the once romantic lover. The European tradition thus lives on, but its function is changed. Terry Goldie adds another note to the Scottian aspect of *Wacousta* by pointing out that 'the Cornish heritage and Scottish experience of the title figure make it possible for him to join the Indians. He, like Clara, his love from the Scottish highlands, is asserted to be a child of nature, perverted by the intrigues of their sophisticated English friend, De Haldimar.'[33]

As mentioned above, Scott's influence is not the only important one in Richardson's work, and Richardson – although possibly the first Canadian adaptor (or parodist) of Scott – is clearly not the first North American writer of historical novels. Among his predecessors in the field, and the most important example of the depiction of the atrocities of the Seven Years' War (or in this context, rather, the French and Indian War), was James Fenimore Cooper in his Leatherstocking novels, above all *The Last of the Mohicans*. David R. Beasley emphatically stresses Cooper's influence on Richardson: 'By his own admission James Fenimore Cooper's *The Last of the Mohicans* was the lightning bolt which turned him to the writing of Wacousta.' Even nineteenth-century reviews of *Wacousta* draw parallels between the two novels. For example, L.E. Horning sees Cooper's Cora and Alice Munro as prototypes of Richardson's Clara and Madeline Beverley.[34]

Wacousta and *The Last of the Mohicans* both show the Seven Years' War from the English side, but whereas Cooper has Indians fighting on both sides, so that Magua's evil character is balanced by the virtues of Chingachgook and Uncas, most of Richardson's Indians appear in a negative light. This seems to be consonant with the traditional Canadian concepts of *survival* and of the *garrison mentality*, especially as they are illustrated in Gaile McGregor's recent theory of a *Wacousta syndrome* in Canadian literature: Canadians – or here their British predecessors – have to take refuge in the fort because they are threatened not only by the forces of nature but also by Indians unwilling to be absorbed into a European society (unless we define the Indians as just one type of the evil forces of nature). What such an interpretation does not take into account is that the evil character of the Indians is largely a result of the influence of Wacousta, who is not an aborigine but an English nobleman in disguise, and after all the phenomenon is called the *Wacousta syndrome*. For this reason, Beasley's argument that Richardson's 'depiction of Indian strategy and cunning is probably what keeps Richardson's Indian from being romantic like Cooper's' does not hold in this case. While many nineteenth-century writers, such as Susanna Moodie, have been accused of using inadequate European metaphors to describe Canadian nature, Richardson even goes so far as to turn Canadian Indians into Europeans whose minds are easier to read than those of the real natives.[35] For these reasons, McGregor's *Wacousta syndrome*, while it may still be a valid concept, does not really mean what it is supposed to mean in her book.

T.D. MacLulich also identifies *Wacousta* as 'in some measure a Canadian reply' to Cooper, but he supports the point made above about the evasion of a real confrontation with the North American environment and peoples by taking Richardson's 'counterpart to Natty Bumppo' to be 'not a true North American frontiersman but a thoroughly European character – a Byronic hero. The deepest conflict in *Wacousta* is the opposition between the two European attitudes embodied in the punctilious Colonel De Haldimar and the impetuous Reginald Morton ...'[36] Morton's alter ego, De Haldimar, tries to suppress the free-ranging Byronic hero, but he can only do so at the cost of his own death and that of two of his children. The garrison turns from a fruitful idyll into the beleaguered seat of barren incest and death. Even the remaining son, Captain Frederick de Haldimar, marries a cousin, so that his future marriage is not wholly untainted by incestuous motives.

Marcia B. Kline thus has a point when she claims that 'the Scottian romance, the saga of man in his natural environment, could not be recast to explain Canadian development.'[37] For her, Richardson's failure in writing a Canadian romance in a truly Scottian vein proves the impossibility of writing this romance without 'probing a kind of evil that is altogether out of place in an orthodox romance.' MacLulich, too, questions the viability and truthfulness of a European type of historical romance in North America:

> The work of several nineteenth-century historical romancers clearly illustrates the difficulties that early Canadian authors encounter when they try to adapt the European literary tradition to a new world social environment. During much of the nineteenth century, Canadian authors treat the North American setting of their historical tales merely as a kind of exotic decor or picturesque stage setting for stories that are thoroughly European in conception. Instead of creating identifiably North American characters and social settings, they habitually imitate the refined manners and the rigidly stratified society that they found in European aristocratic romances.[38]

In his interpretations, MacLulich seemingly inverts chronology by claiming that after Richardson Canadian historical fiction followed Scott's rather than Cooper's model. Cooper, although the first successful historical novelist in America, and even Scott were preceded by Charles Brockden Brown in the practice of writing historical novels. George Woodcock points out that 'Richardson, when he wrote *Wacousta*, can hardly have been unaware of *Wieland* or of Brown's powerful and horrific novel of Indian wars in the American wilderness, *Edgar Huntly*.' Kenneth Hugh McLean shows to what extent Brown's writing as well as some contemporary biographies became important as models on which *Wacousta* was based.[39] Although *Edgar Huntly* deals only implicitly with historical problems such as the rightfulness of the treatment of the Indians by the white settlers who supersede them, some references that its editor, Norman S. Grabo, makes to an essay Brown published in 1799, the year *Edgar Huntly* was published, prove interesting. Under the title 'Walstein's School of History: From the German of Krants of Gotha,' Brown sketches his own theory of historiography. He

> argues that fiction is a perfected form of history, best told as the autobiography of a character worthy of interest and attention. Fictitious history is thus moral, elevating, and even openly didactic. It explores human character by allowing the memoirist to recount his own motivations, so as to reveal the springs of actions as well as their consequences. It may be about ordinary – as differentiated from prominent or great – men and women, by appealing to the two basic areas of moral testing for ordinary readers – the areas of sex and money.[40]

Referring to the same essay, Alfred Weber shows that Walstein's (i.e., Brown's) school of history also includes his pupil Engel, who wants to depict in his novels more of an everyday environment to which readers can relate: 'Engel's principles inevitably led him to select, as the scene and period of his narrative, that in which those who should read it, should exist.'[41]

Although *Wacousta* is not the autobiography of a character (except for the story told by Morton), it would fit into the definitions given by Brown. These formulations are surprisingly similar to Georg Lukács's definition written over a century later and based to a large extent on Scott's historical romances:

> What matters therefore in the historical novel is not the re-telling of great historical events, but the poetic awakening of the people who figured in those events. What matters is that we should re-experience the social and human motives which led men to think, feel and act

just as they did in historical reality. And it is a law of literary portrayal which first appears paradoxical, but then quite obvious, that in order to bring out these social and human motives of behaviour, the outwardly insignificant events, the smaller (from without) relationships are better suited than the great monumental dramas of world history.

Lukács, too, links Scott up with the other important foreign model for a Canadian historical novel. According to him, 'Scott had only one worthy follower in the English language who took over and even extended certain of the principles underlying his choice of theme and manner of portrayal, namely the American, Cooper. In his immortal novel cycle *The Leather Stocking Saga* Cooper sets an important theme of Scott, the downfall of gentile [sic] society, at the centre of his portrayal.' The model has to be accommodated to the North American context, though: 'Corresponding to the historical development of North America, this theme acquires an entirely new complexion ... In America the contrast was posed far more brutally and directly by history itself; the colonizing capitalism of France and England destroys physically and morally the gentile society of the Indians which had flourished almost unchanged for thousands of years.'[42] It may be true that such an accommodation is going on in Cooper's novel, but for Richardson I doubt that there is very much understanding for the role of the Indians. As mentioned above, they are seen in white terms rather than in their own. Cooper's description of Indian cosmology as voiced, for example, by Tamenund indicates more willingness to accept the Indians on their own terms than does Richardson's writing.

What we have here in *Wacousta* is – as I have shown – a repetition with a difference, one might even say, with a vengeance, of European and American narrative themes and structures. Is this repetition with a difference already a parodic historical novel? It certainly stands in the position that would make parodic repetition possible, and the mechanism of parody is in place; but, on the other hand, repetition here still seems to be imitative of British and American literary exploits without being capable of going beyond them. Parody here is still often inadvertent, as is to be expected in the early stages of the development of a national literature.

Douglas Cronk, the editor of the scholarly edition of *Wacousta*, points out another feature that we might interpret as parody. He shows that all editions of *Wacousta* published after the original one of 1832 are faulty insofar as they simplify the characters and the plot. Especially the pirated Waldie edition of 1833 comes in for a lot of criticism: 'By bowdlerizing, Waldie changed *Wacousta* from being probably one of the first realistic historical novels into being just another romance.' Even worse, he 'turned Richardson's pro-British, pro-Canadian historical novel into a non-British, non-Canadian novel which took as its main geographical setting the U.S.A. rather than Canada.'[43] In fact, Waldie re-contextualizes and parodies the novel which may already be interpreted as a parody in its own right. This may be one of the rare cases in which a Canadian novel is parodied by one of the master literatures that are normally imitated by Canadians.

Grove's Ants

> ... in the realm of historical interpretations ... *the past is the outcome of all that has followed it.* F.P.G.[44]

The general direction from foreign model to Canadian parody does not change in the twentieth century. Often immigrant writers bring along new narrative models and ideas with them. Among the leading Canadian novelists of the first half of this century is Frederick Philip Grove, formerly the German author Felix Paul Greve, whose writing is generally influenced by European realism and naturalism. Grove tries to adapt these foreign styles of writing to the Canadian environment in novels such as *Fruits of the Earth, Settlers of the Marsh,* or *The Master of the Mill.* Much of his writing, especially his autobiographical work – as German critics such as Walter Pache and Canadians such as David Williams have pointed out – is also influenced by turn-of-the-century aestheticism. Another style of writing is represented by a novel on which Grove claims to have spent over twenty years of his career: *Consider Her Ways,* which was finally published in 1947. It is the book in the Grove canon that least fits the general image of Grove as the father of Canadian realist fiction; and that is probably why it is rarely discussed in traditional studies, but is more likely to be just mentioned in passing as 'a literary curiosity which, for all its occasional insight, added little to Grove's reputation.'[45] In an oblique manner, *Consider Her Ways* belongs to a specifically Canadian version of the historical novel. While Richardson had chosen the historical romances of Scott and Cooper as models to be parodied, Grove's endeavours finally find their shape in the form of an exploration report.

Grove's personal interest in historiography comes to the fore in his unpublished essay 'Retroaction / Of the Interpretation of History' (ca.

1919), which remained virtually inaccessible until Henry Makow included it in his PHD dissertation of 1982. This essay offers an interesting view of historiography that one might subsume under the theories of emplotment listed above: 'The viewpoint of History, as commonly understood, is wrong, because it is telescopic, if I may coin that word; and its "telos" or fulfilment is the "present" of the historian.' Or, as he puts it some pages later, 'in viewing and tracing history we pick out what we imagine to be the stepping stones or the traces of that which came about; and since we close our eyes to all things else, we think we see a clear line, a distinct river making its way into the present.'[46] As Makow points out,[47] Grove still holds a similar attitude in his pseudo-autobiographical work *In Search of Myself*: 'All interpretation of the past is teleological; it is meant, it is constructed as an explanation of that which is. No matter what happened in the past, its importance is solely determined by its share in moulding the present. It is never what might have been; it is only what happened to happen which decides the value of any deed.'[48]

In his 'autobiography,' Grove reports that he wrote a draft version of *Consider Her Ways* in the early 1920s. However, this early version was not yet emplotted in the form of an exploration report. According to Grove, it turned into 'a grumbling protest' instead of being 'a laughing comment on all life.' Arthur Phelps even referred to it as 'a pretty good sermon.' This version of the novel exists in manuscript form in the University of Manitoba Archives and bears the title 'Man: His Habits, Social Organization and Outlook,' which in itself is a parody of the title of one of Grove's sources, Wheeler's *Ants: Their Structure, Development and Behavior*. But although this 1920s draft is written from the point of view of an ant, an ironic perspective that would offer many possibilities of narrative experimentation, it is organized strictly thematically and is devoid of any narrative content. It may be just a coincidence, but it is still an interesting link between the 'Retroaction' essay on history cited above and *Consider Her Ways* that Grove establishes a connection between humankind and antdom in the essay, referring to human beings as 'curious ants as we are.'[49]

The process of rewriting that the novel underwent before final publication in 1947 involved an emplotment following the normal shape of a narrativized expedition report. As Birk Sproxton puts it, 'Fortunately, when Grove rewrote his Ant Book, he wrote it as a narrative ...'[50] Already in 1933, as Margaret Stobie points out, the text had been completely revised: 'The pulpit thumping is gone. Only the introduction survives from the script of eight years before. This is a new work, new in conception, in tone, and in the quality of the prose. It is a lively narrative of another of Grove's far-travelers. It was this text which was used some fourteen years later, with a few minor changes, for *Consider Her Ways*.'[51] The narrative claims to be an expedition report written by ants from Central America, who travel all over the North American continent: the 'Narrative of an Expedition from the Tropics into the Northern Regions of the Continent ... compiled by Wawa-quee, R.S.F.O.' Its title echoes those of many other reports by such explorers as Hearne, Mackenzie, and Vancouver, and it invites the reader to compare Grove's (or his spokes-ant Wawa-quee's) techniques of emplotment with the original chronology of the expedition that may be reconstructed from the finished product. The techniques used can be analysed according to MacLulich's categories listed above.

As Douglas Spettigue writes in his introduction to the NCL edition of *Consider Her Ways*, the structure of the book is a geographical one: 'The Isthmus' (of Panama), 'The Mountains' (of Colorado), 'The Slope' (of the Rocky Mountains), 'The Plains,' and 'The [Eastern] Seaboard' are the geographical and chronological stages of the ant Amazons' expedition. Spettigue also points out that the exploration report is a ' "popular" account rather than a scientific report.'[52] Its objective is 'to serve as an introduction to the detailed study of special subjects' that exists in the form of 'monoscents' on 'scent-trees,' and to which the scientists among her ant audience may refer. It was the aim of the expedition 'to trace the evolution of the nation Atta from the humblest beginnings of all ants and to make it possible for us to arrange the whole fauna of the globe, or of such portions of it as could be explored, in the form of a ladder leading up to our own kind.'[53] The first step towards an emplotment and a more 'literary' version of the 'original' account is Wawa-quee's divergence from a strictly chronological order of events. At the very beginning of her report, she notes that 'the sequence ... is not strictly chronological; and occasionally a record is introduced in an order the very reverse of chronological' (4). Occasionally she establishes connections between similar thematic units through the use of prolepses, and she admits about several explanations she gives during the narrative that 'in this I shall, of course, anticipate the results of later investigations' (21). At other times, Wawa-quee shows that she is fully aware of her obligation to shorten certain passages in order to avoid tedium: '... in order not to weary by repetition, I shall content myself with this mere statement, omitting the incidents which brought that confirmation' (192). Her fellow ants who are interested in details are referred to the source material of the scent-trees. Even flashbacks do not endanger the homogeneous character of her narrative: 'I must now reach back in time' (70). Instances like this one make it quite clear that Wawa-quee tells her story looking back from a later point in time, re-structuring and re-membering the events re-collected. She is fully aware of the dangers of a too 'myrmecocentric' perspective in writing about lower animals such as human beings.

In Richardson's and Scott's cases, the emplotment of the historical record in the form of a novel invited the invention of a dangerous adversary. The same happens in Grove's book: Assa-ree, the military commander of the expedition, at first supports the exploration of the North American continent, but soon we become suspicious: 'Assa-ree behaved admirably; and when the dangers surrounding us seemed, at the least, to admit of no further escape, it was she who saved our lives, though I almost hated her for it. She was of that type which seems to have all her faculties sharpened by circumstances which deprive others of their power of thought' (50). The tension between Assa-ree and Wawa-quee rises in the course of the expedition. A mutiny can only be averted by using the royal 'perfume of supreme command' (126), and finally Assa-ree is killed as a traitor.

Consider Her Ways has so far been interpreted as an exploration report that makes use of strategies of emplotment. Of course, there is no actual exploration report that is rewritten or parodied by the ants. It is rather Frederick Philip Grove who parodies a type of scientific writing in order to get this political message across. This is not the only level, though, on which parodic strategies work in this book. A specific model that Grove uses is already a parody of the scientific discourse of its own time, Jonathan Swift's *Gulliver's Travels*. Publishers McClelland and Stewart, taking a statement of one of their own authors, Ronald Suth-erland, out of context, quote him on the cover of the NCL edition to the effect that *Consider Her Ways* is 'a tour de force equal to if not better than *Gulliver's Travels*,' leaving out the qualification that this is true 'with respect to suspension of disbelief.'[54]

While parts of *Gulliver's Travels* show us eighteenth-century England as it might have been seen from a foreign or even dissident home perspective, *Consider Her Ways* does the same thing for American society. The similarities between Swift's and Grove's travel narratives often include word-for-word parallels. Many of the ants' 'myrmeco-centric' perspectives reflect Swiftian satire: for example, Grove makes use of Swift's dichotomy of *high heels* and *low heels* denoting Tories and Whigs and applies it to the distinction of men and women; and Gulliver's watch glass is as new to the Lilliputians as Wheeler's test-tubes are to the ants. Gulliver's and Wawa-quee's methods of emplotment have much in common. While Gulliver writes that 'I shall not anticipate the Reader with farther Descriptions of this Kind, because I reserve them for a greater Work, which is now almost ready for the Press,' Wawa-quee refers the readers to the more detailed scent-trees. While Gulliver points out that 'Nothing but an extreme Love of Truth could have hindered me from concealing this Part of my Story,'[55] the ant claims that at one point 'my strict veracity forces me to reveal what I should gladly suppress ...' (54).

The parallels between Grove and Swift are by no means accidental: Douglas Spettigue points to the similarities between the two writers and reminds us that Grove (alias Greve) translated Swift into German. In fact, Felix Paul Greve edited and introduced a German edition of Swift's prose works, including *Gulliver's Travels*, in a four-volume edition published in 1909 and 1910. In his introduction to volume 4, *Gullivers Reisen*, he quotes in German from a letter Swift sent to Alexander Pope in September 1725. The English original of the excerpt had been: '... I have got Materials Towards a Treatis proving the falsity of that Definition *animal rationale*; and to show it should be only *rationis capax*. Upon this great foundation of Misanthropy (though not Timons manner) The whole building of my Travells is erected: And I never will have peace of mind till all honest men are of my Opinion ...'[56]

In this context, it is interesting to note that the ant Wawa-quee, whose perspective Grove uses as the satirical 'frame' in order to parody straight exploration reports, cannot, from her 'myrmecocentric' point of view, identify human satire as such. In the early version of the 'Ant Book,' she describes Swift as one of the few humans who have a positive attitude to animals, because she takes Gulliver's letter to his cousin Sympson at face value.[57]

Consider Her Ways thus proves to be a complex narrative that works on several levels and thus can be interpreted in various ways. Wawa-quee's expedition report illustrates all the different stages of emplotment through which even a piece of non-fiction has to go in order to become readable. In this sense, it is parodic in relation to the genre of exploration writing. Its parodic technique runs parallel to that of a specific work, *Gulliver's Travels*, and it thus also becomes a satire criticizing the American and capitalist way of life in a fashion similar to the one in which Swift had criticized his contemporaries in the eighteenth century.

Combray, Altamont, and Entremont: David Canaan's Remembrance of Things Past

Parodying F.R. Leavis's self-assured tone, Robert Kroetsch once claimed that 'the classic modern novels in the English-Canadian tradition are three: Sinclair Ross's *As For Me and My House*, Sheila Watson's *The Double Hook*, and Ernest Buckler's *The Mountain and the Valley*.'[58] Although the literary importance of Buckler's novel is beyond any doubt, its inclusion in an overview of historical novels may be surprising. Certainly it does not deal with historical events such as the defence of a fort in the Seven Years' War, and it is not based on early historiographical forms such as expedition reports either. On the other hand, it does not only deal with questions of historical consciousness on the level of a narrator who wants to become the chronicler of his tribe; its technique also becomes important in the context of contemporary historical writing: historians have used the structure of an artist's remembrance of things past that we see in *The Mountain and the Valley* and in what I claim is its most important subtext as a model of their revisionary theories of historiography. Besides the romantic revenger's tale and the expedition report, the *Künstlerroman* is a third type of historical novel deserving treatment in this study. A critic like Tom Marshall, for example, also includes Buckler's masterpiece in his study of historical fiction, admitting that it has 'important historical contexts without being historical fiction in quite the same explicit way that MacLennan's novels and *The Diviners* are.'[59]

My aim in this section is to elucidate intertextual and parodic relationships between the third Canadian classic in Kroetsch's triad and an internationally recognized classic of modernism, Marcel Proust's *A la recherche du temps perdu*. I intend to show that Ernest Buckler is not only influenced by Proust but that he also reacts against him. The technique in which the parodic relationship between Buckler and Proust becomes most obvious is the use of epiphanies. David Canaan's failure to turn his own recapturing of the past in the final epiphany of Buckler's novel into his own 'remembrance of things past' could be interpreted as another example of the typical Canadianization of a traditional theme, typical according to the inventors and perpetuators of concepts such as *survival* and the *garrison mentality*. As I will suggest, however, the relationship between Proust and Buckler can also be defined – and more profitably at that – in terms of literary parody.

Both *A la recherche du temps perdu* and *The Mountain and the Valley* are portraits of an artist's coming of age, of his being reconfirmed – at least in his own mind – in his ability and vocation to write a novel. Both novels are thus overtly metafictional, and Buckler and Proust both make use of one of the most obvious forms of textual self-consciousness: narratorial commentary. Especially their epiphanies, as we will see, are explicitly commented upon, and their contribution to the process of writing is stressed.

In Morris Beja's definition, an epiphany is a 'sudden spiritual manifestation, whether from some object, scene, event, or memorable phase of the mind – the manifestation being out of proportion to the significance or strictly logical relevance of whatever produces it.' Beja distinguishes between 'retrospective epiphany' and epiphany of 'the past recaptured': 'The retrospective epiphany is one in which an event arouses no special impression when it occurs, but produces a sudden sensation of new awareness when it is recalled at some future time.' Such an epiphany of 'delayed revelation,' of 'mere recollection,' examples of which Beja finds in Joyce, is differentiated from a Proustian 'actual recapture of the past,'[60] a type of epiphany that we find in Buckler's novel.

Throughout his life, Marcel, Proust's first-person narrator, has felt an artistic vocation. At various points of his life, works of art have stirred his emotions and shown him what art can achieve. His own attempts at artistic creation, however, have so far not been crowned with success. Only late in his life does he sense a new confidence in his ability to create his own work of art:

> Et je compris que tous ces matériaux de l'œuvre littéraire, c'était ma vie passée; je compris qu'ils étaient venus à moi, dans les plaisirs frivoles, dans la paresse, dans la tendresse, dans la douleur, emmagasinés par moi, sans que je devinasse plus leur destination, leur survivance même, que la graine mettant en réserve tous les aliments qui nourriront la plante. Comme la graine, je pourrais mourir quand la plante se serait développée, et je me trouvais avoir vécu pour elle sans la savoir, sans que ma vie me parût devoir entrer jamais en contact avec ces livres que j'aurais voulu écrire et pour lesquels, quand je me mettais autrefois à ma table, je ne trouvais pas de sujet. Ainsi toute ma vie jusqu'à ce jour aurait pu et n'aurait pas pu être résumée sous ce titre: Une vocation.

> And I understand that all these materials for literary work were nothing else than my past life and that they had come to me in the midst of frivolous pleasures, in idleness, through tender affection and

through sorrow, and that I had stored them up without foreseeing their final purpose or even their survival, any more than does the seed when it lays by all the sustenance that is going to nourish the seedling. Like the seed, I might die as soon as the plant had been formed, and I found that I had been living for this seedling without knowing it, without any indication whatsoever that my life would ever witness the realisation of those books I so longed to write but for which I used to find no subject when I sat down at my table. And so my entire life up to that day could – and, from another point of view, could not – be summed up under the title, *A Vocation*.[61]

The grasp of his own past, enabling him to write his autobiographical work, is achieved through various epiphanies, and Proust provides detailed commentaries upon these illuminations. In *Du côté de chez Swann*, at the very beginning of the *Recherche*, he records the episode of the *madeleine*. Whereas an act of volition had been unable to bring back the childhood memories of Combray, this is achieved through the epiphany. Marcel takes his tea in which he had dipped a biscuit:

Mais à l'instant même où la gorgée mêlée des miettes du gâteau toucha mon palais, je tressaillis, attentif à ce qui se passait d'extraordinaire en moi. Un plaisir délicieux m'avait envahi, isolé, sans la notion de sa cause. Il m'avait aussitôt rendu les vicissitudes de la vie indifférentes, ses désastres inoffensifs, sa brièveté illusoire, de la même façon qu'opère l'amour, en me remplissant d'une essence précieuse: ou plutôt cette essence n'était pas en moi, elle était moi. J'avais cessé de me sentir médiocre, contingent, mortel. (*Recherche*, 1:45)

No sooner had the warm liquid, and the crumbs with it, touched my palate than a shudder ran through my whole body, and I stopped, intent upon the extraordinary changes that were taking place. An exquisite pleasure had invaded my senses, but individual, detached, with no suggestion of its origin. And at once the vicissitudes of life had become indifferent to me, its disasters innocuous, its brevity illusory – this new sensation having had on me the effect which love has of filling me with a precious essence; or rather this essence was not in me, it was myself. I had ceased now to feel mediocre, accidental, mortal. (*Remembrance*, 1:34)

Through the influence of the epiphany, caused by the most trivial process of eating a *madeleine* and drinking tea, Marcel's feelings of mediocrity, contingency, even mortality are replaced by pleasure, optimism, and bliss (*plaisir délicieux*).

A comparable experience takes place towards the end of the *Recherche* at the 'matinée Guermantes,' where Marcel, after a lengthy period of isolation in a sanatorium, meets his former acquaintances, the members of Parisian high society. Here the sounds, sensations, and books that he encounters produce in him a 'miracle d'une analogie,' which evokes the past once again, so that he can recapture 'les jours anciens, le temps perdu, devant quoi les efforts de ma mémoire et de mon intelligence échouaient toujours' (*Recherche*, 3:871).[62] The past that is recaptured is actually relived, reborn. Thus what Marcel experiences is not just the remembrance of things past, whatever the title of the English translation may suggest:

> Rien qu'un moment du passé? Beaucoup plus, peut-être; quelque chose qui, commun à la fois au passé et au présent, est beaucoup plus essentiel qu'eux deux. Tant de fois, au cours de ma vie, la réalité m'avait déçu parce qu'au moment où je la percevais, mon imagination, qui était mon seul organe pour jouir de la beauté, ne pouvait s'appliquer à elle, en vertu de la loi inévitable qui veut qu'on ne puisse imaginer que ce qui est absent. Et voici que soudain l'effet de cette dure loi s'était trouvé neutralisé, suspendu, par un expédient merveilleux de la nature, qui avait fait miroiter une sensation ... à la fois dans le passé, ce qui permettait à mon imagination de la goûter, et dans le présent où l'ébranlement effectif de mes sens par le bruit, le contact du linge, etc. avait ajouté aux rêves de l'imagination ce dont ils sont habituellement dépourvus, l'idée d'existence, et, grâce à ce subterfuge, avait permis à mon être d'obtenir, d'isoler, d'immobiliser – la durée d'un éclair – ce qu'il n'appréhende jamais: un peu de temps à l'état pur. (*Recherche*, 3:872)

Merely a moment from the past? Much more than that, perhaps; something which, common to both past and present, is far more essential than either.

How many times in the course of my life had I been disappointed by reality because, at the time I was observing it, my imagination, the only organ with which I could enjoy beauty, was not able to function, by virtue of the inexorable law which decrees that only that which is absent can be imagined. And now suddenly the operation of this harsh law was neutralised, suspended, by a miraculous expedient of nature by which a sensation ... was reflected both in the past (which made it possible for my imagination to take pleasure in it) and in the present, the physical stimulus of the sound or the contact with the stones adding to the dreams of the imagination that which they usually lack, the idea of existence – and this subterfuge made it possible for the being within me to seize, isolate, immobilise for the duration of a lightning flash what it never apprehends, namely, a fragment of time in its pure state. (*Remembrance*, 2:995–6)

This long quotation characterizes Proust's concept of epiphany and especially this theory that there are two kinds of memory, only one of which is fruitful for his artistic purposes: *mémoire volontaire* and *mémoire involontaire*. Voluntary, deliberate memory had deceived Marcel, and only the contingent, involuntary kind had given him artistic bliss and reconfirmed his artistic vocation, which in turn encouraged him to complete the novel. The German critic Hans Robert Jauß explains the importance of the Proustian epiphany as follows:

> Thus 'Marcel's' story receives its unity only a *posteriori*, when he realizes what he had not yet discovered in the *madeleine* experience: that his search for the lost time can only be successfully completed
> through art, because this successful completion at the same time suspends and sustains the distance between reminiscing and remembered self as well as the contingency of its path through this distance, a path which we now recognize as the path leading toward the work of art.[63]

This epiphanic way of restructuring a narrative about the past has also been reflected in historiographical discussions. After modern history-writing – such as that of the *Annales* school in France – left behind the chronological structure of historiography, alternative ways of structuring historiographical texts have been explored, and Proust's name comes up every now and then even in the discussions of professional historians and historiographers, although Siegfried Kracauer admits that the consequences of 'Proust's unique attempt to grapple with the perplexities of time' have not yet been realized.[64]

The 'involuntary' kind of memory establishes a strong link between Proust's portrait of an artist with that drawn in *The Mountain and the Valley*. Several critics have mentioned Buckler's acquaintance with Proust's work, and J.M. Kertzer draws an explicit parallel between Marcel and David. But Kertzer also states the most important difference between the two novels: in *A la recherche du temps perdu*, Marcel 'has found a future for himself and a way of making up for the time he has lost. He finds a timeless world of essences – time in its pure state – in art, not death. But David turns to death and embraces his past at the expense of any future.'[65]

Before commenting upon David's inability to fulfil his vocation, I will draw attention to some basic parallels between David's and Marcel's stories. David Canaan had discovered the miracle of art and the magic of writing early in his life. Whereas Elstir's paintings and Vinteuil's music stirred Marcel's artistic interest, David's was awakened by the stories his grandmother told, by the school play, and by the book that Dr Engles left for him. Reading this book,

> he had the flooding shock of hearing things stated exactly for the first time.
>   Suddenly he knew how to surmount everything. That loneliness he'd always had ... it got forgotten, maybe, weeded over ... but none of it had ever been conquered. (And all that time the key to freedom had been lying in these lines, this book.) There was only one way to possess anything: to *say* it exactly. Then it would be outside you, captured and conquered.[66]

But although he experiences the bliss that a literary work of art produces in the reader, David cannot yet write such a work himself. At least, the 'cleansing cathartic of the first accurate line' (196) does not last long. Like Marcel, he must learn, and – confronted with the problems of real life – his attempts at writing turn out to be failures, although he seems to inhabit a word-shaped universe:

> He took the scribbler from under the pillow and reread the lines he'd written. They had the same stupid fixity as the lines of cracked plaster in the ceiling. There was nothing in them, to come alive as often as they were seen. They were as empty as his name and address scribbled across the white spaces of the catalogue cover in a moment of boredom. (199)

Only years later, when he is thirty, his vocation too is confirmed, as Marcel's is confirmed at the 'matinée Guermantes,' by an epiphany that comes rather late in the novel. While climbing the mountain that dominates the valley in which he has lived all his life, David relives episodes of the past, episodes that culminate in his conviction that he is or can be the greatest writer in the world, that he is able to write the story of his own past and that of his community:

A cloud skimmed the sun. With it, a wide skirt of shadow slid swiftly along the road, then disappeared. He had seen a momentary undulation ribbon through the oatfield like that on a still summer's afternoon.

And suddenly a breaker of exaltation rushed through him in just such a way.

It was the thing that comes only once or twice ever, without hint or warning. It was the complete translation to another time. There is no other shock so sweet, no transfiguration so utter.

It is not a *memory* of that time: there is no echo quality to it. It is something that deliberate memory (with the changed perspective of the years between changing the very object it lights) cannot achieve at all. It is not a returning: you are there for the first time, immediately. No one has been away, nothing has changed – the time or the place or the faces. The years between have been shed. There is an original glow on the faces like on the objects of home. It is like a flash of immortality: nothing behind you is sealed, you can live it again. You can begin again ... (289)

This description of David's epiphany has so many important features in common with Proust's of the *mémoire involontaire* that pure coincidence can almost certainly be excluded. Buckler insists that the memory triggered off by a rather trivial visual stimulus is not at all an instance of deliberate memory (*mémoire volontaire*), but rather a reflection of a Proustian 'temps à l'état pur' – the years have been shed – and a flash of immortality. Reliving his youth, David feels an exaltation or transfiguration, in Proust's terms, a *plaisir délicieux*. Despondency is replaced by optimism, the fear of death is suspended. Nevertheless, this description of an epiphany already contains some hints that such moments of exaltation are not without danger: the breaker of exaltation are not without danger: the breaker of exaltation, even though it brings a 'shock so sweet' and a 'transfiguration so utter,' is also a potential threat, as the reminiscing subject cannot control it.

The mechanism of memory in the epiphany can also be compared in the two novels. The past has been spatialized: Marcel describes in *Le Temps retrouvé* that normally our memories are enclosed in *vases clos*:

le geste, l'acte le plus simple reste enfermé comme dans mille vases clos dont chacun serait rempli de choses d'une couleur, d'une odeur, d'une température absolument différentes ... (*Recherche*, 3:870)

> ... the most insignificant gesture, the simplest act remain enclosed, as it were, in a thousand sealed jars, each filled with things of an absolutely different colour, odour and temperature. (*Remembrance*, 2:994)

Only through the *mémoire involontaire* can a connection between these distinct sections of memory be established, can the memories be made into a coherent plot. This connection is achieved through what Proust calls a metaphor, but which today would probably be referred to as a metonymy:

> Ce que nous appelons la réalité est un certain rapport entre ces sensations et ces souvenirs qui nous entourent simultanément ... quand, en rapprochant une qualité commune à deux sensations, [l'écrivain] dégagera leur essence commune en les réunissant l'une et l'autre pour les soustraire aux contingences du temps, dans une métaphore. (*Recherche*, 3:889)

> What we call reality is a certain relationship between these sensations and the memories which surround us at the same time ... when, like life itself, comparing similar qualities in two sensations, [the writer] makes their essential nature stand out clearly by joining them in a metaphor, in order to remove them from the contingencies of time ... (*Remembrance*, 2:1008–9)

Proust's connection between the remembered sections of the past finds its counterpart in Buckler's epiphany. On his way up the mountain, shortly before his final epiphany or translation, David has a feeling of synaesthesia and a first epiphany:

> He could think of anything now. Everything seemed to be an aspect of something else. There seemed to be a thread of similarity running through the whole world. A shape could be like a sound; a feeling like a shape; a smell the shadow of a touch ... His senses seemed to run together. (287)

This emotion resembles that which Marcel had commented upon in the quotation above, and it prepares the reader for another moment in which connections are established. Buckler describes how his process of 'remembrance' functions:

> It was as if the time were not a movement now, but flat. Like space.

> Things past or future were not downstream or upstream on a one-way
> river, but in rooms ... You could walk from room to room and look at
> them, without ascent or descent. (287)

Here, during his first epiphany, the spatialized past consists no longer
of *vases clos*: one can penetrate from one room of his past into the
next.[67] But David's memories are still of the 'as if' kind, copies of
original experiences: 'he heard again ... felt again ... tasted again ...'
(287). After the final epiphany quoted above, however, the translation
is total, and the past is the present:

> A spring of tears caught in David's flesh. He wasn't standing on the
> road at all.
>   He was waking that clean April morning and touching Chris's face
> to wake him too and tell him that the very day was here at last – the
> day they were going back to the camp on the mountain. (289)

Here he recaptures the past, reliving it rather than remembering it,
making the step from 'retrospective epiphany' to a 'recapture of the
past': 'there is no echo quality to it.'
    Merely reliving or 'becoming' the events of the past, identifying with
them through an epiphanic experience, is not sufficient, though, as
David soon finds out: while Marcel's recapturing of the past is an
entirely positive experience, Buckler's protagonist is persecuted by the
voices of the past that the epiphany has awakened. These are first of
all the voices of the elements of his surroundings, but also those of
his fellow citizens from whom he – the budding intellectual and artist
– had kept quite aloof most of the time. These memories are subcon-
scious reactions created without any interference of his volition, and
so he cannot control them either: 'And now the fact of exactly the way
that *faces* happened to be – exactly that way because of exactly all the
feelings behind them – added its cry to the voices of the objects about
him. It was a more exquisite accusing still' (292–3). All the voices he
has roused – they develop into a threatening crescendo – show him
where he failed to establish the true contact with the fellow members
of his community that would have validated his artistic mission: for
example, he missed the chance to establish a closer relationship with
his brother Chris (294); and he used his girlfriend Effie in order to
impress his friends rather than really loving her for her own sake (295).
    Only on top of the mountain is David rescued by another illumi-
nation:

> I will *tell* it, he thought rushingly: that is the answer ... He saw at last
> how you could *become* the thing you told ...
>
> He didn't consider *how* he would find it ... Nor how long it might
> take ... He knew only that he would do it ... It would make him the
> greatest writer in the whole world. (298–9)

In a work of art he will be able to 'reassemble his past'[68] and retell
the memories awakened by the epiphany, but he arrives at this insight
only after the frightful confrontation with all the voices he had roused.
In the same way that Marcel makes artistic use of his 'metaphor,' David
must find his own method of 'becoming' what he tells, of eliminating
the distance in time as well as in space. Whereas Marcel succeeds,
David dies without having become an artist. As A.T. Seaman puts it,
'That he is dying is important for two reasons: his vision comes to him
only in death, and very possibly, it comes to him *because* of impending
death.'[69] This may have something to do with his egotistical motives
for wanting to be a great writer: the isolation into which he – like
Proust – withdraws is quite unnatural in his environment. Even his
first attempts at producing literature – in the 'applied' field of drama
– had shown that he, who wanted to be 'the greatest actor in the whole
world' (82), was tempted to use art in order to 'take [the others] with
him always, in their watching. Closer somehow *because* they followed'
(81). It is not surprising that this attitude to art afterwards causes him
'shame of having spoken the foolish words in this goddam foolish
play' (82). Ironically, it is his grandmother who creates a truly Canadian
work of art (i.e., one which is useful for the community) out of old
rags which stand for and 'become' her memories. In the end it is Ellen,
the grandmother, who – even without an epiphany – can transform
her memories into a coherent 'narrative.'

The comparison of Proust's and Buckler's epiphanies has shown that
they are structurally almost identical in both novels up to the moment
when David shows that he is not really capable of coping with the
memories awakened during his illumination: two would-be writers,
who for years have felt unable to write the work of art they are certain
they have the vocation to write, have a sudden intuition that interprets
their memories in such a way that they might form the coherent plot
of a novel. Both authors 'know' that they can write their books, but
the realization of these dreams, which in Proust's case turns out to be
the *Recherche* itself, is denied David Canaan: he dies. Although, as
Douglas Barbour remarks, he at least dies happy, he leaves his creator,

the implied narrator (or Buckler himself), the task of finishing the portrait of the artist *manqué*.

The failure of the Canadian rural artist where the European urban author succeeds might tempt us to interpret Buckler's version as the 'typical' Canadianization, à la Atwood, of a traditional plot; once again, the garrison fights for its survival and does not succeed: 'In Ms. Atwood's view, it is an inevitable concomitant of the Canadian imagination that people will fail: they cannot escape, they even die, whether or not the story demands such an ending.' But David's failure can be explained differently and – I think – in a more satisfying manner. Most recent critics, such as Alan Young and Douglas Barbour, have seen David's failure as ironic rather than purely tragic, and Buckler himself refers to 'the whole dramatic irony' of his death and final delusion of being the greatest writer in the world.[70] Even though an author's comments upon his own writing should not be privileged, this supports Barbour's and Young's view.

I would like to take their interpretation, which sees a distancing process between the narrator and his hero, even further, to show that *The Mountain and the Valley* is a parody – a repetition with a difference – of Proust's *Recherche*. Buckler parodies Proust's model of the *Künstlerroman*: he makes use of the Proustian model and applies it to David Canaan's situation. At a certain point, he deviates from his model: the epiphany, his most important borrowed element, works for both authors, but in Buckler's novel, its result, the recapturing of the past, is shown to be illusory; Buckler denies David the victory over death that enables Marcel to write his novel.

Buckler's parody, while it does not ridicule the traditional use of epiphany in the portrait of an artist, questions its value as a technique of artistic creation as well as the artist's solipsism that it seems to entail. A sudden intuition does not seem to be the usual mode of artistic composition for a writer who says about himself that he does not believe in inspiration in the process of writing:

> I think that inspiration, by and large, is one great big myth. What really happens: you work and work toward an idea, and some sort of mold of the thing desired forms in your mind. Then – while you're chopping, or hoeing, or whatever – the subconscious gets going: fitting images against this mold, and when one of them – phrase, incident, or whatever – slips into it, that tiny click you hear, that's what's mistaken for inspiration.[71]

Here Buckler's scepticism meets with that of Thomas Wolfe, who found that 'you can't go home again' to Altamont and came to 'a substantial rejection of his reliance on his own recollected epiphanies, which till then had been one of the bases of his work.'[72] But Proust himself had been aware of the restricted value of epiphanies. Marcel makes it clear at various points that the epiphanies give him flashes of illumination, but that the realization of his novel, the transformation of the insights gained through an epiphany, depends on work. Furthermore, only the epiphanies, not the ensuing act of transforming them into a work of art, are exempt from the dangers of mortality:

> Maintenant, me sentir porteur d'une œuvre rendait pour moi un accident où j'aurais trouvé la mort, plus redoutable, même ... absurde ... Je savais très bien que mon cerveau était un riche bassin minier, où il y avait une étendue immense et fort diverse de gisements précieux. Mais aurais-je le temps de les exploiter? (*Recherche*, 3:1036–7)

> Now the feeling that I was the bearer of a literary work made an accident in which I might meet death more to be dreaded, even absurd ... I knew very well that my brain was a rich mineral basin where there was a vast area of extremely varied precious deposits. But would I have time to exploit them? (*Remembrance*, 2:1115–16)

Marcel withdraws from the life of Parisian high society in order to write his book in the isolation of his room. His Canadian counterpart undergoes a similar ordeal, isolating himself – at least spiritually – from society, but his withdrawal into the 'garrison' is as unproductive as Colonel De Haldimar's was. Readers, who realize that in fact the book they have just finished is the book that David would have written, know that someone else has completed the work. When he finally overcomes the limitations of the valley of Entremont and reaches the summit, it is too late for David to write about it. He lives out the dictum of the writer from the other summit, Altamont, who stated that you can't go home again. As David Williams writes, 'When Ernest Buckler decided to set his portrait of the artist in a town called Entremont, he might as well have been inviting deliberate comparison with Wolfe's Altamont.'[73] Although both the American and the Canadian writer parody the European artist novel, the Canadian position differs from the self-confident rejection of the European model from the top of independent American heights, and it leaves the aspiring Canadian writer in the forever compromising situation between the mountains: *Entre*mont.

Buckler's parodic strategies in *The Mountain and the Valley* underline the status as narrative models that Proust's and Wolfe's novels have for the Canadian writer. His parody has the function of criticizing, not the process of remembrance that takes place in an epiphany, but rather the creative force with which it endows the prospective author. The illumination as technique is not questioned, nor is its cognitive function, but Buckler's narrator is even more critical of its importance for the actual act of writing than Marcel was. The recapturing of things past succeeds in both novels by means of epiphanies, but – and perhaps also because of his egotistical and anti-social attitude – the artist in *The Mountain and the Valley* is denied the fruit of his epiphany, the satisfaction of becoming the greatest writer in the world as well as the voice and historiographer of his community. Taking into account his attitude towards this community, one might be grateful for not having to read his own emplotment of the history of Entremont.

3 Timothy Findley's Metafictional Histories: Modernist Parodies or Parodies of Modernism?

Timothy Findley is without doubt one of the foremost contemporary Canadian writers of 'fictive history.' Two of his novels, *The Wars* and *Famous Last Words*, centre on the greatest political conflicts of this century, the world wars. *The Wars*, winner of the 1977 Governor General's Award, is not the first of Findley's novels to draw upon historical facts, but here for the first time he deals explicitly with the problem of writing about these facts and integrating them into an artistic whole. The novel thus becomes an instance of historical metafiction. Whereas, in Simone Vauthier's words, 'all historical fiction strives to supplement history, *The Wars* goes one step further by thematizing its reason for doing so.'[1]

Findley uses parody in order to call attention to the 'metahistorical' aspects of his writing. He adopts types and structures of traditional war literature and repeats them within a new context; that is, he subsumes them under a new perspective in which there is not only an awareness of the absurdity of war but also an emphasis on the inherent companionship of all living creatures. The latter possibility offers an escape route from a world tending towards total entropy, a world in which – according to Robert Kroetsch – 'what we witness is the collapse, for North American eyes, of the meta-narrative that once went by the name Europe.' Findley's parodic technique illustrates 'how the value of past experience is a function of the skill with which we recreate it imaginatively, transcending the chaos of time and history.'[2]

Findley chooses the First World War – rather than Heller's absurdities of the Second World War – as a military and historic event that lies so far back in the past that – except for the odd eye-witness account of then very young and impressionable persons who today 'can still be met in dark old rooms with nurses in attendance – it is only through records such as photographs, letters, and official histories that the pres-

ent-day narrator can try to arrive at the truth. Memory for him exists
in the form of textual and photographic documentation only, and as,
in Robert Kroetsch's words, 'the traditional authority of the novel itself
begins to falter,' he has to find his own method of emplotting the
material found in this documentation in order to produce a coherent
version (if we are willing to call *The Wars* that). The First World War
seems to have been one of the major points in world history at which
the possibility of achieving such a coherent vision was doubted. Paul
Fussell claims in his *The Great War and Modern Memory* that 'the Great
War was perhaps the last to be conceived as taking place within a
seamless, purposeful "history" involving a coherent stream of time
running from past through present to future.'³

Instead of being able to begin with textual sources in the form of
reliable, coherent narratives, Findley's narrator has to work in the Fou-
cauldian archive, in the same way that the researcher and archivist in
the novel have to work in a real one. Michel Foucault defines the
archive in *L'Archéologie du savoir* (The archaeology of knowledge) as

> ce qui fait que toutes ces choses dites ne s'amassent pas indéfiniment
> dans une multitude amorphe, ne s'inscrivent pas non plus dans une
> linéarité sans rupture, et ne disparaissent pas au seul hasard d'acci-
> dents externes; mais qu'elles se groupent en figures distinctes, se com-
> posent les unes avec les autres selon des rapports multiples, se
> maintiennent ou s'estompent selon des régularités spécifiques; ce qui
> fait qu'elles ne reculent point du même pas avec le temps, mais que
> telles qui brillent très fort comme des étoiles proches nous viennent en
> fait de très loin, tandis que d'autres toutes contemporaines sont déjà
> d'une extrême pâleur.⁴

The historian, even the historian of twentieth-century affairs, becomes an archaeologist, and his or her situation corresponds to one of
the poles between which Robert Kroetsch sees Canadian literature taking place: 'the vastness of (closed) cosmologies and the fragments found
in the (open) field of the archaeological site.'⁵ Sense and meaning can
only exist in this jumble of facts if they are imposed by a narrator, and
part 1 shows us the narrator in the archive trying to reconstruct an age
from its fragments. Although the sections are not always arranged in
chronological order, they still provide enough information that by the
end of this part, the reader has a good impression of the Canadian
past that Robert Ross leaves behind when he embarks for the battle-
fields of Europe. But this reconstruction can only be a reconstruction

in our time, taking into account and reflecting the present context in which it is undertaken. We, the readers, live after all in the age of Star Wars rather than in that of trench warfare.

The Prologue to *The Wars*, which later turns out to be the proleptic repetition – outside and well in advance of its context within the plot – of a scene occurring towards the end of the novel, has been criticized by Laurie Ricou for not being a 'prologue at all, no address to the audience, no summary of theme.' And no introduction to a historical novel, one might add. Ricou criticizes the narrator within the novel – not the author, Timothy Findley, of course – for terminological inaccuracies. It is the narrator whom he sees desperately trying 'to superimpose some shape on his frightened stammering.'[6] But this technique of taking a scene out of its original context and embedding it in a new frame (which – as in this case – may be a contextual vacuum) illustrates very well the narrator's own situation. Working with stories or story elements, photographs and letters that he finds in his archive or taped conversations, he himself has to reconstruct the context of the events he wants to narrate. And in the same way that the reader is capable of finally better understanding the Prologue once he or she comes upon it for the second (or, as far as the chronology of events is concerned, the first) time later in the novel, he or she will be able to fit other plot elements into a greater context and make some more sense of a seemingly absurd situation. The reader will have participated in the parodic act of history-writing.

Three of the novel's five parts – the first (relating the prehistory of Robert Ross's engagement in the Great War up to his arrival in Britain), the second (describing Robert's life in the trenches), and the fifth – consist of numbered sections told in different styles from different points of view. Part 3 consists of chronologically arranged descriptions, most of them set on 28 February 1916; and part 4 is a longish transcript of a tape. Obviously, we are dealing with different approaches that the narrator makes to his material in order to arrive at a coherent vision of historic events. Coherence is not given *per se* in the chapters consisting of numbered sections: the sections are divided by large white spaces suggesting the separateness and non-chronological order of all the items of information gathered from the archives. The narrator admits that his work is unscientific and haphazard: 'In the end, the only facts you have are public. Out of these you make what you can, knowing that one thing leads to another. Sometime, someone will forget himself and say too much or else the corner of a picture will reveal the whole' (10–11).

Right from the start readers can observe several – sometimes contradictory – methods of coming to terms with chaos through emplotment. In certain versions, events such as deaths which might otherwise have been absurd, are reinterpreted so that they then correspond to well-known myths. Or they become so famous that they become myths in their own right in 'a world of reinvigorated myth.' As Paul Fussell writes, 'At the same time the war was relying on inherited myth, it was generating new myth, and that myth is part of the fiber of our own lives.'7

Since in times of war official propaganda can hardly ever be trusted, word-of-mouth communication becomes the breeding-ground of new myths. In *The Wars,*

> what you have to accept at the outset is this: many men have died like Robert Ross, obscured by violence. Lawrence was hurled against a wall – Scott entombed in ice and wind – Mallory blasted on the face of Everest. Lost. We're told Euripides was killed by dogs – and this is all we know. The flesh was torn and scattered – eaten. Ross was consumed by fire. These are like statements: *'pay attention!'* People can only be found in what they do. (11)

John F. Hulcoop has pointed out the importance of *paying attention* to Findley's words.8 In this case the narrator does not really have to draw readers' attention to the rather obvious mythical connotations of Ross's ordeal by fire, but we should 'pay attention' to the sentence following the reminder, which at first seems to be a truism: it is, however, not necessarily true that people can only be found in what they do, as such an empiricist view does not take their motivation into account. Actions, as well as passivity, can be seen from many perspectives and can be interpreted in many different ways; they can be emplotted into various versions of the same story.

The unreliability of documents (whether genuine or invented) that forces emplotment strategies upon a narrator is also illustrated by the use of photographs. When the narrator tries to analyse one, he cannot abstract from the quality of the paper on which it has been printed: 'The year itself looks sepia and soiled – muddied like its pictures' (11). Another photograph seems to exist nowhere but in his imagination. His commentary is set apart from the rest of the text, and the fact that it is given *here* in our time is indicated by its being set in italics:

Robert Ross comes riding straight towards the camera ... There is mud on

his cheeks and forehead and his uniform is burning – long, bright tails of
flame are streaming out behind him. He leaps through memory without a
sound. The archivist sighs. Her eyes are lowered above some book. There
is a strand of hair in her mouth. She brushes it aside and turns the page.
You lay the fiery image back in your mind and let it rest. You know it
will obtrude again and again until you find its meaning – here. (12–13)

As indicated, it is quite doubtful whether the photograph exists outside
the narrator's imagination. And as he mentions, it is here, in the present, that he has to come to terms with the past, and all the more so
as the realism of even documentary photographs has become doubtful
during the Great War: soldiers who had been avid photographers before gave up on this supposedly objective way of rendering reality after
their experience of trench warfare.[9]

Another aspect of the unreliability of photographic documentation
exists even in peaceful times: because handicapped children are not
part of life as it should be, Robert Ross's hydrocephalic sister Rowena
is never shown 'in photographs that are apt to be seen by the public'
(13). Photographs may speak for themselves and they may form 'the
main structuring principle of the novel and the source of Findley's terse
and strikingly visual style,'[10] but most of the time someone has selected
the pictures we are given.

Yet another type of quasi-factual information dealt with in *The Wars*
is the transcript of a tape recording. The transcript as such may be
deemed accurate, but the lady interviewed has to admit that her memories are not: 'At least that's my memory of it – the way it was,' she
says. 'You get them all mixed up, after so long a time ...' (16). She is
introduced as Marian Turner, the nurse who took care of Robert Ross
after his arrest (15), and this reference is the first one in the novel
pointing forward to the ostensibly 'criminal' offence he committed later.
The sections following the transcript fill in the reasons for which Robert
has left his home – his shock at his hydrocephalic sister's death, the
dominating personality of his mother – and describe his military train-
ing and sexual initiation on the Prairies. In the same way that Robert
had become very much attached to animals at home – his sister's rabbits
– and on the Prairies – the horses as well as the wild coyotes – on the
voyage to Europe he feels a close kinship to the horses accompanying
the Canadian soldiers. This motif of companionship between man and
animal, probably the Canadian counterpart to the 'Arcadian recourses'
typical of First World War English literature,[11] shapes the whole novel,
of course, and in a way it justifies the murder or manslaughter that

Robert commits later on, when he tries to save a number of horses from senseless destruction.

While so far documentation belonging to ostensibly non-fictional genres has been shown to be the structural underpinning of *The Wars*, Robert Ross's departure from a world of tradition and innocence is also reflected in such literary references as his dead sister's Scottian name, Rowena (the purity of the Middle Ages can only be found in Canada), and his fellow officers' reading of books such as George Alfred Henty's *With Clive in India* or – even more fittingly – *With Wolfe at Quebec*. Paul Fussell counts Henty's books among 'the tutors' in the special diction associated with 'the quiet action of personal control and Christian self-abnegation.' Within *The Wars*, Captain Ord's commentary after having been criticized for reading such childish fare as Henty's books adds to the irony of the situation: 'Ord said hoarsely that since he was going to do a boy's work he must read the "stuff of which boys are made" and smiled' (58). Like many others, Robert himself is unable to sum up his feelings on the way to Europe in an adequate way. In a letter to his father, he reverts to such false phrases as 'So – adios! as the bandits say' (52), which is somewhat reminiscent of (and perhaps parodies) the tone of such patriotic writings as Ralph Connor's *The Sky Pilot in No Man's Land*. Later he sums up the transatlantic passage in about a dozen lines (68), sustaining Fussell's judgment that 'any historian would err badly who relied on letters for factual testimony about the war.'[12]

Part 2 of the novel starts with another reference to an imaginary picture that readers have to compose themselves, ideally a picture that is not just a repetition of the cruelties of war but a repetition implying an active response: 'There is no good picture of this except the one you can make in your mind' (71). Pictures are inadequate, and so is language. When the narrator tries to describe the Flanders mud, it turns out that 'there are no good similes. Mud must be a Flemish word' (71). The other human senses have to respond to new and unknown impressions, too: 'There was a smell that Robert could not decipher' (74), the smell of chlorine gas. Surprisingly a new section starts with the statement that 'the front, after all, was rather commonplace' (83): life in the dugouts in a way succeeds in shoring up the rest of civilization into a parody of home life, including pictorial fragments from a church window and the animals (amongst others, the toad) that Captain Rodwell keeps alive. His fellow soldier Levitt tries to convince himself – through Clausewitz – that ' "the whole war can be carried out as a serious, formal minuet ..." ' (92). A repetition this would be, too, perhaps also a parody, but not the progressive/positive kind that we are looking for.[13]

The first half of part 2 is set in Flanders and develops more or less chronologically, but before section 13 relocates Robert in Belgium on the eve of a devastating battle, several sections fill in important information about the acquaintances he has made during his preceding stay in England: his Canadian idol, Captain Taffler; his friend, Harris; his future lover, Barbara d'Orsey, then still accompanied by Taffler; and her young sister, Juliet d'Orsey, later to be the companion of his last years, without whose help the reconstruction of Robert's life would have been impossible for the narrator.

Trying to establish connections between the documents in the archive, the narrator has to admit to certain problems in the imposed chronology. His alternative view runs into difficulties: 'The dates are obscure here – but it must have been mid-January, 1916 since Robert's tour of duty began on the 24th of that month' (94). Even the first meeting between Robert and Barbara d'Orsey clearly must have been reconstructed from a later point of view from which it has become clear that their acquaintance developed into a love relationship. Otherwise a remark such as 'Nothing happened this first time they met' (97) would not make much sense. Section 11 introduces another voice, that of Barbara's younger sister, Juliet, who – as a young girl – also fell in love with Robert. The narrator's voice is still discernible in this section, introducing Lady Juliet, and so it helps the reader locate him in our present time (at least later than 1969) by the remark that, having finally located Lady Juliet in London, 'you feel like Aldren [sic] on the moon' (99).

The following transcript of Lady Juliet's reminiscences is full of references to Victorian and Edwardian literature and society, showing how society in the novel sees itself and is seen through a literary perspective and to what extent such a literary point of view influences the historical perspective. The homoerotic relationship between Juliet's adolescent brother and his friend is mirrored in their nicknames, Oscar and Bosie (102), which, referring back to Oscar Wilde and his homosexual lover Lord Alfred Douglas, opens up a whole realm of historical and literary connotations, mixing the novelistic version of 'real life' with 'real' aspects of the literary world. In this context, the protagonist's name, Robert Ross, is an interesting choice, as – in addition to being Wilde's literary executor – the Canadian Robert Ross was one of the first of his male lovers.[14] Inserted into the transcript are 'editorial' bits of information which tie the action of the novel in with historical facts and establish connections with real and imagined writers involved in the fighting. For example, on 1 July 1916:

> *This is perhaps as good a place as any to point out that Lord Clive Stour-*
> *bridge, Juliet and Barbara's eldest brother, was one of the Cambridge poets*
> *whose best-known work – like that of Sassoon and Rupert Brooke – had its*
> *roots in the war. Other poets who were present on the First of July, be-*
> *sides Stourbridge and Sassoon, were Robert Graves and Wilfred Owen.*
> *Both Sassoon and Graves have written accounts of the battle.* (103)

Art and war have uncanny connections here: the fictional action of the novel is interspersed with actual names and facts which are easily recognizable as such, so that a new, parodic perspective is created that – although false – can serve to elucidate the truth. We hit again the problem of reference discussed in chapter 2: although the text uses fictional characters in a fictional situation, it is also meant to refer readers to a real historical situation and to the problem of writing about it.

Juliet's references go beyond contemporary literature, however, and include ancient mythology. Speaking about her sister's consecutive love affairs with soldiers doomed to die, she compares her to Ariadne: 'Ariadne and Dionysus. Well – it's not a bad analogy. Yes? Deserted by one god – she took up another.' One might wonder, though, whether the next sentence is not (on Juliet's part) an inadvertently parodic connection of the Dionysus myth with the mythical phoenix figure: 'Every year, Dionysus was destroyed and every year he was born again from ashes' (105).

While a photograph in the archives co-opts Robert Ross for the imperial tradition expressed in Benjamin West's painting *The Death of General Wolfe* (49) – a painting, by the way, which seems to have developed into a 'pan-Canadian icon'[15] in literature – a conversation between him and Barbara d'Orsey shows that he has grown wary of such a tradition:

> ... Barbara said to Robert: *you may not realize, Lieutenant Ross, that*
> *General Wolfe was born at Greenwich.* No. Robert hadn't realized. *Yes,*
> said Barbara. *Then he grew up and got your country for us.* Robert said:
> *No,* ma'am. I think we got it for him. *We?* Barbara asked. *Soldiers,* said
> Robert. It was the first time he'd truly thought of himself as *being* a
> soldier. (108)

And as being a Canadian, one is tempted to add.

The end of this section, the narrator insists, already points forward to 'the end of the story' (108). This remark should be taken as another hint that, in spite of the sometimes unorthodox order of the book's sections, there is a narratorial instance – what Vauthier would call a *scriptor* – controlling all the different styles and voices and controlling also the establishment of narratorial frames.

The third part of the novel takes a different approach to the description of historical events in that it covers a much shorter duration of time in a minute fashion that is often reminiscent of the film technique of slow motion. The part stretches from 4 A.M. on Monday, 28 February, to Wednesday, 8 March, but most of the action takes place on 28 February between the explosion of a devastating land-mine at 4 A.M. and Robert's unfortunate killing of an apparently friendly-minded German soldier around 1 P.M. Whereas there had been a discernible – though not an identifiable – narratorial voice so far, Simone Vauthier points to the relative absence of the organizing voice of the narrator as a characteristic feature of part 3. This part of *The Wars* is thus the only one that corresponds to reader expectations concerning historical novels. It is 'la seule *séquence* qui vise à la transparence du récit historique, la seule donc qui immerge le lecteur dans le passé et sa folie sur une assez longue durée de lecture.'[16]

In spite or because of the rather detailed descriptions, it is difficult to arrive at a coherent view of trench warfare: 'everything was out of sync' (114); ski poles are to be found at the bottom of mine craters (122). Still, some life-forms succeed in surviving: Robert's soldiers even live through a chlorine gas attack by making use of organic substances (i.e., their own urine). When, at the end of his tour of duty, Robert returns to England, he has with him Captain Rodwell's sketch-book, and he finds that he himself is the only human being that his friend had thought worthy of inclusion together with the animals he had drawn. Once again, Robert Ross is included in a frame, put in a perspective, that goes beyond the narrow and destructive concerns of human beings at war.

Part 4 of *The Wars* consists of a rather long transcript of a present-day recording of Lady Juliet reading from and commenting on her journals. She refers to herself at the time of the First World War as a *'malapert dwarf with a notebook'* (143). Her perspective on the affair between Robert Ross and her sister is that of a young inexperienced girl, so that it cannot be surprising that personalities turning up in the background, such as a certain Mrs Lawrence and a Mrs Woolf, are mentioned in passing only, although such personalities would invite further comments/emplotments to be made during the reading of the old journals. Lady Juliet's comments while reading from her notebooks indicate that some of the information given earlier about Robert's meeting Captain Taffler in Alberta probably came from her in the first place. The existence of the narrator in the background, arbitrarily arranging and rearranging bits of information, whether they be important or not, becomes blatantly obvious in the laconic commentary at the end of this part of the novel: 'So far, you have read of the deaths of 557,017 people – one of whom was killed by a streetcar, one of whom died of bronchitis and one of whom died in a barn with her rabbits' (158).

Resembling in its structure the first two parts of the novel, part 5 of *The Wars* consists of fifteen numbered sections and an epilogue. At the beginning, we see Robert setting out for the trenches again, and at the end he is dead, having 'died of wounds' inflicted on him not while fighting against the Germans but while fighting to uphold his companionship with his fellow creatures, the horses. By raping him in the baths at Désolé (a harsh parody of the Arcadian motif of 'soldiers bathing'?),[17] his fellow officers had proved to him that companionship amongst human beings was not to be counted on. When several horses have to die because of a captain's obstinate and wrong orders, Robert kills him and deserts: 'Then he tore the lapels from his uniform and left the battlefield' (178). Here the piece of the narration that also serves as prologue to the novel (re)appears at its proper place in the book.

One sees how the story of the rebel develops into myth: 'Here is where the mythology is muddled' (183). There are supposed to be various versions of what happened; they are corroborated by 'witnesses,' but none of them appears in the transcript of the court martial against Robert. He was almost killed when the soldiers pursuing him set fire to the barracks where he and the horses that he had liberated were hiding. The horses were 'all of them standing in their places while they burned' (186), but 'Robert turned the mare and she leapt through the flames – already falling – with Robert on her back on fire.'[18]

What is corroborated by his nurse is that later, when given the chance to end his life painlessly, he rejects the offer. While Barbara d'Orsey obeys the mythical model and leaves him for another good-looking hero from the 'colonies,' the dashing 'Lieutenant-Colonel Albert Rittenhouse – an Australian who had won much praise and two decorations for valour at Gallipoli' (189) – Juliet takes care of him until he dies. The gravestone inscription devised by Juliet unites him with the four elements, 'EARTH AND AIR AND FIRE AND WATER' (190).

The epilogue of the novel presents Robert in a photograph holding 'the skull of some small beast – either a rabbit or a badger' (190): a new version of the old *et in Arcadia ego* theme. A quotation by a – probably fictional[19] – author reinforces the importance of the experience of death. It seems to address the reader or researcher directly:

> Then you remember something written long after Robert Ross was dead. It was written during another war – in 1943 – by the Irish essayist and critic Nicholas Fagan. This is what he wrote: *'the spaces between the perceiver and the thing perceived can ... be closed with a shout of recognition. One form of a shout is a shot. Nothing so completely verifies our perception of a thing as our killing of it.'* (190–1)

This quotation (which may be invented like most of the documentary material used here) also widens the scope of the novel so as to include other wars. But, seen from Robert Ross's point of view, which was all in favour of life, especially of animal life, this quotation – which almost works as a caption to the photograph of Robert and the skull – is wrong, if not bitterly ironic. What Robert had wanted to establish was peaceful coexistence of human being and animal, certainly not verification that equals extermination. We have already seen that photographs can be integrated into a parodic perspective in family histories, and, of course, archivists can do the same thing when they establish connections between one 'archaeological' find and another.

At the end of Findley's idiosyncratic and humane view of 'The Wars,' the narrator observes the archivist closing her book, but a last document is to be seen, and it is not a public, historical one: it is a private photograph, as it shows Rowena, who was always hidden away from the public eye, and it shows life: 'Look! you can see our breath!' (191). What overcomes the destruction of war is the personal caring for other living beings.

In her elaborate analysis of the 'narrative stances' in *The Wars*, Simone Vauthier differentiates between the novel's first-person narrator (her *I-narrator*), a historian who addresses an anonymous researcher as well as his readers, and an impersonal narrator present in the overall narrative. Behind the scenes she posits the existence of a *scriptor*, an 'authority superior to both narrators,' who arranges and numbers the sections of the novel in 'gestures of appropriation.'[20] She compares his method of taking bits and pieces of information and rearranging them into something new to that of Lévi-Strauss's *bricoleur*, but of course it is also that of the parodist.

There is no doubt that *The Wars* is a novel dealing with the private life of Robert Ross and the response of this sensitive young man to the Great War. But in the context of this study, it should first and foremost be seen as a historical novel about the inhumanities of war and the casualties it inflicts on human beings and nature, as a novel, too, which 'implicitly claims that it illuminates the past better than history' by showing how life (human and animal) is really affected. As the references to Paul Fussell's *The Great War and Modern Memory* have shown, it exemplifies and integrates into itself many of the outstanding features of First World War literature. Sister M.L. McKenzie, in her essay 'Memories of the Great War: Graves, Sassoon, and Findley,' illustrates to what extent Findley follows the model set by these English war poets, whose names have already been mentioned by Lady Juliet. In fact, in the early manuscripts of *The Wars* Findley mentions Robert Graves's *Goodbye to All That* as one of the models on which his writing is based.[21]

By imitating texts like this one and by integrating their features into a Canadian perspective – in short, by parodying them from a Canadian point of view – *The Wars* becomes a moving document – albeit a fictional one – of Canadian participation in the Great War and also of rising Canadian nationhood. The Canadian point of view was already present in some of Findley's material: among the sources that he lists are wartime letters from his uncle and a book written by one of his fellow soldiers, Raymond Massey's *When I Was Young*. By integrating these materials into his narrative, Findley shows us to what extent war memories are subjected to the same 'literary' forces of remembrance, conventionalization, and mythologization as other memories that are written down in order to be transmitted to later generations.

Sister McKenzie's analysis of novels of the Great War also justifies the reading of Findley's novel as parodic. She speaks of 'Findley's debt to the tradition that Graves and Sassoon helped to initiate,' and also of 'his own contribution to that tradition,' of the way 'Findley adapted these motifs to his own fictional purposes,' thus of repetition with a difference. Robert's companionship with animals mentioned at the beginning of this chapter may be based – as she points out – on Robert Graves's 'own sympathy for animals in the midst of war.' But it is also the intensity of this companionship that turns Findley's text into a repetition with a difference: the North American coyote does not have its counterpart in European literature and mythology. Thus, McKenzie claims,

> the coyote is perhaps the best indicator of an important difference between Findley's novel and the earlier accounts. While the animal

world is a cherished reminder of a past that is lamented by Graves and Sassoon, the figure of the coyote brings into play the reader's hopes and fears for the future ... The strong link between Robert, the preserver of horses, and the coyote, adapter and deft pupil of his own experience, encourages us to conclude that the novel's view of the future is more optimistic than the author's gloomy musings in the interview might otherwise suggest.[22]

As writers such as Timothy Findley obviously cannot have first-hand experience of the Great War, all documents that they can work with have to be dealt with in the same manner as any other textual material: 'by purely literary means, means which necessarily transform the war into a "subject" and simplify its motifs into myths and figures expressive of the modern existential predicament. These writers provide for the "post-modern" sensibility a telling example of the way the present influences the past.'[23] Simone Vauthier shows how and why Findley, as such an author with a 'post-modern sensibility,' influenced by his contemporary environment, rewrites a traditional war story from an unusual point of view, which gives him a new perspective on aspects of warfare that are not generally mentioned in politically oriented histories: 'History excludes what is extrasystemic in relation to a given system of interpretation, i.e. of values. Just as the military account of the tragedy could not but leave out much that was important, so the dominant narrative concerned with Canadians in World War I naturally tended to suppress the disturbing memory of an aberrant violence which followed neither the approved channels of patriotic murder nor the customary ways of resistance to "the wars." '[24] There are, Vauthier suggests, other forces behind historical movements than those acknowledged.

Although modernist poets such as T.S. Eliot and Ezra Pound wrote their masterpieces in the aftermath of the Great War, their cosmologies could still be held together through the parodic rather than straightforward use of myths, especially in the case of Eliot's 'mythical method.'[25] While this mythical method worked for these 'modernist' writers whom Findley parodies, it no longer works in the world of his own narrator and scriptor, who has to combine the elements of various Greek myths (of the phoenix and Dionysus) into yet another parody.

Parody as the re-working of a genre, or parody as the rereading of history, is the technique employed by Timothy Findley in this novel. The traditional war novel is repeated not only with a difference but certainly with a vengeance.

In a remark that seems prophetic if we consider Timothy Findley's subsequent writing of *The Wars* and *Famous Last Words*, Paul Fussell comments on the literary tradition that First World War writers could fall back on in their search for models. For us, '... the literary scene is hard to imagine. There was no *Waste Land*, with its rats' alleys, dull canals, and dead men who have lost their bones: it would take four years of trench warfare to bring these to consciousness. There was no *Ulysses*, no *Mauberley*, no *Cantos*, no Kafka, no Proust, no Waugh, no Auden, no Huxley, no Cummings, no *Women in Love* or *Lady Chatterley's Lover* ...'[26] As if to respond to Fussell's comment and to show how at least one of the works mentioned has influenced the contemporary perspective on 'The Wars,' Findley's book on the Second World War, *Famous Last Words*, is Hugh Selwyn Mauberley's report on an international Fascist conspiracy before and during the Second World War, or – more precisely – it is his version of events as it is read by two American soldiers. *Famous Last Words* is not Findley's first novel to refer to Nazi Germany: in *The Butterfly Plague* he had already described some aspects of the Nazi regime, including its attractiveness for some Americans. Like *The Wars* and most of the other Findley novels, *Famous Last Words* gives its readers an unusual perspective on the action portrayed. While *The Wars* had focused on the cruelties of the First World War and their effect on a young Canadian, in his later *Not Wanted on the Voyage*, Findley's main interest changes from recent history to the mythological story of Noah's ark, but once again as seen from a new, now feminist, point of view. In a sense, Findley here takes up the tendencies that existed already in the transcripts in *The Wars*, because Simone Vauthier identifies yet another – and, in terms of this study, parodic – strand in the narrative of *The Wars*: while the narrator represents the perspective of a younger generation, the two women interviewed bring in a female point of view, a perspective that is often neglected in writing about war: '... they can re-define Robert Ross's gesture and through their combined (re)telling, make available to the present day its positive affirmation within negation.'[27]

Famous Last Words is the most disturbing of Findley's novels, as it so clearly mixes the spheres of literature and history, rewriting history and the writing of history as we know it. The name of Robert Ross in *The Wars* may well have been chosen to remind us of Oscar Wilde's Canadian homosexual lover, but this kind of knowledge is not necessary for an understanding of the novel as parody. The mixing of fact and fiction – what Simone Vauthier, speaking about *The Wars*, calls '(the fictional use of) the non-fictional'[28] – reaches a new quality in

Famous Last Words. It becomes nowhere so obvious as when Ezra Pound and Hugh Selwyn Mauberley discuss politics together. And whereas the subsumption of old stories and the arrangement of parodic layers had still been relatively easy to detect in *The Wars*, *Famous Last Words* leaves many more structural and thematic questions open than the novels treated so far, although at first sight it seems to make things easy again by filtering everything through the single perspective of Mauberley's writing. Findley, on the one hand, clearly goes back to 'scientific' historical sources and writes a novel that resembles a history book with a popular appeal, while on the other hand he makes it blatantly obvious that *Famous Last Words* is everything but such a history book. While *The Wars*, however false and unreliable its 'documents' were, delivered a picture of history that did justice to the general historical development, *Famous Last Words* is more radically revisionist.

Because it integrates elements of both factual history and the world of fiction, *Famous Last Words* – following the example of *The Wars* and radically surpassing it – parodies two different types of writing. While it has always been permitted in historical fiction to invent characters and let them interact with real-life politicians and statesmen, Findley's Mauberley is a new and special case because he, although never having existed, has become a mythical figure who evokes the leading representatives of literary modernism, especially, of course, his original creator, Ezra Pound: Hugh Selwyn Mauberley as a myth is a *fictional fact*[29] more tangible than many real persons may ever have been. The mythical figures in *The Wars* had only served as a backdrop, but here the mythical persona through whom everything is (or, rather, seems to be) seen in the novel differs from other figures who were invented by their authors only to reflect a certain point of view in a certain literary work. Findley here perfects a technique that Marie Vautier sees at the centre of the fiction written by other Canadian novelists such as Jacques Godbout and Rudy Wiebe:

> While commenting upon two important historical and political events, the narrators of both novels [*Les Têtes à Papineau* and *The Scorched-Wood People*] are working *within* a given mythological system and *working out* a new mythological system. The act of myth-making is central to their texts: they self-consciously blend fiction and history to create or recreate myth. The textual flaunting of historical allusions and ahistorical illusions, however, goes one step further: the narrators present *themselves*, as well as their texts, as a mixture of fictional elements and historical personnages [sic].[30]

Narrators such as Swift's Gulliver and Grove's Wawa-quee, both mentioned above, were similarly created with the express purpose of allowing their creators to shed some oblique light on their own societies. Beyond being incorporated into *Famous Last Words* for such direct purposes, Mauberley also brings along with him into the new work a whole range of intertextual and mythical associations. These intertextual relations can be exploited and to a certain extent modified, but intertextual characters and plot elements also live lives of their own, which – while still under the control of the writer – can no longer be reduced to what they were in the original sources. As Coral Ann Howells puts it in her excellent essay on Findley's historical novels, 'they are fictions that rewrite history in order to give significance to past events by creating patterns which reveal essential truths about human nature that can only be distilled through time and presented through art.'[31]

In *Famous Last Words*, Ezra Pound's Mauberley is a decadent and disillusioned would-be artist mostly known for the film (a parody?) *Stone Dogs* based on one of his novels. He is involved (so at least he claims in his 'famous last words' engraved on the walls of an Austrian hotel) in a worldwide conspiracy – or *cabal*, as he calls it – of business and society leaders with pro-Fascist leanings, who want to form a totalitarian Europe without condoning Hitler's excesses. The Duke and Duchess of Windsor, that is, the former King Edward VIII of England and his American-born wife, Wallis, were – knowingly or unknowingly – at the centre of these plans.

As the novel *Famous Last Words* integrates much factual information into its re-working of historiography, my interpretation will first combine a short summary with the analysis of such parodic integration of non-fictional models; that is, it will not stress the use of fictional and invented documents. Later, the parodic reaction to literary models, especially Pound's *Hugh Selwyn Mauberley*, will come into focus. Taking into account some of the non-fictional works about the main 'real' characters in *Famous Last Words*, such as the Duchess of Windsor's *The Heart Has Its Reasons*, her husband's *A King's Story*, Walter Schellenberg's memoirs, or Frances Donaldson's *Edward VIII*,[32] one is first of all struck by the factuality of much of the contents of Findley's work. The story of King Edward VIII's abdication for Wallis Simpson is generally known and can be verified in many different sources. The inclusion of episodes set in China in the 1920s is 'justified' by the fact that Wallis Simpson spent some time in Shanghai and Peking in the early 1920s, meeting some of the leading Italian Fascists there. Most

of the novel's principal characters are drawn from real life: Hess, Ribbentrop, Schellenberg, Ciano, Churchill, Pound, Oakes, Christie, Bedaux. Many of the actions reported really took place: King Edward VIII
sailed on the *Nahlin*; after his abdication, he visited Nazi Germany;
he and his wife went to Spain and Portugal before being persuaded
to accept their posting on the Bahamas.

Some of the most improbable and seemingly fictionalized incidents
in *Famous Last Words* stem directly from the author's ostensibly non-
fictional sources. In these historical, biographical, and autobiographical
works, several elements are to be found that are just waiting to be
woven into the plot of an international conspiracy. For example, the
duke and duchess's pro-German tendencies and their acquaintance
with leading Fascists were well known: in his recent book, *The Duchess
of Windsor*, Charles Higham even claims that 'it was widely believed
... that Wallis was by now [1936] having an affair with Ribbentrop and
that he was paying her directly from German funds in Berlin to influence – as if that were necessary – the king.'[33] The Duchess of Windsor
herself points out that Churchill was afraid – and if Higham's information is true, rightly so – that her husband might be abducted from
Portugal by the Germans and put back on the English throne as an
English counterpart of Quisling or Pétain. As for the duke's thoughts,
she mentions that 'it is David's conjecture that the Germans were behind the Spanish Government's offer; that they had in some way learned
of, or suspected, the dispute between him and Churchill; that they
hoped in some way to exploit his mood of dissatisfaction.'[34] That sus-
picions such as Churchill's can be integrated into historical visions that
seem almost as fantastical – if not more so – as Findley's is proved by
sensationalist 'non-fictional' works published both before and after
Famous Last Words; in the latter category are such works as Peter Allen's
The Crown and the Swastika and Charles Higham's biography of the
Duchess of Windsor.[35]

The new perspective from which Findley, or rather his narrator, sees
the story of the Duke and the Duchess of Windsor serves the integration
into a coherent whole of many so far inexplicable incidents and occurrences lifted from historical sources. Even events that did not seem
to have anything to do with Edward and Wallis's role in the cabal –
such as the murder of Harry Oakes, which according to Findley was
the original nucleus of the novel – are irresistibly drawn into the net
of the Penelope conspiracy, as is the anti-Fascist demonstration of a
young Italian poet, which – to abide by the 'facts' – had taken place
a decade earlier.[36] In this latter case, the inclusion of a 'real' character

into the action serves in fact to undermine the claim of the novel to be a 'real' historical fiction.

It is Hugh Selwyn Mauberley who claims that all the incidents that he writes down on the walls of the Grand Elysium Hotel in the Tyrolean UnterBalkonberg belong together and form parts of the one great cabal. He becomes the archaeologist of his own past, the historian highlighting certain elements, suppressing others. Mauberley is one of the few characters in the novel whose existence is obviously fictional. All the information that the reader gets from the walls is his (as long as we are willing to accept that no subsequent reader, neither the apologetic Lieutenant Quinn nor the adversarial Captain Freyberg, has tampered with the 'facts'). Mauberley has imposed the narrative perspective on the events, but he also claims that he is only an ignorant lowly member of the cabal, and that even politicians of Ribbentrop's calibre were not yet at the top echelon of the conspiracy. Still, the perspective he imposes on history is much more coherent than that achieved by the scriptor of *The Wars*. And as David Williams mentions, he seemingly draws all other narratorial instances (except for Freyberg) into his plot: 'Now, narratively speaking, Mauberley himself must be the whole cabal, since he is the only one who knows everything that is going on.'[37]

The only certainty we have about Mauberley is that – literally and literarily speaking – he is a creation of Ezra Pound; in fact, one who is now surrounded by an almost mythical aura. And in the writing that Mauberley leaves behind, he tries to enhance this aura: the second of his epigraphs that Quinn discovers represents an existential truth in addition to being a tongue-in-cheek comment of an artist on his own work of art:

> ... a sentence scrawled outside the disciplined alignment of the others and set there like a bear trap to catch the reader unaware.
> 'All I have written here,' Quinn read, 'is true: except the lies.'[38]

It is not surprising that a novel dealing with the attractiveness of Fascism for leading figures, especially in American society, has as its protagonist a character created by Ezra Pound, who himself is the most notorious American writer to have come under the spell of the totalitarian regimes in Europe. In addition to also being a character in the novel, Pound becomes important on a parodic level, because it is his literary work that is used as a model parodied in order to provide Findley's novel with a structural underpinning. Mauberley, the American expatriate novelist, who dabbled in aestheticist poetry but never wrote the true work of art that was in him, now finally writes a text that shows something that the aestheticist poetry he produced in London (and his two novels that were quite successful otherwise) could not: human concern. And 'so after years of silence, Mauberley was a writer at the last' (58).

While the order of the sections in *The Wars* seemed more or less arbitrary, so that the reader accompanied the researcher in the *process* of writing, and while no clearly dominant voice was discernible, the events depicted in Mauberley's 'fresco' are printed in the order that they (the *product* of Mauberley's memory or fancy) are read by Quinn, one of the American soldiers who discover his mangled corpse in the Grand Elysium Hotel at the end of the Second World War. This demolitions expert is an intellectual who had admired Mauberley's writing even before being confronted with his famous last words and who is thrilled by this last literary (?) production of his idol. Originally, these events seem to have been written down in their chronological order, dating back to 1924, but even though the connection between the events depicted is not necessarily obvious to the reader from the beginning, Mauberley has clearly chosen them for a purpose: generally, they show him in contact with other members of the cabal known under the code-name Penelope; sometimes, however, he writes about goings-on between other members, and one wonders from whom he, the supposedly lowly member of the group, would have got this kind of information. As Mauberley had said, 'All I have written here is true; except the lies,' and so the description of conversations between the Duke and the Duchess of Windsor may be based on inside information or just pure imagination. The same goes for meetings between German Nazis such as Schellenberg, later to be the head of Hitler's intelligence service, and the Reich's foreign minister, Ribbentrop (e.g., 380–2), the latter of whom clearly is a member of Penelope, and the former of whom may be one, if he has not taken over the whole doomed organization in a way similar to the one in which Mauberley has taken over narratorial control of the novel itself.

The text that the reader may or may not believe to be a true transcript of the writing on the wall is commented upon by Quinn and Freyberg, the American soldiers. Quinn, the artistically interested intellectual, reads it as the last and monumental statement of a great writer gone astray, whereas Freyberg is doubtful about its veracity and reads it with the distance of a historian looking for proof and documentation. However, whereas Quinn 'does not distinguish what may or may not be taken at face value'[39] and thus is willing to let himself be persuaded or convinced of Mauberley's innocence of Nazi crimes, Freyberg – aware of the danger of apologetic writing – has in fact prejudged the writer and is reading the text only for corroborating evidence. Thus neither of them will be able to abstract an unbiased view from the material: probably no unbiased history can be written about these times; at least not by any 'historian' presented in the novel. We see, too, that a parody of historical documents can be accepted by some readers and rejected by others.

Quinn and Freyberg's discovery and reading of the writing on the wall takes place after Mauberley's death and is obviously part of the text that is not filtered through Mauberley's perspective. Thus the existence of an omniscient narrator must be posited, a narrator whose reliability is of course as uncertain as Mauberley's or, for that matter, that of the narrative voice in *The Wars*.[40] This omniscient narrator provides the frame of the story, starting with a prologue entitled '1910' (1–2), which shows the suicide of Mauberley's father, who leaps off the roof of the Arlington Hotel in Boston. Mauberley, the only witness, is forever marked by the experience and is convinced that this suicide was a purposeful act: ' "*He who jumps to his death has cause*," [a message addressed to him by his father] said. "*He who leaps has purpose. Always remember: I leapt*" ' (2).

The main part of the novel consists of eight parts grouped around sections of Mauberley's text as they are read by Quinn and as they take the reader from 1924 to 1945 and from China to London, Berlin, Paris, the Mediterranean, and the Bahamas. While Quinn's reading of Mauberley's epigraph from the Book of Daniel is included in the omnisciently told part 2, starting with part 3 the sections written by Mauberley are typographically set apart from the 'omniscient' narratorial text. At the end of part 8, after Mauberley has finished the history of the conspiracy named Penelope, the omniscient voice takes over again, showing how Mauberley is killed by the Nazi and/or Penelope henchman Harry Reinhardt and how Freyberg's version of history that focuses on the Nazis' guilt is already – in May 1945 – replaced by a postwar anti-Communism that is no longer interested in discovering Nazi crimes and connections. The novel ends with Quinn's reading and dating Mauberley's epilogue:

Thus, whatever rose towards the light is left to sink unnamed: a shape that passes slowly through a dream. Waking, all we remember is the awesome presence, while a shadow lying dormant in the twilight whispers from the other side of reason; I am here. I wait. (396)

The history that is written but not read lives on as a trace at best, left to be written about by poets and novelists, not by historians.

The fact that Quinn dates the epilogue suggests that he sympathizes – if only for aesthetic reasons – with Mauberley's interpretation of history: this document, which was seen only by a handful of American soldiers, will 'sink unnamed' and be forgotten as if it had never existed. But what we are left with is the uncanny feeling of having witnessed evil. Quinn's narrative frame has been sucked into Mauberley's, which it was meant to contain. On the one hand, he has accepted Mauberley's point of view and, by dating or practically signing it, parodically integrated it into his own perspective. On the other hand, Mauberley seems to foresee and parody in advance any future reader's (in this case, Quinn's) attempts at justifying his ways by integrating that reader into his version of events, making him 'a belated, if inadvertent, member of Mauberley's narrative cabal.'[41]

Dennis Duffy distinguishes between three streams of narrative in the novel, two of which coincide with those identified above: 'Mauberley's wall diary; the account of Mauberley's earlier life and the activities of Quinn and Freyberg after his death; scenes appearing alongside the diary passages but which Mauberley could never have known or witnessed.' There can be no objection to the first two levels of narrative mentioned, and a lot speaks in favour of an omniscient narrator in charge of those 'scenes appearing alongside the diary passages.' If we are looking for a coherent reading of the novel and do not want to postulate the existence of 'an invisible creator convey[ing] implicitly a sense of himself as the unmoved mover behind the briefer narrative of Mauberley,' these scenes become a problem, because they seem to lead us back to a looser structure reminiscent of *The Wars*, in which not every section could be allocated a narrator. But such a reading would be too dependent on strategies of writing that are based on literary realism, a mode that Findley – and many modernists before him – have long left behind. Seeing that most of these passages take place well before Mauberley's death in May 1945, and taking into account Mauberley's not necessarily reliable perspective, one might interpret these scenes as unintentional hints on Mauberley's part at his much deeper involvement in the cabal. Furthermore, as E.F. Shields points out, 'rather than succeeding in spite of the inconsistencies in point of view, *Famous Last Words* in good part succeeds because of them.' Dominick LaCapra would presumably welcome the difficulties that the novel offers its interpreters, for he claims 'that one way a novel makes challenging contact with "reality" and "history" is precisely by resisting fully concordant narrative closure ...'[42]

While Mauberley's ambition was 'to describe the beautiful,' Dorothy Pound had discovered with her husband by the end of the Second World War that 'down went all the old necessities for literature; all the old prescriptions for use of the written word; all the old traditions of order and articulation fading under the roar of bombast and rhetoric' (5). For this reason, Pound had replaced literature with pro-Fascist propaganda, leaving poetry behind for politics. But propaganda is not the only form of writing that can become important, even deadly, as Mauberley is soon to find out. Making his way through Italy to the relative safety of the Austrian border, he is hunted by the Nazi agent Estrade, who wants to get hold of 'his notebooks, his years and years of jottings and annotations' drawn from his 'privileged relationships with people whose lives could now be ruined': 'The woman in the moleskin coat wanted not only to kill him; she wanted to kill his words as well' (21).

Estrade, though, has not been able to get hold of the notes which, in whatever form – embellished, rewritten, or revised – have been turned into Mauberley's fresco, which is introduced by the arguably most famous epigraph to ever have foreshadowed doom, the quotation from the Book of Daniel (5.5): 'In the same hour came forth fingers of a man's hand, and wrote over against the candlestick upon the plaister of the wall of the king's palace ...' This quotation (52) sets the tone for Mauberley's text, and the ensuing biblical words of judgment – 'MENE, MENE, TEKEL, UPHARSIN' (Daniel 5.25) – are written into the sky and into Mauberley's text by the young Italian poet whom Findley has transplanted from 1931 Fascist Italy to 1941 Nassau (ironically the date is 4 July). With the biblical motto 'Thou art weighed in the balances, and art found wanting' (Daniel 5.27) in mind, one does not necessarily have to agree with Captain Freyberg that 'this ... whatever story it tells, will end with an apology' (54). Nevertheless, at the outset Quinn is 'absolutely certain he would exonerate Hugh Selwyn Mauberley' (58).

Starting with his biblical epigraph, Mauberley has emplotted his story in a certain way: putting himself in the tradition of a biblical prophet is a way of shunning all responsibility for what one may have brought about; but emplotment, the manipulation of historical data so as to make them fit a certain interpretation, is also a parodic strategy – another repetition with a difference. Furthermore, the biblical overtones and the surroundings of the *Nahlin* cruise in the Mediterranean

tempt Mauberley to instil even more literary elements into his emplotment of chronologically arranged historical data so as to arrive at
'the coherence of myth' and finally at an 'interpenetration of fiction
and fact, history and mythology.'[43] Mauberley is arguably more adept
at this than Juliet d'Orsey had been in *The Wars*:

> And yet I liked this coast – its legendary cast. This place was once *Il-
> lyria*, Lady. *Mythic*. Well chosen for the king in hand, since this was
> where they had deified Pan. Well chosen, too, for my sake, I thought
> – since somewhere south of Dubrovnik was the cave where Cadmus
> had been transformed into a serpent (dragon?) who was made the
> guardian of myth and literature.... Folklore had it that Cadmus was
> the Phoenix, or a sort of lizard-Lazarus, rising from the flames of
> some forgotten human rebellion; an assurance that, in spite of fire, the
> word would be preserved. And it was then I decided what my dis-
> guise might be for that incognito rendezvous. I should play the ser-
> pent's part. (62)

In the end, Mauberley dies, and doubts are in order as to whether he
(or even only his message) will be reborn from the ashes of the Second
World War. Anyway, Mauberley supposedly writes – or rewrites? –
this text in 1945, and so this may well be an *ex-post facto* mythification,
especially since he – or rather his creator – seems to have read Frances
Donaldson's 1974 remarks on the *Nahlin* journey: 'For this journey
was the beginning of what would so shortly be the end, the point at
which every historian writing of the Abdication must inevitably start.'[44]

But even by the time about which he writes here, he has become
aware of the existence of the international conspiracy, and Isabella
Loverso has called him '*one of us*' (93). Talking about the 'mythical
couple' of 'the golden king' and his lover, he remarks, 'This was the
new mythology, I thought. Homer might have written it' (63). Findley
here uses his own 'mythical method' in having Mauberley structure
his narrative according to Homeric myth. In an interview, he himself
says:

> I'm interested in icons. It is the repose of an icon that interests me.
> Somewhere in *Famous Last Words* there is a moment where a character
> says that if this were the Trojan War you would choose your icons
> this way. And that's what Mauberley is doing. He's saying that if this
> is the Trojan War, 'Who is Helen?' Okay, it's Wallis Simpson ... Now,
> a lot of people no longer recognize Wallis Simpson as being as power-

ful as she actually was. They think, 'What a silly creature to have chosen!' But, ironically, Wallis Simpson was one of the great icons of that age, without any question, and there is no question she pulled together the focus of what was going on in Britain.[45]

The first longer excerpt from the fresco that Quinn reads – 'Dubrovnik: August 17th, 1936' (60–4) – thus already points to the various levels of parodic emplotment that can be identified in the novel: on one level, we have Mauberley emplotting his own life so that it becomes an apology (in Freyberg's reading) or an exoneration (in Quinn's reading); on a second level, there are Quinn and Freyberg in the act of interpreting this material; and on a third level – which is in fact the deepest-reaching one – there is the author rearranging the historical 'facts' according to his artistic plans. This combining of historical events with the fictional character of Mauberley still reflects the model of the narrative situation of a Scottian or Lukácsian historical novel: although the hero is drawn into the main historical process – he receives a telegram from Wallis Simpson, his former lover and now the lover of the English king, inviting him to join the two on their cruise – he remains at the margin of the important political decisions. Soon, however, his parodic integration will become much deeper.

The second excerpt that the readers come across in the Grand Elysium Hotel – 'China: August, 1924' (66–76) – deals with Mauberley's 1924 love affair with Wallis in Shanghai, the Eastern city that stands for the uprootedness of post–First World War Western societies and for the lost generation: 'in this microcosmic hell the age I lived in was being defined ...' (68). The excerpt provides us with an intriguing free variation on certain bits of information about Wallis's obscure activities in the Orient. Was she a spy or a whore? Was she involved in drug peddling or politics?

After the report on Mauberley's relationship with Wallis in China there is a twelve-year gap in the chronology of Mauberley's text before he writes about a 1936 visit with the Pounds in Rapallo (77–83), during which Pound's reaction to the German re-occupation of the Rhineland and the general political evolution of Europe are summed up in one sentence: 'Let them march and make their wars and get it over with ... Then we can finally come to the only subject that matters: *money*' (79). Mauberley denies Pound his originality, claiming that he is an 'intellectual poacher' (80), but Pound's poaching would be just another instance of parodic thinking. Wrong-headed as Mauberley's former mentor may be, he knows about the power inherent in writing, even in Mauberley's: 'You done pretty well with your words,' he remarks. 'Seems to me I've seen a few corpses floating in your wake from time to time' (82).

In the next excerpt, set first in Venice (84–94), presumably fictional English friends criticize Mauberley for his pro-Fascist views, but Isabella Loverso, widow of a former associate of Mussolini's, informs him of the existence of 'friends with whom I think you should speak' (93) and thus opens the world of the Fascist, but probably anti-Hitler, cabal to him. Now Quinn has caught up in his reading with the events leading to the invitation to join the royal couple at Dubrovnik, so that from now on almost all entries are read, with some exceptions, as they were supposedly written by Mauberley, that is, in their chronological order. Mauberley describes his meeting Edward VIII and Wallis and then goes on to depict – from an omniscient perspective that he should not have – a most intimate scene between Edward and his mother, Queen Mary, that involves a dressmaker's dummy representing 'the Queen' (103).

The next section Mauberley finds worthy of inclusion in his version of history is Wallis's Paris meeting with her husband, Ernest Simpson, during which she asks him to agree to their divorce, which will free her to marry the king (106–8). Mauberley once again plays a role subservient to the real actors: as when he had qualified his own relationship to Wallis as 'the way dogs have of loving the feet at which they lie' (64), he again uses a canine metaphor in order to describe himself in relation to her (106).[46] In Mauberley's view, Wallis finds out for the first time that there may be large stumbling blocks in her way. When Simpson tells her that his only reason for not suing her is that 'the law does not allow [him] to name the King as co-respondent,' she has to admit to herself that 'history might have aces up its sleeve' (107).

Mauberley's description of a meeting between his former friend Edward Allenby, the fictional parliamentary under-secretary of state for foreign affairs,[47] and Charles Lindbergh (108–21) is once again based on facts insofar as Lindbergh did indeed visit England during Edward's reign. These facts are then emplotted in such a way as to turn Lindbergh, who had been the Nazis' guest at the Berlin Olympics, into an agent of the cabal who wants to convince Allenby to join Hess and Ribbentrop in the conspiracy: ' "There's more at stake than England," he said. "And more at stake than Germany." For the first time, he looked directly into Allenby's eyes. "And more at stake than America" ' (114).

In Paris (121–56) Mauberley is meanwhile reeling from Julia Franklin's devastating criticism in the *New York Times* under the title 'HUGH SELWYN MAUBERLEY: OUT OF KEY WITH HIS TIME' (128). This is the first time that a direct quotation from Pound's *Hugh Selwyn Mauberley* is parodically integrated into the text. Although he is shocked, Mauberley has to admit that 'very much of it was true' (129). Unbeknownst to the intellectuals, he rises in the ranks of the cabal: Isabella Loverso introduces him to Charles Bedaux, the American businessman with close Nazi connections, in whose château Wallis and Edward finally get married. The American wants Mauberley, Wallis's old and trusted friend, to draw her (and her future husband) into the cabal: 'And that is where you come into the story' (139).[48]

This is the moment when the frames of narrative clearly lose their distinctness because we recognize that Hugh Selwyn Mauberley knows much more than a lowly member of the cabal would be expected to know. He goes to Cannes and on his way is photographed in his Daimler as 'what appeared to be the late King Edward VIII riding in the back seat. In fact it was nothing more than his picture, blown up to cover the entire front page of *Le Monde*. Smiling' (143). Mauberley here gets caught in an obvious blunder in his emplotment, as *Le Monde*, in addition to never having photographs on its front page,[49] was founded as late as 1944 and thus did not even exist in 1936. The attempt at increasing the respectability of his plot by making reference to a well-respected newspaper fails. We may even interpret this anachronism as another marker of parody, like the young Italian pilot mentioned above, reminding us that emplotment is always possible and that no text is trustworthy.

Mauberley asks Wallis to overcome the momentary hate she feels for Edward, who – by abdicating for her – has deprived her of the chance of ever becoming a queen, and he convinces her to marry him anyway: 'There is nothing now that is impossible. Only so long as you marry the King' (144). While she is more or less aware of the cabal, according to Mauberley 'the Duke in no way knew of the other forces at work around him' (147). He still thought that he was dealing with Hitler only. To Quinn, however, '... now it was clear that a force more potent than the fleeting Nazi forces of that moment had been involved in using him – and through it was clear both Bedaux and von Ribbentrop had pulled the strings for whatever that potent force had been – and *was* – someone, too, was pulling *their* strings. And the reach of the cabal was becoming truly alarming – precisely because its edges could not be seen' (148). Quinn is relieved, though, that 'Mauberley's only role had been to play the messenger.' Still, Mauberley is also the narrator of what he has intentionally emplotted as a myth, and Quinn correctly states that 'mythology can have two meanings, that's all. I mean ... I mean – *The Iliad, The Odyssey* ... I mean ... there *was* a Trojan War. The Trojan War did happen' (150). What we know and remember of the Trojan War today, though, is not the war that happened, but rather the war as it is depicted in Homer's epics.

In his discussions with Freyberg, Quinn sticks to his position that Mauberley's version is truthful (*'Tell* the truth. About himself. Including the mistakes he made' [154]), but Freyberg continues to insist that what Quinn does is 'whitewash' Mauberley's past. The position of the readers is of prime importance in the interpretation of historical documents, and this is especially so when these texts are not documents proper but memoirs written with all kinds of personal motivations in mind. Freyberg formulates the dilemma of the readers succinctly: ' "... Like you said, the story's only half been told ... By the way – I'm assuming you mean we've only just *read* half: not that he's only told us half" ' (155).

At the beginning of part 4, Isabella Loverso tells Mauberley what she thinks about historical myths and legends such as Mussolini's famous *March on Rome*: 'It is all a legend, you see? A story – though people who were there and *saw* him riding *tell* you that he walked ...' (160). She, too, has started weaving herself into a mythical story, referring to herself as 'the spoils of war' (162) and inviting Mauberley's comment: 'Andromache.' She, too, knows about the power of written texts, as her murdered husband had been a poet who became proof 'that mere human beings can be so afraid of the written word they will kill to be rid of it' (166).

In Madrid in 1940 (176–86), Mauberley finds a live example of a people rewriting its history and trying to find a suitable method of emplotment: 'My suspicion was they had not yet decided how to tell their stories: how to relate what had befallen them' (176). Here he also rejoins the Duke and Duchess of Windsor. With a quite tumultuous past behind them, they have found ways of reshaping their personal histories:

> One night, Wallis told the story of her life and left out China. I was very hurt. Then the Duke told the story of his life and left out having abdicated. Wallis was very pleased. Nonetheless these stories told the temper of the times and the motto we had adopted: *the truth is in our hands now.* (177)

This motto might of course be that of Mauberley's complete writings on the wall and of Findley's book as a whole. Judging by what Frances Donaldson has to say about the duke's 'small adjustments to the past which render his version of it unreliable,'[50] it is also true of the real-life duke in his postwar French exile.

In Madrid, at a party, Mauberley overhears Ribbentrop and the Windsors and finally realizes that the cabal to replace the Fascist leaders with the duke and the duchess is the outcome of words he had written himself without being aware of their power. He had called for *a new kind of leader ... whose very presence makes us rise'* (180). It is his cabal after all, or maybe a parody of it. He has written it into existence, and now the characters take off on their own. 'So this is history as she is never writ,' he comments, and predicting studies such as the present one, he continues, 'Some day far in the future, some dread academic, much too careful of his research, looking back through the biased glasses of a dozen other "historians," will set this moment down on paper. And will get it wrong' (180). While he has not yet taken any direct responsibilities for the actions of the cabal, Mauberley claims the credit for having come up with its name – a mythical one, of course – *Penelope* (182).

In the following sections, Mauberley once again relates events at which he obviously was not present. The short excerpt entitled 'Berlin: July, 1940' (186–7) shows the SS agent Walter Schellenberg setting out from Berlin to 'kidnap the Duke and Duchess of Windsor and bring them back into Spain' (187). Schellenberg, in this version, is certain that he is fulfilling a task handed down from Hitler himself, a task the fulfilment of which will increase his and his boss Himmler's prestige at the expense of Ribbentrop's Foreign Office. The section on the foiled kidnapping incident in Portugal (187–217) seems to be based on historical facts so far as Schellenberg's involvement is concerned, but the abduction of the duke and duchess by British soldiers cannot be substantiated. Although somewhat unwillingly, Edward finally accepted the post of governor general on the Bahamas and agreed to leave on a boat rather unsuitably named *Excalibur*. The rumour of a kidnapping by the British intelligence service that Schellenberg had invented in order to motivate the duke to fall in with German plans seems, however, to have impressed the Windsors.[51] Mauberley turns it into a full-fledged episode, which in its turn can be used to explain some of the duke's unorthodox behaviour later on.

Frances Donaldson claims that the Schellenberg episode made it quite obvious that the Windsors could not have had close connections with the Nazis. By integrating this episode into an even larger frame, that of Penelope, Findley (or is it Mauberley?) relativizes Schellenberg's importance (for the time being) and thus disqualifies – in his fictional (?) universe – Donaldson's 'more positive evidence.'[52]

At the ensuing meeting in Berlin of Schellenberg, Estrade, and Ribbentrop (222–36), Schellenberg has to realize that in Portugal he had been playing Ribbentrop's game, too. Such an interpretation of the events in Portugal has in fact, although with a different emphasis, also been made by Peter Allen, who claims in his book *The Crown and the Swastika* – published after *Famous Last Words* – that '... Schellenberg's mission for Ribbentrop was to be something of a side-show, a bit of window-dressing for Ribbentrop's benefit, while the real business in Portugal was going on with top Nazis involved in far-reaching peace negotiations arranged by the ss/sd, of which Ribbentrop was largely unaware.'[53] Schellenberg (the character within the novel, that is) does not know that the Duke of Avila, the prospective host of the Windsors in Spain, is a member of the cabal. The German is, however, in possession of a slip of paper bearing the word *Penelope* in Wallis's hand as well as a drawing of Ribbentrop's coat of arms. This discovery causes much nervousness in the German wing of Penelope.

Describing another visit to the Pounds (255–64), Mauberley relates their reaction to Trotsky's murder, a death that foreshadows his own at the hand of Harry Reinhardt. Trotsky's notebooks were burned, another ominous parallel to the fate of Mauberley's notes, but fortunately, at first sight, the burning did not have the same consequences for Mauberley's work that it had for Trotsky's because, unbeknown to his murderer, Mauberley had copied all the information onto the walls of the Grand Hotel. In the end, however, his writing will be lost, too, because this loss proves to be politically expedient.

While Wallis's activities on the Bahamas for the Red Cross and other organizations are well documented, the *Spitfire Bazaar* (265–98) is probably Findley's invention, as are de Broca's biblical writing in the sky and the Dickensian Little Nell, who lived by the 'theory ... that you could sum up the age you lived in by reading its walls' (275).

In some events described in part 7 of *Famous Last Words*, Mauberley is personally involved, whereas in others he acts as a kind of omniscient narrator. Rudolf Hess's flight from Augsburg to Scotland took place, of course, as did his interrogation by MI5 agents. In order to tie this event into his story, Mauberley claims that one of these agents turns out to be Harry Reinhardt, who in the course of the novel acts as a henchman for Penelope and the Nazis as well as the British secret service.[54] Mauberley himself, while visiting the widow of his former friend Ned Allenby (309–16), discovers for the first time that the information contained in his notebooks may endanger private life: when she finds out about his connection with Fascist sympathizers who were responsible for her husband's death, she suggests he commit suicide. He has a more pressing duty on behalf of Penelope, though: Sir Alan Paisley, whom Hess had tried to contact in Scotland, sends him to the Bahamas to contact the Windsors in order to arrange for their return to Europe. While the cabal still seems to be working on this level, the description of its German wing (317–22) shows that Schellenberg is on the verge of dismantling or taking over Ribbentrop's organization.

In the last part of the novel, Mauberley finally cannot avoid giving up the stance of an uninvolved artist who acts only as a go-between without being actually involved in the cabal: in order to keep the Canadian millionaire Harry Oakes from finding out about the planned departure of the duke and duchess from Nassau for Europe, he orders Harry Reinhardt to kill Oakes. He realizes that by ordering a murder he abandons his stance as an observer and becomes deeply involved in shady dealings: 'Hugh Selwyn Mauberley – poet, novelist, critic, polemicist and winner of prizes, including both the Pulitzer and the Concordia – sat amongst the whores and lighted a cigarette' (359). Having killed Oakes, Reinhardt illustrates Mauberley's depravity by making him lick Oakes's blood off his hands, thus finally drawing the poet into the criminal actions involved in the cabal. The rest of the story about the Windsors' aborted return to Europe is told from a European perspective, as a discussion between Ribbentrop and Schellenberg. Schellenberg now has gained the upper hand and tells the foreign minister that Edward and Wallis are not coming to Europe because 'we have other plans, now' (380). It does not become clear whether – as Ribbentrop fears – 'Schellenberg had found the upper echelon' (381), or whether the SS had taken over the lower echelons of Penelope in order to further plans to make Himmler the new führer.

There is no happy ending to the story of Wallis and Edward as it is told by Mauberley; of course, neither is there one for Mauberley himself. He knew that Schellenberg's agents were following him, and the last thing he could hope for was to finish his text. The omniscient narrator describes his death, but the readers within the novel as well as the outside reader wonder, 'Had all the truths been told? Had everything been said?' (385). As Freyberg and Quinn find out, it does not really matter. Before we can understand the past, we have to get used to the fact that it is constantly being reinterpreted, put into new frames that make old ways of looking at things obsolete. One parody being integrated within the frame of the next, it seems impossible to arrive at any truth that is not a parody. Eugene Benson points out that the literary frames can often contribute more to a truthful picture of the past than the authorized histories or biographies. In the case of the Duke of Windsor's autobiography, for example, 'even the most casual reading of ... *A King's Story*, demonstrates that he left "most of the story out"; *Famous Last Words* puts it back in and in playing games with the evidence Findley's duke becomes more real than the duke of unedited History.'[55]

So far, it has been stated that Mauberley's voice, which claims to be marginal to the political actions involved, is the dominant one in the novel (except for that of the omniscient narrator, of course). Timothy Findley himself remarks that 'Mauberley didn't come in until about the third draft, as the unifying voice, to keep the whole thing in one voice.' According to Benson, Findley had first tried to write the novel through the perspectives of the duke and the duchess: he 'seems originally to have intended using them as personae through whom he could reach into the international capitals of Europe to explore the nature of fascism and its influence.' But finally, Findley states, having gone through five different modes of writing, 'I came upon Mauberley and realized I had found the perfect voice to narrate the story.' The only way to make the necessary connections was probably through Findley's invention of a fictional character, for – as he says – 'you can't grab from real people what you can from people whose lives have been put down in this organized way, and that is the value of the novel.'[56] Whereas other contemporary writers provide several voices in their novels, at least the writings on the wall in *Famous Last Words* are clearly dominated by this one perspective. The scriptorial scaffolding is different from that erected in *The Wars*, because here the scriptor (if he exists) is not the only element to keep the parts of the narrative together.

According to Findley, once he had discovered Mauberley's voice, clearly a purely literary influence, 'then I put in everything that Pound had put into Mauberley.' At this level, the literary work becomes as important as the historical data analysed so far, if not more important, as the underlying model to be parodied in *Famous Last Words*. Findley says that 'I was slavish to the poem sequence, to the detriment of the book, so I'm told. I wanted to get every bit of that poem in there.'[57] Far from being detrimental to the general structure of the book, this combination of non-fictional and fictional models integrated into one coherent work keeps readers on their toes questioning every 'fact' mentioned as well as every literary allusion, disorienting them insofar as they never know how to read the text and what level to emphasize in their reading.

The parodic style of *Famous Last Words* differs from that of other novels in that the literary model imitated is often not prose fiction but rather poetry. The language of poetry, depending on verbal constructs different from straightforward prose, poses several problems for the parodying novelist, as poetic constructions cannot always be easily imitated in prose; on the other hand, poetical constructs such as metaphors offer the parodist the chance of parodying them through literalization, especially when the real-life background of the Bahamas lends itself to such a technique.

Stephen Scobie contributes to the study of intertextual connections between Pound's poem and Findley's novel by pointing out that 'what distinguishes Findley's Mauberley, ultimately, from Pound's is the greater strength, thoroughness, and ... heroism of his bearing witness.' Scobie points out that the repetition of part of Pound's 'Envoi' at the beginning of the China section is 'the longest quotation from Pound's poem in Mauberley's own text,' and that the title *Stone Dogs* of Mauberley's novel refers back to a line in *Hugh Selwyn Mauberley*. The novel (within the novel) became a success in its film version (thanks to Bette Davis), but in the context of the poem such a 'prose kinema' is probably nothing more than a valueless parody (in the generally accepted sense) of real life, 'a mould in plaster, / Made with no loss of time.'[58]

Coral Ann Howells calls Findley's method of incorporating Pound's Mauberley into his own writing, of using Pound's original text as a 'catalyst' for his reinterpretation of history, 'allusive,'[59] but the term *parodic* is more adequate in the context of this study. Her identification of Findley's appropriation and literalization of Pound's metaphors is fascinating, and the following interpretation owes much to her essay ' "History as she is never writ": *The Wars* and *Famous Last Words*.' Howells has produced a solid contribution to the debate that Hulcoop had foreseen, 'as to whether Findley's Mauberley, hunted and haunted inscriber of "the ultimate graffiti" ... bears any resemblance to the fastidious fragments of Pound's imagination immortalized in the poem-persona with the unforgettable name of "Hugh Selwyn Mauberley." '[60]

Pound's *Mauberley*, the parodic foil of *Famous Last Words*, is of course a series of intertextual parodies in its own right, as critics such as John Espey, Hugh Witemeyer, Jo Brantley Berryman, and many others have shown. It is based on the *Odyssey* in a way similar to Joyce's 'parodic' use of Homer.[61] One has to admit, though, that Findley's Mauberley himself is hardly an Odysseus character: born in a Boston hotel, he does not have an ancestral home to return to, and his Penelope leads him into death.

Pound's poem also contains parodic reference to Gautier, Flaubert, Gourmont, and to many classical sources. It thus becomes a good example of what Pound himself had called 'criticism in new composition,' proving that 'every literary composition may become ... an explicit or implicit commentary upon some part of the existing literary tradition.' In addition, one can establish parodic relationships between the two parts of *Mauberley*, the second part of which 'is almost a mirror image of the first, revisiting it and sometimes quoting directly from it.'[62]

Quotations referring to English poets of the 1890s and to Pound's (Mauberley's) contemporaries in the first part return in the second part, 'Mauberley (1920),' in order to compose a picture of Hugh Selwyn Mauberley as the conventional, unimaginative, and unproductive poet of the early twentieth century. Especially the 'Envoi' section of the first part, which parodically subsumes the history of English verse, can be seen to be parodically reflected in Mauberley's 'Medallion,' in which 'the scene of the *Envoi* is rehandled with unconsciously ironic emphasis on bookish precision lacking any awareness of invitation and passion.'[63]

Since the artistic cooperation of Ezra Pound and T.S. Eliot in their writing is a well-documented fact, and since both have created long poems about artist figures, it seems quite natural to draw parallels between J. Alfred Prufrock and Hugh Selwyn Mauberley in relation to their creators. At least according to some critics, there are close parallels between Eliot's voice and that of his persona. Mauberley, on the other hand, is rather an antithetical product of Pound's imagination, however far one is willing to extend his own voice – to the detriment of Pound's – in the poem. Pound insisted, 'Of course, I'm no more Mauberley than Eliot is Prufrock.' For this reason, the existence of both Pound and Mauberley in Findley's universe and a discussion between the real Pound and his 'ironical foil' seem rather appropriate, especially in a context involving parody which can easily be interpreted not only as a technique of misprision within literary history but also as a mechanism of an author's expurgating his own earlier kinds of writing. Pound himself, for example, remarked about the first part of *Mauberley*, 'E.P. Ode pour l'Election de son Sepulchre,' that 'the worst muddle [the critics of *Mauberley*] make is in failing to see that Mauberley buries E.P. in the first poem; gets rid of all his troublesome energies.'[64]

In *Famous Last Words*, Mauberley does not bury his mentor; he is even survived by him, and as he is survived by him, it becomes clear that – as in real life and to the detriment of his political reputation – Pound overcomes that phase in his work and life in which he was like Mauberley. But although Pound survives, David Williams is certainly right in pointing out that in the poem 'Pound is the one who comes to know himself through his character's failure, while in the novel it is Mauberley who is thought to have found himself through his summing up.'[65] Even if he found himself, it was too late for him to do penance, though.

Speaking about the real Ezra Pound outside the novel, one can identify the Mauberley phase in his career with the imagist phase of his writing, which was followed by the vorticist phase, in which he grew tired of the poetry of his fellow imagists (and Amygists) and insisted on the difference between the active conception of poetry (vorticism) and the mere reception of an impression (imagism). John Espey, for example, in his book on *Mauberley* makes the distinction between the latter phase in which Pound became 'the active instigator,' the man who left poetry for politics in the end, namely, the Pound we meet in *Famous Last Words*, and the former one of 'the passive aesthete,' which is Mauberley in *Famous Last Words*. Espey distinguishes between 'Pound, the poet of "love, passion, emotion as an intellectual instigation," and Mauberley, the poet of "aesthetic receptivity of tactile and magnetic values, of the perception of beauty in these relationships." '[66]

Hugh Witemeyer equates Mauberley's passive aestheticism with Walter Pater's impressionism of the 'aesthetic critic' who regards 'all the objects with which he has to do, all works of art, and the fairer forms of nature and human life, as powers or forces producing pleasurable sensations.' It is Mauberley as opposed to Pound, Witemeyer claims, who 'falls victim to a Paterian aesthetic based too exclusively on a "special impression of beauty or pleasure." ' Still, as Berryman points out referring to Flaubert's and Joyce's 'impressionist' technique that influenced Pound, Pound 'does not oppose Impressionism *in toto*, only certain phases of it.' Mauberley stands for the negative aspects of impressionism and becomes 'what Pound terms the inferior impressionist.' While part I of *Mauberley* 'criticizes and rejects the milieu it describes, in part II Mauberley himself accepts it and tries to survive in it without combating its faults.'[67]

Even the sometimes difficult question as to whose voice we hear in the Mauberley poems finds its parallels in the critics' varying and uncertain responses to the 'omniscient' parts of Mauberley's writings on the wall in *Famous Last Words*. 'E.P.,' who, according to almost all critics of *Hugh Selwyn Mauberley*, is something like the persona that Ezra Pound had sloughed off by leaving London, had been 'for three years, out of key with his time' trying 'to maintain "the sublime." ' Findley transfers these characteristics to his Mauberley in the newspaper article that the journalist Julia Franklin writes about him. Franklin states that Mauberley 'appears to be totally unaffected by the march of events. Instead, he avoids all confrontation with his diminishing talents by spending an inordinate amount of time with the dissolute aristocracy of faded England and with the morally bankrupt crew that mans the élite but sinking lifeboat of a Fascist-dominated Europe ...' (128). Except for the last sentence, this might be a prose version of what Pound – in the voice of his Mauberley – has to say about 'E.P.,' who equally 'unaffected by "the march of events," ... passed from men's memory'[68] thirty years earlier, while the real Pound left London for Paris and finally, as we see in the novel as well as in real life, for political action in Italy.

Sections 2 to 12 of the poem, which generally are assumed to rep-resent Pound's London contemporaries and predecessors whom he decides to leave behind, provide Findley with more models inviting parodic inclusion in *Famous Last Words* – on the level of contents as well as on the level of formulation. Pound's references to the First World War (sections 4 and 5) might as well refer to the Second World War. Coral Ann Howells has shown the multi-layered meanings of Pound's line about those who 'walked eye-deep in hell,' which is 'a metaphorical description of Mauberley's situation as he writes in the prison of the Hotel Elysium and also finds its hideous concretisation in the manner of Mauberley's death in the novel, from an ice-pick through his right eye ...'[69] But first Mauberley sees himself 'caught in the eye of one who cannot lie' (129), Julia Franklin.

Mr Nixon in the ninth section of *Mauberley*, generally identified as the commercially successful Arnold Bennet, gives the advice to 'butter reviewers ...,'[70] which in *Famous Last Words* is taken up, not by Maub-erley himself, but by Hemingway. After being insulted in public by a Spanish aristocratic lady whose Fascist relatives had been killed by the Loyalists, Hemingway bribes all journalists present by inviting them for drinks, so that the event blows over unreported (125–9).

In the second part of *Hugh Selwyn Mauberley*, which is the part entitled 'Mauberley (1920),' Pound indulges in parodic self-quotation ('His true Penelope / Was Flaubert') and then continues, 'And his tool / The engraver's.' While Pound's 'self-depreciative sexual emphasis ...

undercuts the posturing of the opening "Ode" it echoes and parodies,' Howells points out that ' "his tool / The engraver's" becomes Mauberley's silver pencil ... used to write his story on the walls of the four rooms in the Grand Elysium Hotel ...' Section 3 mentions 'the coral isle, the lion-coloured sand,' which become 'the scenarios for the Duke and Duchess of Windsor's story,' but here we have also a sketch of Mauberley's growing 'isolation,' of his 'Olympian *apathein*,' 'his final / Exclusion from the world of letters.' In Pound's poem Mauberley's writing ends up being nothing more than 'maudlin confession,'[71] and this evaluation is more or less the same as Captain Freyberg's judgment of the writing on the wall.

There seems to be a Pound influence on *Famous Last Words* even beyond the framed story told by a Pound character. The writing on the wall is read and interpreted by two Americans: Freyberg and Quinn. Quinn is clearly more literarily and artistically inclined than his fellow soldier, and he is willing to give Mauberley's writing an unbiased and unprejudiced reading. Eerily enough, his role as a friend of art in un-artistic times is reminiscent of the actions of his namesake John Quinn, the 'New York Irish lawyer and art collector who was patron and financial godfather to old Yeats' and also an anti-Semitic acquaintance of Pound's.[72] This John Quinn is also mentioned in Pound's poetry – not in *Hugh Selwyn Mauberley*, but in the *Cantos* (12, 80, 103).

Canto 80 is one of the *Pisan Cantos* written in the Disciplinary Train-ing Center, in which the Americans held Pound at Pisa (see also page 291 for a reference to his cage in the frame story of *Famous Last Words*), and according to John Espey, there is a close relationship between these cantos and the earlier Mauberley poem: 'Pound, held in a prison en-closure, once again under personal pressure, with almost no books, turns repeatedly to the period of *Mauberley's* composition and to the years of which *Mauberley* was the culmination.'[73] In Canto 80, Quinn turns up in the company of many Fascists of the time but is clearly not identified as such himself and is only mentioned as a friend of the Yeatses. Quinn's perspective in the novel is slightly more reliable than Mauberley's own, but on the other hand, although he is willing to give Mauberley's writing a fair reading, he shows that an unbiased position is impossible when one's personal appreciation of political writing that also figures as art is involved. The only way of shielding oneself from these influences is to embed everything in the frame of a set political interpretation in the way Freyberg does. But even Freyberg has to admit that his version of parody may easily be subsumed in another one.

Thus the various levels of emplotment, the various parodies from

Mauberley's, Quinn's, Freyberg's, and the narrator's point of view, give us different versions of the same 'historical' events. Every one of these interpreters adds another interpretive frame to the emplotment undertaken by his predecessor. As pointed out in chapter 2, Hayden White differentiates among four modes which the emplotment can follow: romance, comedy, tragedy, and satire, a terminology adapted to the Canadian context by T.D. MacLulich as quest, ordeal, or odyssey. Mauberley himself emplots his story so that he becomes a major figure in the international game. While he writes his text, he does not yet know that he will be killed by the German henchman: his story seems to belong to MacLulich's category of the quest. Quinn believes this version, but as he knows the outcome, the emplotment turns into an ordeal. Freyberg does not accept the quest version proposed by Mauberley; he remains sceptical, but his own quest finally turns into an ordeal, when his beliefs, which had provided the impetus for the fight against the Nazis, become inopportune.

The narrator finally fills in additional information, but he refrains from taking a position. Parodying a point of view means, as I have shown in chapter 1, incorporating it into one's own view of things and repeating it with a difference. An intention to change the text (and indeed the environment into which it is implanted) is inherent to parodic strategies. In the case of the outermost frame of *Famous Last Words*, unless one assumes that not emplotting elements of a story is a form of emplotment, too, there does not seem to be an ultimately privileged point of view in the novel, even though I tend to agree with Stephen Scobie that 'Findley does insist on the moral dimension of the *truth* of Mauberley's testimony.'[74] There is no obvious intention visible, and this leaves Findley's non-emplotment open to criticism, because the principle of 'parodic glue' mentioned above gives the parodied text (in this case, Mauberley's/Quinn's) a certain amount of power. If the narrator does not counteract this effect, and here he does not, he (and maybe even the author) exposes himself to criticism such as John Melmoth's, who is unhappy with Findley's view of history-writing because he does not answer the most important underlying question: 'how could one "whose greatest gift had been an emphatic belief in the value of imagination" be so misguided or self-deluding as to "join with people whose whole ambition was to render the race incapable of thinking"?'[75] The answer to this question may very well be that his quest was the quest for the work of art, whether it be in the form of writing or politics, and that he, Mauberley, the aesthete, did not see the evil purposes to which beautiful art could be put, or that, if he knew them, he did not care. Quinn succumbs to the same temptation as Mauberley, and the narrator does not make his own position clear enough in the frame elements that surround Quinn's statement. After all, it is Quinn who signs Mauberley's last words in *Famous Last Words*.

Among the novels discussed so far, Findley's are clearly the most sophisticated ones in parodic terms. He rewrites historical as well as literary texts, combining them into a new kind of writing that may be less accurate than purely factual non-fiction, but he arrives – in the manner of D.M. Thomas's *The White Hotel* – at an artistic vision that is able to render the human dimensions of recent history more tangible than many scholarly books do. *The Wars* succeeded in illustrating the historic events of the First World War in a novel about the writing about the Great War. Although these events are accessible only through archives and documentary sources, they can be re-created sixty years later. The models that Findley integrates into his own works are real and fictional persons, real and fictional documents, real and fictional quotations (such as Fagan's) and motifs. *Famous Last Words*, the novel dealing with even greater problems of Nazism and the Second World War, is the ultimate example of parody as a re-functioning of textual models. It stands out from the novels discussed so far because it combines in a new manner fictional and non-fictional sources. Going beyond *The Wars*, it includes and integrates not only fictional characters and motifs but also their own acts of narration. The novel becomes metafictional also in the sense that it takes a long – albeit, in John Melmoth's perspective, shifty – 'look at literature's responsibilities.'[76]

Findley may not answer all questions concerning literature's responsibilities in this novel (as pointed out, there is no finally privileged perspective on the events), but he provides a new, fascinating, and provocative context, which gives his readers a new path of access to historical and ethical problems that might otherwise be lost in sterile history books, dealt with – as Mauberley had feared – by nobody but 'dread academics.'[77]

Findley is, so the title of this chapter suggests, a modernist. Can such a classification be upheld in the light of an approach that claims that most narrators of *The Wars* are clearly our contemporaries lost in the maze of Foucault's archive; and that *Famous Last Words* is an inextricable labyrinth of sometimes illogically intercalated narrative perspectives that could well claim to be part of the postmodern species of what John Barth has called the 'literature of replenishment'?[78] This question can be answered in the affirmative because, even if he cannot help living in a postmodern world, Findley still strives for a coherent universe and a coherent cosmology, in which inherent values such as life, caring, and commitment do exist. This coherence then finds its expression in the parody of contemporary history being based on a reinterpretation of one poem. Just as Pound's Mauberley had placed himself in the tradition of Greek mythology, Findley's narratorial voice strives to subsume all the other ones as if it represented the monologic structure of a classical epic or of a stylization in the Bakhtinian fashion. Findley's primarily monologic way of using parodic structures is clearly different from that of a committed postmodernist such as George Bowering, the next author to be treated in this study.

4 Bowering: Postmodern Parodies

There is no relationship between time & history.

There is lots of time. It goes on & on. Dont worry there is lots of time. Just look at it anywhere & you'll see. There is so much time no one has ever seen more than a little of it.

But history. There is only so much history. History has a beginning middle & end. It ends when someone angrily throws his typewriter into Lake Ontario. *George Bowering*[1]

A part of this coast, prior to our visit, had been seen by different navigators, and the position of certain head lands, capes, &c. given to the world. Several of these I have found myself under the necessity of placing in different latitudes and longitudes, as well those seen by Captain Cook, as others laid down by the different visitors who have followed him. This, however, I have not presumed to do, from a consciousness of superior abilities as an astronomer, or integrity as an historian; but from the conviction, that no one of my predecessors had the good fortune to meet so favorable an opportunity for the examination ... *George Vancouver*[2]

At one time history was an art. Historians got deflected into thinking of history as a science, probably around 150 years ago. I think it was a lot more interesting when history was an art. *George Bowering*[3]

Timothy Findley's metahistorical parodies, his variations on the possibility of writing novels about the writing of history, were based on texts by the modernists and their predecessors. They incorporated literary and non-fictional texts (such as Pound's *Hugh Selwyn Mauberley* and Raymond Massey's or the Duke and Duchess of Windsor's autobiographies) into their own universe, re-working history from an artistic point of view that could be sustained in 'real' literary works of art, although it met with defeat on the political level in the end. Even though they clearly depended on a 'postmodern' environment – such as that of the archives in which they were written – Findley's novels very much restricted themselves to those types of incoherence that were already available before Canadian writers such as Robert Kroetsch, George Bowering, and Frank Davey not only denied the universe we live in any coherence but also seemed to relish this vacuum. Findley's novels show that Walter Pache was right to include the qualifying adverb in his statement (in an essay on Bowering and Kroetsch) that 'in Canada, postmodernism is *partly* synonymous with related terms like "post-colonial" or "post-European."' '4

George Bowering's novels did not receive very much critical attention before *Burning Water* won the 1980 Governor General's Award, and a fellow writer of historical fiction, Chris Scott, even denied this latter work the status (if there be any attached) of being a historical novel.[5] Still, although they do not show the coherence of a modernist work for which Findley strives in his novels, Bowering's novels contain many – seemingly casual – insights into the act of writing historical texts, including historical fiction, and into the workings of parody in this context. Bowering expresses his personal views on historical writing in his essay 'A Great Northward Darkness: The Attack on History in Recent Canadian Fiction': 'In Canada our most popular prose writers write popular history. Our readers prefer it to fiction. When they read fiction they like to read fiction that obeys the rules of historical narrative, the sense that character and setting and event combine to lead to a conclusion, that there is a force something like necessity, that language is the normal link between pre-linguistic history and drama.'[6]

Bowering's interest in historical themes and historical fiction did not start, however, with *Burning Water*. As for his theoretical musings, his own attitude towards historical novels is best illustrated in his 1977 'novel' *A Short Sad Book*. This 'historical-geographical'[7] novel has an epigraph which at once sets itself and its attitude towards history and the telling of history apart from any realist type of writing and also from some tendencies in modernist writing, even though modernism and realism should not be generally equated. The quotation is from Alain Robbe-Grillet, the father of the French *nouveau roman*: 'Under our gaze, the simple gesture of holding out our hand becomes bizarre, clumsy; the words we hear ourselves speaking suddenly sound false; the time of our minds is no longer that of the clocks; & the style of a novel, in its turn, can no longer be innocent' (5).[8] We should, in other words, not expect a novel to sound 'real' any longer, and we cannot expect a historical novel to re-create the past as it was but should rather admit from the start that we can only create it as we imagine it. Bowering voices similar thoughts in a 1979 interview: 'James says in *The Art of the Novel*, I think, that the novel is to history as painting (he's talking about realist painting) is to nature – an imitation. His assumption was that the rules we have of history are the rules that we're going to have when we get into fiction. We've come around and changed the rules of fiction and at the same time changed the rules of history. Maybe we changed the rules of history first. We look at history in a much different way now.'[9]

As far as Bowering's attitude towards history in *A Short Sad Book* is concerned, the novel has a part entitled 'Canadian History,' which, in Bowering's typical style of writing-as-process, illustrates one of the maximum underlying the whole argument of this study:

> Canada is the country in which writing about history is history.
>   Let me try again.
>   I meant to say that Canada is the country in which writing history is history. (74)

As pointed out earlier, it is of course not just in Canada that one might say that the writing of history is history, that history is text rather than facts. *A Short Sad Book* claims to be a historical novel, and its parodic character is already obvious in its title, which parodically alludes to that of Gertrude Stein's story 'A Long, Gay Book.' Although Smaro Kamboureli's resigned admission that 'it is a work that resists summation and challenges generic classification' is probably an adequate way of dealing with this text, an attempt at summarizing at least some plot elements should be made. In Kamboureli's own words, 'Bowering's excursions take him from his personal landscape and history, including his criticism and fiction, to the Canada Council offices and to the top of the mountain where Sir John A. MacDonald [*sic*] and Evangeline make love, the reality of his act of writing and the Canadian publishers' world to Margaret Atwood and Louis Riel.'[10] All in all, *A Short Sad Book* plays with many of the clichés that have dominated the study of Canadian literature and history, the most important of which are already named in the titles of the book's six parts: 'Canadian Geography,' 'The Exile of Evangeline,' 'Canadian History,' 'The Black Mountain Influence,' 'The Pretty Good Canadian Novel,' and 'The Return of Evangeline.'

The title of part 1 hints at the precedence that geography normally takes not only in introductions to Canada but also in introductory studies of Canadian literature – such as Margaret Atwood's *Survival*, which is omnipresent as a model parodied in Bowering's text – as well as in the literature itself. Among the most important features of Canadian geography is of course – in addition to the arctic character of much of Canada's land mass – the long (and undefended) border with the United States, with the ensuing consequence for Canadians that it is very difficult for them to develop the sense of 'a country of their own.' So, although Bowering starts with the statement that 'I was going to write a book about love, & one time I woke up & said I love this country,' he admits on the same page that it was difficult for an eight-year-old boy growing up in British Columbia to identify with Canada, and that the main identification model was to the south: 'When I grew up I was going to be an American boy. I loved that country. That was human nature not my mind' (15). On the next page, he even talks about 'all us Americans' (16), turning his younger self into a naïve imitation of American gunslingers, preferring American stereotypes to Canadian ones such as hockey players, which he as a resident of the temperate West Coast has trouble visualizing.

Seen from the perspective of the adult writer, such a youthful (or juvenile) imitation of American values turns into a repetition with a vengeance, that is, a parody. Whereas in the earlier Canadian parodies mentioned, such as Richardson's *Wacousta* or Findley's *The Wars*, the first models to be parodied had been British, Bowering's narrator remarks that

> I found out I was not American first.
>   Long before that I knew I was not British & I thought I must be American. (33)

Only after the mention of non-Canadians such as a famous poet like 'Walt Whitman the American,' who 'had walkt' in the Canadian forests from which 'we lived a block away' (26), and of a European explorer such as de Soto (27) – both of them trying to include Canada within their own versions of manifest destiny – do some Canadian figures creep into the first part of the novel. They try to stand up to a comparison with obvious heroes such as Stan Musial (33) and thus to help the young Canadian writer find his own national models. Among them are Bill Barilko, a vanished pilot (30), Claire Trevor, and the Métis leader Gabriel Dumont, who is lost in the Eastern Canadian National Art Gallery (35) and later turns into the writer David McFadden, as well as the nineteenth-century painter Paul Kane (36). The last Canadian, one of mythical proportions, to be mentioned in the first part of *A Short Sad Book* is Evangeline, the archetypal Canadian eighteenth-century myth, who ironically is the creation of a nineteenth-century American poet.

Part 2 of *A Short Sad Book* is entitled 'The Exile of Evangeline,' and intermittently shows Evangeline on her parodic way, not to Louisiana, but rather to the West Coast: 'Evangeline packt up her few possessions & got on the train never to see her homeland again. The train pusht west, into Upper Canada, & then out, as they say, west' (49). Travelling through the Prairies and experiencing a Saskatchewan winter, Evangeline finally arrives in Vancouver. Here she takes up with John A. Macdonald (64), the nineteenth-century Eastern Canadian myth, who is present in order to commemorate the fulfilment of the national dream of the transcontinental railway by driving in the last spike. The two mythical Canadians, one Franco- and the other Anglo-Canadian, go up Grouse Mountain together.

Interspersed into the rather confused and confusing text are narratorial remarks on writing, on Canadian clichés such as snow, on Canadian cities such as Fredericton and Montreal, and on meetings with Canadians such as the poet Al Purdy, who 'went by without a word' (44). Metafictional remarks about the novel that is being written and about beavers are linked with names like that of Carleton McNaughton, of such archetypal figures as the ice-skater Barbara Ann Scott, or of the radio program 'The Happy Gang' (47). The narrator writing his historical novel is permitted to create such confusion that we can and should assume it to be planned. But having delivered a long list of seemingly incoherent ingredients, Bowering (or is it 'Bowering,' the narrator?) gives the following warning to those thematic critics à la *Survival* who have not yet given up on sifting through *A Short Sad Book* image by image and who may want to integrate this material into a thematic interpretation of Canadian texts:

> Confuse setting & person confuse landscape & characters & you wind up with thematic criticism not a novel.
> Anthropology not fiction. (53)

Part 3, bearing the title 'Canadian History,' starts out with the love-making of presumably John A. Macdonald and Evangeline. Their discussion of positions parodies Margaret Atwood's victim (or here, rather, virgin) positions as they are described in *Survival*. Victim position number four (i.e., to be a creative non-victim) is rendered as: 'You have to be a creative non-virgin' (72). But, as the narrator remarks on the same page, the novel 'is beginning to parody itself.' He still has not found out where exactly Canadian history begins: 'Now I cant help thinking who was the first Canadian, someone had to be the first Canadian' (77). Pointing forward to his novel *Burning Water*, he already excludes a famous explorer from his list:

> Captain George Vancouver has a city & an island in Canada but he has a city in the United States & a rock in Australia & an arm in New Zealand & a mountain in Alaska.
> No, Captain Vancouver was not the first Canadian. (78)

Before the search for the first Canadian focuses on John A. Macdonald himself – 'You are the first Canadian, Mac, so it does have a beginning. It is a classic case of Confederation' (93) – the two dead heroes of the Battle of the Plains of Abraham are thrown in for good historical measure and mixture. Linking the different layers of history that we find in the archives (now thoroughly postmodern, when compared to Findley's),

> General Wolfe's bullet went thru the brain of a dray horse & continued west over Lake of the Woods until it passt thru the body of Evangeline, making a ninety degree turn at her left hipbone. (89)

For even better measure, selfsame bullet

> came out of Evangeline & entered a beaver, it came out of the beaver & entered Big Bear, it came out of Big Bear & entered the Carr Brothers, it came out of the Carr brothers & entered Lee Harvey Oswald.
> Now that's interesting.
> Lee Harvey Oswald has just entered Canadian history. With a bang. (90)

Interesting it is, no doubt. Needless to say that 'Lee Harvey Oswald was cold stone sober when he shot John A. Macdonald' (100).

But one wonders if something did not go wrong when the narrator tried to reassemble the shards of Canadian history, the 'broken beer bottle glass' that is to be found 'all over the Canadian Shield' (27) and probably also on the West Coast, since there the narrator finds 'a stone carved by Alexander Mackenzie,' the first to cross Canada by land,

and 'a bottle thrown overboard by Archibald Menzies,' the surgeon and botanist on George Vancouver's expedition (93). More interesting, though – unless one wants to read even more outrageous parodies that are not really of the type I have been looking for in this study – are his theoretical ruminations in his 'chapter about the relationship of time & history' (98) from which I have quoted in the epigraph to this chapter. Later on he also writes, 'He sat at his desk & wrote history. What he wrote was George Bowering sat at his desk writing history. He didnt make the mistake, so something is playing games with history here' (101). Here the writer is caught in the game of the metafictionist – or metahistorian – writing about the writing of history and problematizing his own situation. He even introduces – without mentioning its function – the Quaker Oats box which is perennially used by theorists in order to illustrate the effect of unlimited mirror effects in writing, of the so-called *mise en abyme*: 'He was filled with more energy than usual. That morning he had sat at his table eating Quaker Oats & reading the Quaker Oats box. What he read was not of historical interest but it was something like history' (102). Evidently he was not reading at all, but looking at the picture on the Quaker Oats box.

Television and film as new media in which the 'writing' of history takes place become important, too, in a postmodern society, in which the old documents that are integrated into new ones (i.e., parodied) can also be supposedly objective pictures. Here, as always, the frames play an important role in the interpretation of the 'texts'; on television, films like that about the Kennedy assassination can even be played backwards, an effect already used by Kurt Vonnegut in *Slaughterhouse-Five* when the bombing of Dresden was shown backwards:[11]

> One time they played it backward & Jack Ruby pulled a bullet out of Lee Harvey Oswald & Lee Harvey quit grimacing & so on & you know it continued so that there was Jack Kennedy's head all in one piece & the Americans leaving Cuba & that is how American history happens on television.
>
> But in Canada history consists of writing history. For that reason history is filled with mistakes & most of them are written by poetry. The novel can only sit back & try to understand. (102–3)

The topic of part 4, 'The Black Mountain Influence,' is of course the *bête noire* of all fervently and narrowly nationalist students of Canadian literature who have been fighting against the influence of the American Black Mountain poets in Canada in the wake of Robert Creeley's teaching at the University of British Columbia. This influence culminated in the publication of the magazine *Tish* by UBC students such as George Bowering, Frank Davey, and Fred Wah. Right from the beginning, Bowering has the insight that 'if I want this to be a post-modern novel I'd better forget about history' (107), since postmodernity and the idea of history probably exclude each other. But he concludes that 'this is not Canadian literature I'm writing. I'm making post-modern Canadian history' (114).

Since the Black Mountain influence is an American phenomenon – or perhaps not, since the narrator suggests that there may be a Black Mountain near Vancouver, 'on the north shore or just beyond' (120) – he proceeds to a comparison of American and Canadian literature, surprisingly and ironically enough on traditional thematic grounds. He makes fun of those who draw too rigid a line between the two countries, mostly because – as he suggests – they have been educated in the United States anyway. Imitating the thoughtless rigidity with which strict rules for the Canadian-ness of Canadian and the American-ness of American literature are created, he arrives at his own definition: 'That in American literature they are all above the water or on the water. Chasing the great white whale or two years before the mast, & in Canadian literature they are in the water or underwater' (110). Canada's answer to Melville and Dana is obviously to write about submarine victims: 'One is walking into the lake & becoming an ancient fish, one is hitting an iceberg & going down, one is looking for her father's words on a rock face under the surface, it was a Canadian publisher, business as usual' (111). His favourite enemy – one of those who might have insisted on the importance of the Canadian theme in poems such as F.R. Scott's 'Lakeshore' or E.J. Pratt's *Titanic*, or in novels such as Margaret Atwood's *Surfacing* – is 'the Canadian nationalist professor from Ottawa name of Sparrow, who is 'paid by the CIA to give Canadian nationalism a bad name' (113). The fact that there is, or was, a nationalist professor in Ottawa whose Christian name is not Sparrow, but Robin, is certainly no coincidence.[12]

The narrator realizes, though, that he – like the anthropologically minded nationalist critics concentrating on phenomena such as 'the Immigrant Experience' (131) – cannot restrict himself to literary matters in his writing of 'post-modern Canadian history.' Consequently, post-modern history books appear within his historical novel, too: at the bottom of Lake Ontario, a character discovers a copy of 'the Tercentenary History of Canada, Volume III, From Laurier to King, MCMVIV [sic]–MCMXLV' (136), this supposedly being the follow-up volume to the book written by the anonymous historian who promised to re-member Evangeline in his book that was to be called 'The Tercentenary History of Canada, Volume II, From Champlain to Laurier, MDCVIII–MCMVIII ... publisht by P.F. Collier & Son' (39). If critics fall prey to Bowering's playful 'critic-mocking' that would allow them 'to congratulate themselves that they have discovered the secrets of the work,'[13] a stroll to the library shows them that the name of the anon-ymous historian is Frank Basil Tracy, and that the title of his three-volume opus is *The Tercentenary History of Canada from Champlain to Laurier, MDCVIII–MCMVIII* (New York and Toronto: P.F. Collier 1908). But although a second edition of the history was published in 1913, there is no trace to be found of a volume extending to 1945. One might also wonder if an anglophone prime minister of Canada such as King would really appreciate being (parodically?) subsumed under the per-spective of a tercentenary edition commemorating the foundation of the French-Canadian capital of Quebec.

As the title of part 5 indicates, Bowering and his sleuth Al are willing to settle for 'The Pretty Good Canadian Novel' if The Great Canadian Novel cannot be found. A sense of bi- or multicultural compromise seems to take over: publishers such as the Alberta Doukhobor Stan do not have to be very literate as long as they love books (140); French Canadians such as Laurier Lapierre prove more British than Canadians of English stock; second-generation Americans with the mythical Métis name of Gabe Dumont have become so Americanized as never to have seen a beaver. Stan follows Evangeline through the archetypal snow towards canonization: 'They were headed east. Toward the text books' (151). What they meet there is a series of parodies or pastiches of famous Canadian novels. In front of a certain house they meet David Canaan from Buckler's pretty good Canadian novel (and parody), *The Mountain and the Valley*, who just woke up:

> David opened his eyes. April air pluckt at the curtains like breath be-hind a veil. It held a hint of real warmth to come, but the linen chill of the night still sharpened it. Clean limb shadows palpitated with precision & immaculacy on the breathing ground outside. The whole morning glistened fresh as the flesh of an alder sapling when the bark was first peeled from it to make a whistle. It glinted bright as the split rock-maple, flashing for a minute in the sun as it was tost onto the woodpile. (152)

One would be tempted to say that Buckler's overwritten style is parodied quite effectively, but that of course Bowering cannot sustain this kind of writing for long ('Have you noticed, said one of the characters to another one of the characters, that we characters all talk a lot like the author' [177]), so that he has to continue: 'Jesus, I feel shitty in the morning, thought David.' But the paragraph turns out to be an exact quotation – except for Bowering's typographical and orthographical mannerisms – of the third paragraph of the second chapter of *The Mountain and the Valley*.[14] Bowering's own continuation of the quotation provides a parodic frame, though, which shows in what light the reader is meant to see this example of a pretty good Canadian novel.

The next Pretty Good Canadian Novel Bowering incorporates into his writing – and once again he does it wholesale, copying a whole paragraph – is Hugh MacLennan's *Two Solitudes*: on his way 'down the St Lawrence River where Canadian history happened in the text books' (155), he comes to Saint-Marc where

> spring leapt quickly into full summer that year. One day people woke & saw that the buds had become leaves & the mud dried into friable earth. There was great activity over all the parish as the planting was completed. Before it was finisht the first blackflies appeared in the spruce of the distant forest; then they were in the maple grove on the ridge behind the Tallard land. By the Queen's birthday or May twenty-fourth it was almost as hot as mid-summer. The heat simmered in delicate gossamers along the surface of the plain, cloud formations built themselves up thru the mornings, & by afternoon they were majestic above the river. The first green shoots of the seeds that had been consecrated on Saint Marc's Day appeared above the soil in the sunshine. *Quebec was really being described.* (155, my emphasis)

Except for the archaic mannerisms of spelling and the typographical error ('or May twenty-fourth' instead of 'on May twenty-fourth'), the beginning of chapter 14 of *Two Solitudes* has been copied verbatim.[15] Only the ironic metafictional comment at the end has been added by Bowering, thus erecting a whole new parodic frame around the quotation, turning it from one of the seminal texts of 'mainstream' Canadian literature into just a 'pretty good Canadian novel.'

After the description of the Quebec landscape of *Two Solitudes*, we meet the Doukhobor publisher at 'the edge of a Goyish lake' (158) with Richleresque overtones and see him ending up at Brother André's shrine in Montreal 'under the black shadow of the Mount Royal Influence, among the discarded crutches' (159), finally finding the PGCN 'about a detective who, after following a false lead to a mountaintop in British Columbia, confronts the slayer of Tom Thompson [sic] in London Ontario' (165). And one wonders if this is really the story one has been trying to read so far.

Part six finally gives us 'The Return of Evangeline,' which is announced to the prime minister by the actress Claire Trevor, who returns from women's heaven and – as an American – has some trouble adapting to Canadian political realities, first addressing him as Mr President. While Bowering shows his postmodern powers by omitting a chapter (LII) from the novel and philosophizing about the three-sided houses of realist fiction, the prime minister (Trudeau), Robert Fulford, and Sparrow discuss whether Evangeline should be readmitted from heaven into Canada. For Sparrow, she – as 'the figment of an American poet's imagination' and, as such, 'another agent of U.S. imperialism' (176) – should not be admitted. Although finally offered repatriation as a correction of 'a sad political misdeed of the past,' she, the muse, tells the narrator that 'myth is a truth of repetitive time. It is a blot that bleeds thru all time' (184). Then she kisses him goodbye – so that he is 'from this day markt' (185) by the kiss of the half-American muse – and returns to women's heaven. So much for myth criticism written by Easterners who 'are from a text book, they are admythical in short' (184).

All in all, the parodies in *A Short Sad Book* are rather loosely organized humorous satires on some aspects of the Canadian literary and historical scene, including a lot of personal gibes at exposed nationalists such as Margaret Atwood and especially Robin Mathews. Although the metafictional comments about the writing of a novel and the metahistorical comments about the writing of history go in the same direction as some of the conclusions drawn from Timothy Findley's writing, there does not seem to be the same kind of commitment and seriousness behind the persona of Bowering's narrator. This may well be due to the different – more ludic – attitude that a confessed postmodernist such as Bowering has towards questions of history and historicity, especially in the context of his writing. In a recent interview, he admits to having a rather lackadaisical attitude to historical sources and events. When interviewers discussing his works with him accuse him of 'not taking into account ... the social implications' and of not 'tak[ing] on the political at all as content,' Bowering's assertion in his own defence may not sound convincing to every reader: 'What you've got there is a male-female relationship that involves power, so you have Scotch-English-Canadian versus French Canadian, man versus woman, powerful versus not so powerful ...'[16] What he does clarify in the course of his elaborations, though, is his parodic relationship to Gertrude Stein, whom he had already indicated in the novel as the important influence behind his stream-of-consciousness mannerisms: '& people say why are you doing archaic avant-garde writing. This is warmed over Gertrude Stein there I said her name why are you doing it?' (154).

Still, there are a lot of important insights into the act of writing and remembering included in the banter of *A Short Sad Book*, not the least of them being the importance of the act of writing history, which here takes precedence even over the act of making history. In a postmodern novel which denies its author and its readers a coherent cosmology, the process of constructing story and history becomes an everlasting task. Parodies here serve the purpose of constructing and deconstructing one's own identity in a situation of perpetual intertextuality, of constantly shifting paradigms: the concepts floating around always have to be integrated into a semi-coherent historical view: 'This world was made a few moments ago, & what we call the past is our memories creating history' (123).

Whereas in *A Short Sad Book* George Bowering discussed the question of the relationship between the postmodern novel and the writing of Canadian history, *Burning Water* now is such a postmodern novel in which we observe a contemporary Canadian writer – called George Bowering – trying to write a historical novel about the exploration of his own country. Of course, this country did not yet exist as a nation in its own right when the events depicted took place, so that the exploration was undertaken on behalf of the imperial mother country, Great Britain. As his exemplum, Bowering chooses an expedition of the early 1790s under the command of Captain George Vancouver. He bases his version of events on Vancouver's original exploration report and on his crew's journals, but he breaks up the original order of this source material. Then he rearranges the events so as to make his readers lose any sense of chronology based on the European calendar, a standard foreign to the regions Vancouver explored. It is obvious that Bowering had to select from writings covering a five-year voyage of exploration that touched four continents, including the coast of what is now the Canadian province of British Columbia, and the crowning of which would have been the discovery of the Northwest Passage.[17]

The novel is a reconstruction of imperial history from the colonized point of view, an 'attempt to subvert the perceived clichés of his predecessors': *Burning Water* can be interpreted as a model case of the postmodern, postcolonial reaction against the structures and strictures of imperial master narratives that are imposed upon new literatures. Bowering's 'metahistorical' reaction to European models differs from the use that a more modernistically inspired writer such as Timothy Findley makes of historical metafiction; it is typical rather of the postmodern version of metahistorical parody, the beginning of which we saw in *A Short Sad Book*. Canadian reviewers in general were not very happy with Bowering's attempt, showing that in the view of some readers Bowering's postmodern kind of parody may be somewhat too blatant, lacking true commitment. Consequently, not a few critics and reviewers must have been shocked when the novel was awarded the Governor General's Award. W.H. New, for example, admits that the concept lying behind the novel 'constitutes a clever idea in technique,' but he doubts that any of it is 'transformed beyond cleverness into literature.' Chris Scott calls *Burning Water* 'a truly ugly book' by 'just another deadbeat academic scribbler.' Anthony S. Brennan comes to the conclusion that 'Bowering aimed to write a novel about George Vancouver and ended up with notes for a novel,' and only Smaro Kamboureli responds positively to 'Bowering's main accomplishment,' which is 'his usage of historical documents in composing his novel.'[18]

It is not surprising that in a country that shares some important postcolonial features with Canada, its fellow Commonwealth country New Zealand, the reception of *Burning Water* was quite positive. In the New Zealand quarterly *Landfall*, Reginald Berry suggests that Bowering is representative of his literary culture, and Gary Boire (a Canadian then teaching in New Zealand) chooses a quotation from *Burning Water* as his starting-point in an editorial dealing with New Zealand–Canadian relations. Boire sees close parallels between the writing in both countries, which – as he also points out – were both explored by the hero of *Burning Water*, Captain George Vancouver: both countries are 'ex-colonies struggling to resist neo-colonizing neighbours; both countries enjoy and brood upon the delicate balance of heterogeneous "regions" within a homogeneous state; both cultures share the burden of historical settler-guilt mollified by liberal democratic ideology.'[19]

Burning Water plays with the problems of history-writing and thus provides an interesting example of the rewriting of an imperial historical document. Metafictional comments 'imply that history is a provisional construct which resembles fiction ... but it also automatically foregrounds the writing self in a dialogue with history ...' As pointed out above, exploration reports such as the one on which Bowering's novel is based are the Canadian version of early historiography, written of course from the point of view of the British colonizers, so that they have to be reread from and through a Canadian perspective. As Bowering himself is the first to admit, his fanciful novel about George Vancouver's exploration of the Canadian west coast relies to a large extent on the captain's journals and those of his surgeon, Archibald Menzies. In an interview with Reginald Berry, Bowering claims that in a context such as that of British Columbia, 'you can do something wonderful in an area in which the history is not well known. And if you confront history in your writing, you will do it in different ways. The method with which we write probably has to do with the fact that each of us has to go out at the very beginning and be our own historian rather than read what historians do.'[20]

In the same interview, Bowering describes how in the 1960s he came upon the subject of Vancouver's exploration, which turned into the main subject of *Burning Water*: in an Eastern Canadian library, he found a copy of Menzies's journal, on which he based his first version of the story, the long poem *George, Vancouver*. The most important source of *Burning Water*, however, is to be found in Vancouver's journal. Comparing this source with what Bowering has made of it, one is struck by the surprising faithfulness with which Bowering follows – and often quotes – some parts of Vancouver's journal and also by the outrageous liberties he takes with others. Often there is just a slight shift in perspective – a new frame into which the old picture is integrated – which leads to a parodic vision; sometimes, however, Bowering explodes the coherence of the eighteenth-century cosmos.

The framing of older texts which takes place in *Burning Water* is indicated even before the main text starts. While the elements from other writers were integrated without any acknowledgment into the *Short Sad Book*, Bowering alerts the readers of *Burning Water* to the parodic or intertextual nature of this novel. On the acknowledgments page he writes: 'As well as the obvious passages from the writings of George Vancouver and other officers of his expedition, I have made short quotations from the following books: *Vanity Fair* by William Makepeace Thackeray; *Duino Elegies* by Rainer Maria Rilke; *G.* by John Berger; *Mardi* by Herman Melville; *The Tempest* by William Shakespeare' (7). Typically, the most important and blatantly obvious literary source, Coleridge's *Ancient Mariner*, is not worth a mention.

In a prologue and three parts ('Bring Forth a Wonder,' 'The Devil

Knows How to Row,' 'The Dead Sailors') containing altogether fifty-nine chapters (or rather fifty-eight, for – as in *A Short Sad Book* – there is no chapter 52), Bowering – or rather the writer 'George Bowering' within the novel – tells the readers his version of the history of George Vancouver's exploration of Canada's west coast, of how Vancouver inscribed his own and other British names all over a foreign continent; but – on a metafictional level – he also tells the readers about the process of his own writing the story and history two hundred years after the fact, with all the problems this act implies. Thus the quotation from Robbe-Grillet that Bowering had used as an epigraph in *A Short Sad Book* applies to *Burning Water* as well.

The Prologue of *Burning Water* establishes the frame in which the 'two equally important (and closely intertwined) strands'[21] of the novel – the story of George Vancouver and the metafictional story of George Bowering writing the story of George Vancouver – are linked together: here already we see the beginning of the appropriation by a Canadian of the story of the appropriation of Canada (if we take this Amerindian term to be the original name of the country rather than one imposed by the British) on behalf of the British Empire. And to appropriate a story means to integrate it parodically into a new narrative.

As Bowering himself has shown in *A Short Sad Book*, the easiest way of incorporating a parodied text into the new perspective of a parodying text is to use a quotation: this quotation is then integrated into a frame that makes clear that we are not dealing with just a repetition, but rather with a repetition with a difference. In a way, Bowering's Prologue already serves this function of a frame, as the Vancouverite Bowering warns us:

> When I was a boy I was the only person I knew who was named George, but I did have the same first name as the king. That made me feel as if current history and self were bound together, from the beginning.
>
> When I came to live in Vancouver, I thought of Vancouver, and so now geography involved my name too, George Vancouver. He might have felt such romance, sailing for a king named George the Third. What could I do but write a book filled with history and myself, about these people and this place? (9)

Bowering himself refers in the Prologue to the 'poetry book about Vancouver and me' (i.e., *George, Vancouver*) and to a radio play, but neither seems to have had the epic quality worthy of the 'story of the greatest navigational voyage of all time' (9). In order 'to do it for real this time, their story,' Bowering even 'went back to Trieste, as far eastward as you can go in western Europe, among seafaring Europeans or their descendants' (10). And, especially in a novel that is largely based on parodic echoes, Trieste, as Eva-Marie Kröller points out, is more than just a city in Italy: 'Yet Trieste and the territory surrounding it are so strongly associated with crucial developments in modern history and literature as to make its very name into a quotation.' Bowering himself leads us to the same direction when he comments on an earlier draft of Burning Water entitled 'The Dead Sailors': '... [the novel] starts off I went to Trieste, right? So it starts off with a parody of the beginning of a realist novel, which goes something like, "he was residing in a hotel in blah-blah-blah" ...'[22]

Commenting on the complicated narrative situation of a novel in which 'we Georges all felt the same sun,' Bowering concludes his Prologue: 'We cannot tell a story that leaves us outside, and when I say we, I include you. But in order to include you, I feel that I cannot spend these pages saying I to a second person. Therefore let us say he, and stand together looking at them. We are making a story, after all, as we always have been, standing and speaking together to make up a history, a real historical fiction' (10). This introduction already puts everything told within the novel into a certain perspective: from now on, pronominal reference is shaky at best – he may be Vancouver as well as Bowering at almost any time – and the least one can do is agree with Ronald Hatch that Burning Water 'directs us to reflect on the way in which every historian becomes a part of his creation.'[23]

After the title page of part 1 has flaunted the novel's metafictional character by reproducing the engraving on the Chinese notebook in which the manuscript of the novel was supposed to have been written, chapter 1 starts with the discussion by two West Coast Indians of a 'vision,' in fact Vancouver's ships, approaching an inlet on 10 June 1792. Only the younger, inexperienced Indian takes the incoming ships to be giant birds, though, while the other one is more pragmatic and knows European boats to be facts rather than visions and teaches his student in good rationalist eighteenth-century European manner to make use of his imagination, which is based on fact, rather than this fancy, which is not. In his essay 'Imagining History: The Romantic Background of George Bowering's Burning Water,' Edward Lobb points out that this distinction between fancy and imagination that pervades the novel 'is an ambitious and largely successful treatment of the nature of imagination in Coleridgean terms.' Vancouver himself later defines the distinction between fancy and imagination, between 'idle dreaming and real perception':[24]

> 'The imagination,' he said. 'You speak of it as if it were the opposite of facts, as if it were perhaps the enemy of facts. That is not true in the least, my two young friends. The imagination depends upon facts, it feeds on them in order to produce beauty or invention, or discovery. The imagination is never the enemy of my eleven feet. The true enemy of the imagination is laziness, habit, leisure. The enemy of imagination is the idleness that provides fancy.' (155)

Reginald Berry points out another literary echo in the first chapter, a Joycean parallel, which itself may have been caused by the partial setting of the contemporary strand of the story in Trieste, the city where Joyce taught: 'In some aspects the first section of Burning Water (two Indians discussing a vision on June 10, 1792) reads like a parody of the first section of Ulysses (Stephen Dedalus and Buck Mulligan conversing in the Martello tower on June 16, 1904).'[25]

Although it is not his official mission during his exploratory travels, Vancouver wants to appropriate the coast; he 'loved to jump out of a boat, stride a few paces up the beach, and announce: "I claim this new-found land for his Britannic majesty in perpetuity, and name it New Norfolk!"' (26–7). Only Quadra, a captain sailing for the Spanish empire, can serve as a less imperially oriented 'European' voice in the novel because, for obvious reasons, he identifies with the colonies rather than with the mother country: '"It is just that I was born in Lima, you should remember. I am a European only by virtue of the stories and traditions I always heard from my parents and their friends"' (28). Quadra has already integrated the European tradition into a 'parodic' frame and can look at the European view of history in a detached way of which Vancouver is incapable. When Vancouver anachronistically reminisces about his 'friend' James Wolfe, who was killed by the French on the Plains of Abraham (before Vancouver could have ever met him), Quadra reminds him of the place that Wolfe has won in history. Of course, he does not forget either to allude to Benjamin West's painting The Death of Wolfe, which seems to haunt most Canadian historical novels:[26] '"But try to look at it this way, George. He will have a secure place in history. They will paint pictures of his triumphant death, with his body fully-clothed in the colours of his homeland. They will write great poems and perhaps songs about him. His name will live forever in that land. Have they decided on a name for it yet?" ' (29).

While writing the novel in Italy, Bowering comes upon buildings and monuments that are so old that the historical discussions about the naming of the New World – which form a major part of this novel written by a New World author – seem absurd, or at least inconsequential: 'He walked all the way round the Santa Maria del Fiore and thought that it had been standing a few hundred years when Vancouver sailed, that in fact it was a couple of hundred years old when, in 1592, Juan de Fuca, real name Apostolos Valerianos, claimed that he had found north of latitude 48° a vast inland sea' (30).

The story of Juan de Fuca leads Bowering back to the theme of history-writing and plagiarism or parody. His George Vancouver, who had already been to the west coast on earlier expeditions with his mentor, James Cook, questions not only de Fuca's claim to have reached the Strait of Anian but also the existence of the strait: ' "I have been there, you'll remember, and I believe that Juan de Fuca never reached the water given his name by Meares" ' (31). In his own journal, the real George Vancouver cannot withhold a certain satisfaction either at finding proof that earlier exploration reports such as Meares's narrative of Captain Gray's exploits had been nothing but fantasies or uncritical copies of earlier writing. After meeting with the American Gray, he states that 'it is not possible to conceive any one to be more astonished than was Mr. Gray, on his being made acquainted, that his authority had been quoted, and the track pointed out that he had been said to have made in the sloop Washington. In contradiction to which, he assured the officers, that he had penetrated only 50 miles into the straits in question ...'[27] Or, as Bowering's Archibald Menzies disqualifies Meares in a conversation with Gray, 'Our meeting enables us to detect to the world a fallacy in this author which no excuse can justify' (97).

In a dialogue that the George Bowering in the novel imagines while walking through twentieth-century Italy, Vancouver comments on 'the journals of Mr. ex-Commander Meares' that 'reck less of the truth than any you'll find this side of Juan de Fuca, strait or Greek' (31–2). Still, in Florence he hits upon 'a monumental *mappa mundi*' sporting 'a fanciful *Cina* and a fanciful *Giapan*' as well as 'a sea called the *Stretto di Annian*' (36). And later, in chapter 28, Bowering summarizes several of the myths about the existence of a Strait of Anian or a Northwest

Passage, also including the information gathered regarding Gray's supposed exploits:

> Meares said that in 1789 the American Captain Gray, in the *Lady Washington*, sailed past the pillar and into the Strait of Anian. Meares' book published a chart of that lengendary voyage. (But two years later Mr. Menzies with Lieutenant Puget, falling into conversation with Captain Gray, brought up the facts of Meares' book and the fortunate passage, whereupon the Yankee disavowed both. Fancy, we are permitted to see once more, does not hesitate to make its face plain where there is money to be claimed.) (125)

On the metafictional level of the novel, the narrator George Bowering makes fun of the Proustian or Joycean way of overcoming the distance between past and present through an epiphany, the 'historiographic' method that we had already seen fail in Buckler's 'pretty good Canadian novel.' After he sees a seagull, 'a sheet of intuition fell over him. He felt a pressure of memory' (38). Bowering plays with his readers' expectations; after he has described what an experienced reader would recognize as a typical Joycean epiphany, he refuses to emplot the events narrated in the expected way: unfortunately his vision was only the memory 'of his earlier life as a seagull.' Not being 'a mystic' or 'a nineteen-year-old college student,' he does not feel that affected by the vision and does not succumb to any delusions of being a Joycean protagonist, and 'it did not change his life in any way' (38). Bowering here rewrites the story of an epiphany, and – comparable to Buckler – by having it fail, he shows the inappropriateness of this European model in a Canadian context.

The effect in this case is humorous, and, of course, Bowering's novel as a whole is rather humorous; here, as in his other fiction, the ludic element is omnipresent, a quality to which a structural analysis such as this one does not always do justice. That is why some remarks on Bowering's language, the paint on the window-pane within his narrative frame,[28] are necessary, because it so obviously draws attention to itself and repels many critics and readers through flippancy, cliché, and the use of styles which are completely incompatible with the characters of the respective speakers (especially in the case of the natives). Bowering's use of language is as much a parody as his use of earlier texts, whether they be historiographical or literary. If we interpret his appropriation of history that he had already indicated in *A Short Sad*

Book, and which also dominates *Burning Water* from the Prologue onwards, as the act of removing it from the sphere of influence of the
colonial powers, we may discover an analogous attitude towards language. According to John Moss, 'Bowering's principal tool in the constructive demolition he undertakes is language itself. This he mercilessly
deploys to flaunt our apparently obsessive will to accept the unac-
ceptable. Words, phrases, clauses, sentences, paragraphs, in *Burning
Water,* all fall into place according to grammatical convention. And if
they baffle, mislead or confuse, if they amuse, infuriate or impress, so
much the better.'[29]

Vancouver states that language is a means of domination: he uses
language in order to institute government and trade. 'Learning a naked
foreigner's tongue,' Bowering makes him say, 'is the first step in creating some form of government' (42). But sometimes Vancouver even
turns this act of domination into an Adamic act of naming: not only
did he write 'all over the globe,' but 'he never wrote down on his charts
any names that were there before he got there' (63). And he gets there
by means of a boat: 'The ship is the vessel of metaphor, a carrying
across, as they say' (166). He pretends to be the first one to give names
to what he claimed was an as yet unnamed and uninhabited country.
Of course, the country was not uninhabited; the mountains and bays
probably had Indian names already, and many of them had been named
by the Spaniards. In fact, like palimpsests, the Spanish names appear
on some of Vancouver's maps. Still, it is not only Bowering's George
Vancouver but also the real one who prides himself on having been
the first in yet another respect, of having come closer to the South Pole
than anybody else, thus to have boldly gone where no man went
before, gaining the right to indulge in an Adamic Act of naming.[30]
Bowering's Vancouver refers to his role as Adamic when he decides
to spend a night 'on no rocking waves, but where the newmade Adam
himself might lie him down' (110). Dr Menzies, who is somewhat more
apt at deciphering the already existing sign systems of the New World,
tends to be unhappy with the language, if not the contents, of his
captain's decisions.

From the point of view of domination through language, one of the
worst puns in the novel becomes interesting: after Vancouver has proved
his linguistic skills by asking in his pidgin Haida, 'How through forest
it days with canoes many is?' Bowering comments, 'Years later Benjamin Wharf would be built where this aching query was put' (143).
The irony underlying this aching pun is that Benjamin Whorf, the
linguist, was interested in language as a means of communication and

not of domination: Vancouver's interest in language is a parody of Whorf's. The flippant language Bowering uses always has this parodic quality, which detracts from its direct referential, denotative function and points back to the storyteller, who thus affirms his own power over the story.[31]

In Bowering's emplotment of the history of Vancouver's expedition, the centre of which is Vancouver's emplotment of himself, the botanist Archibald Menzies very soon turns out to be the captain's main antagonist. In the source material, the naturalist and doctor generally 'emerges from the multiple references of the various accounts as a most likable character, testy at times with Vancouver's arbitrary commands, but ordinarily a kindly and attentive surgeon.' In the 'Biographical Note' accompanying C.F. Newcombe's edition of Menzies's journal, J. Forsyth writes, however, that 'although Captain Vancouver and Menzies were usually on good terms ... the relationship became strained when the Captain demanded Menzies' journals and the latter refused to give them up until Sir Joseph Banks and the Admiralty had granted permission ...'[32] Thus the episode in which Menzies refuses to hand over his notebook to Vancouver (chapter 58) is historical, but in the context of the novel it gains new significance: he refuses to let his own emplotment of history be subsumed under Vancouver's perspective.

Bowering is clearly not the only one in the novel who regards history as a text that can be altered: Vancouver and his fellow explorers do the same thing. Even in Vancouver's journal, there develops a close relationship between Vancouver and Juan Francisco de la Bodega y Quadra, the Spanish – or rather Peruvian – captain who teaches Vancouver, the 'Puritan on the very edge of the world' (60), a little *joie de vivre*. 'The warm friendship' between Vancouver and Quadra that earlier biographers see shining 'through the impersonal account' turns into a homosexual relationship. The historical Vancouver himself points out that the political differences regarding the handing over of Nootka to the English 'had not the least effect on our personal intercourse with each other, or on the advantages we derived from our mutual good offices.'[33] No wonder that – even if Bowering's fantasies concerning such developments were true – the emplotment strategy of suppression would have been applied in Vancouver's log, leading to 'the absence of his greatest discovery in those pages' (74).

The question of emplotment, even if not called by that name, is on Vancouver's mind when he wonders, 'What kind of fancy fixed their sailing date for All Fools' Day?' (80), and the reference to All Fools' Day as well as a 'ship of fools' (81) might remind readers of another ship of fools setting out on All Fools' Day, namely, Herman Melville's *Fidèle* in *The Confidence-Man*. On this other ship, the reliability of language is also continually questioned, although the context is quite different from that of Vancouver's expedition.[34] A good example of how arbitrarily one can emplot certain events by integrating them into a story or refraining from doing so is given in chapter 18: a storm smashes into the *Chatham* and the *Discovery* and invites emplotment. Bowering the narrator insists on the importance of the parodic frames that he might build around (the textualized version of) the event: the storm 'might have been a test. It might have been a warning. It was probably just a meteorological fact' (82).

While he claims to have abstained from emplotment strategies in the above case, Bowering does not hide the fact that he emplots Archibald Menzies's actions so as to make them fall into the general parodic pattern of the novel. The fact that Menzies shot an albatross and analysed its corpse in April 1792[35] serves as a starting-point at which Bowering can anchor mythological and literary emplotment. Menzies 'brought down the brown albatross that had been following them since they had departed the [Sandwich] Islands ...' (86). The parody here, of course, is that of Coleridge's *Rime of the Ancient Mariner*, and as he does not trust his readers in the same way that Joyce and Eliot had relied on their audience's knowledge of underlying 'classical' texts, Bowering does not hesitate to thematize this intertextual relationship: 'In case anyone was wondering: yes, this happened on the same day that the English poet was composing his Christian ballad.' The 'thoroughly unsuperstitious' doctor, though, may have been fully unaware of his running along thoroughly beaten literary tracks because 'in any event, Dr. Menzies seldom read verse, though he did write commendable prose' (87). This first reference to Coleridge closes the first part of the novel, entitled 'Bring Forth a Wonder.'

Like the doctor, Bowering's seamen also resist their being drawn into the parody unless they are forced or invited to by the naïvety of the emplotting literati: 'They didn't give two hoots about an albatross. Unless there was a literary person about. If there was a literary person about, they let on about how the great spread albatross over the quarterdeck was the source of supernatural calm, and the dead albatross was a source of the supernatural dread' (162). A 'sailor named Delsing,' bearing a name that has often served George Bowering as his own *nom-de-texte* in *A Short Sad Book*, the early novel *Mirror on the Floor*, and other stories,[36] tells a German poet that he had once killed an albatross and had been forced to wear it 'around his neck until it dropped off' (162). Such a parody of Coleridge's story, which reconstructs the situation on which the poet's 'Christian ballad' might have been founded, is of course a special type of parody which almost parallels the interpretation that sees Pound's *Hugh Selwyn Mauberley* as (presumptively?) parodying what Findley or others may later produce as their parodies of itself.

Among the intertextual relationships between Bowering's *Burning Water* and Coleridge's *Ancient Mariner*, there is also the title of the novel, which – whatever else may be alluded to in it – takes up references in the poem to the slimy marine animals present in tropical waters that 'burnt green, and blue and white' (l. 130) and gave a charmed appearance to the sea that 'burnt alway / A Still and awful red' (ll. 270–1). As John Livingston Lowes has shown, Coleridge had based his lines on 'burning water' on the journals of Captain Cook. So we are here confronted with a complex network of parodic relationships: Coleridge artistically re-works (parodies, in one sense of the word) Cook's writing; the real George Vancouver, who had been Cook's apprentice on his expeditions, rewrites what had been erroneous statements in the journals of Cook, 'his chief and best teacher,' 'his father' even (44, 45). Here we have a good example of what Helen Tiffin calls 'canonical counter-discourse': 'This strategy ... is one in which a post-colonial writer takes up a character or characters, or the basic assumptions of a British canonical text, and unveils those assumptions, subverting the text for post-colonial purposes.'[37]

The beginning of part 2 of *Burning Water* (bearing the Coleridgean title 'The Devil Knows How to Row') takes Bowering the writer back to the city of Vancouver, covering the distance of George Vancouver's year-long travels in a matter of hours. The reader is brought back into the company of the Indians, who are discussing the 'vision' that they had of the Englishman's boats. In having them either behave according to white stereotypes of what Indian behaviour is like – thus parodying the stereotypes – or by having them take over wholesale some 'white' locutions and proverbs – thus parodying these traditional locutions by integrating them into a totally unexpected context – Bowering achieves humorous effects whose didactic efficiency as a parodic shock treatment should not be ruled out. An example of the first case is the comment on the older Indian's patient behaviour towards the young Indian as an artist: 'The third Indian's efforts to be creative were noted by his friend with approval. That is why he wasn't impatient with him. A lot of people think that Indians are just naturally patient, but that's not true. Before the white "settlers" arrived there were lots of impatient

Indians. It's only in the last two hundred years that Indians have been looking patient whenever there were any white men around' (92). The acceptance of white clichés by Indians and their parodic integration into the fundus of native wisdom becomes clear in the next example: ' "There is an old Haida saying I have heard," said the third Indian, "that says, history will repeat its unhappiest hours upon those who do not remember what happened the first time" ' (94). As Archibald Menzies puts it in an (imagined) conversation with Vancouver, '[The people who live here] deem the mountains to be mountains, that and whatever advantage they can make of that. They are true Western man' (108).

At least in these paragraphs, the perception of the Canadian west coast from a European point of view in the old (i.e., Vancouver's original) text is exchanged for the perception of the European explorers from an 'indigenous' Canadian point of view in the new (i.e., Bowering's parodic) text. I am aware that critics such as Terry Goldie would rightfully quarrel with my use of the word *indigenous* here: Goldie points out in his contribution to *Future Indicative*, the Ottawa symposium on modern theoretical approaches to Canadian literature, that even in exploration reports such as Samuel Hearne's (and this certainly refers to His Majesty's cartographer, George Vancouver), the European is the sign-giver in the semiotic process of naming a new country: 'This semiosis in which native peoples are presented is under the control of the white sign-makers. The signs at play, whether those signs represent repulsion or attraction, reflect the power relationships in the economy of imperialist discourse.'[38] This, however, is the very fact that Bowering makes (and many readers may wish to add, too blatantly) obvious in his parodies. As I pointed out earlier, the indigenous people Bowering describes parodically are not Indians in their own right but Indians as seen by Bowering. Such a blatantly obvious reduction of the natives to comic-book figures can be interpreted as Bowering's criticism of the fact that, as Robin Fisher puts it, 'some of the major themes of Canadian historical writing have perpetuated a limited view of the indigenous Canadian.' It satirically points out what Bruce G. Trigger calls the 'failure of historians and anthropologists to regard native peoples as an integral part of Canadian society.' Commenting on Bowering's parodic technique, Goldie remarks in *Fear and Temptation: The Image of the Indigene in Canadian, Australian, and New Zealand Literatures* that 'George Bowering emphasizes his prenominal relationship with George Vancouver ... but the latter is constantly insensitive to the necessities of indigenization which the text exhibts so strongly.'[39]

Although he communicates and trades with the indigenous population, George Vancouver's interest is – at least in Bowering's view –
primarily to be a surveyor leaving 'no faint lines or white cloudy spaces
on the charts he took back to Europe's scribes,' and to 'become the
name they thought of first' (100) whenever they thought of the Pacific
coast. Vancouver's tendency to inscribe himself into the new-found
landscapes also leaves its traces in *Burning Water*. At a certain point,
Vancouver's original voice takes over, for example in chapter 23, which
is entirely an almost literal transcription of a letter that he sent to
Admiral Stephens on 6 December 1793, and which summarizes events
– such as the death of John Carter after eating mussels – that took
place in the month of August of that year.[40]

The most daring examples of changes of factual information that
Bowering uses with regard to Vancouver's narrative, and which arise
from strategies of emplotment, are without any doubt the suggestion
of a homosexual relationship between Vancouver and Quadra throughout the novel and a dream in chapter 30, which would have been the
absolute centre-piece of the novel, arithmetically speaking, if the book
had not been thrown off balance by Bowering's omission of chapter
52. The strange vision in which Vancouver sees his boats flying across
the continent from the west coast to Hudson Bay may be traced back
to one of the 'moments of excitement' in Vancouver's narrative 'when
he was sailing up Howe Sound, thinking for a few hours that he had
breached the barrier of the coast mountains' and found the Northwest
Passage. In his published journal, Vancouver writes that on 15 June
1792, 'towards noon I considered that we had advanced some miles
within the western boundary of the snowy barrier [of the coastal moun-
tains], as some of its rugged lofty mountains were now behind, and to
the southward of us. This filled my mind with the pleasing hopes of
finding our way to its eastern side.'[41] Leaving all pretensions of writing
a realistic work of historiography behind, Bowering develops these
pleasing hopes into a full-fledged visionary dream.

At the beginning of part 3, 'The Dead Sailors,' Bowering has fulfilled
the vision he had in a dream in part 2 of 'unexpectedly flying to a
strange Central American city with his wife' (118): 'He had gone east
to Trieste because the Europeans had come west, and now he was
going south to Guatemala because they had come north' (173). Still,
Vancouver himself finally moves south to California and Hawaii in
order to meet Quadra and ultimately return home to England.

For obvious reasons, we might expect Bowering, who in the Prologue
elaborates on his personal connection not only with the person George

Vancouver but also with the city of Vancouver, to concentrate on the Canadian content of Vancouver's text. But one of the scenes he high-lights is set on his way south in the Pacific Ocean, seemingly in the middle of nowhere, at the point where an archipelago discovered by the Spaniards is supposed to be: Los Majos. In the published version of his journal, Vancouver just states that there is no land where the Spaniards claimed Los Majos were situated: 'At the close of day there was no appearance of these islands so far as could be seen a head, and as we had now passed some distance to the westward, I concluded they could have no existence in the neighbourhood of the spot assigned to them, and for that reason I relinquished any further search, and made the best of our way to Owhyhee.' His editor, W. Kaye Lamb, indicates the possibility that Los Majos were identical with the Sand-wich Islands and remarks that 'Vancouver makes no mention of this possibility himself, no doubt because he would have been reluctant to admit that the Spaniards might have discovered the islands before Cook.'[42] In Bowering's novel, Vancouver explicitly states that such a 'fact' would run counter to his strategy of emplotment: 'If Los Mojos [sic] are not there, then the Spaniards were visitors to the Sandwich Islands before James Cook landed there, and that would not be an acceptable fact in my view of history' (202).

Whereas the examples of emplotment quoted so far, except maybe for the last one, which moves already in the direction of a falsification of facts rather than just a biased interpretation, are all more or less classifiable as instances of highlighting or suppression, we have in the unexpected and clearly ahistorical ending of the novel a radical change in Vancouver's narrative. Similar to Findley's *Famous Last Words* in this respect, it goes far beyond all strategies of emplotment admissible in historiography: while the historical Vancouver returns to England to write his *Voyage*, Bowering's is killed by Menzies. The antagonism between Vancouver and Menzies is the major strategy behind the em-plotment of the historical data referring to the Vancouver expedition, but in a way the parodic strategies of emplotment develop an energy of their own. In tune with the parodic parallels between the *Ancient Mariner* and *Burning Water*, the dying Vancouver asks, 'Will you want me round your neck till I fall?' (258). In at least one instance (a prolepsis in a reference to the late Captain Vancouver [151]), Bowering has pre-pared the reader for this murder committed by Menzies, or by another, mightier force – 'some strength unwitnessed' (the narrator or author?). At first sight, the murder destroys the historiographic aspirations of the novel, but the alteration should not distract us from the fact that

Burning Water is – amongst other things – a historical novel, at least insofar as it deals with the problems of writing a history. Admittedly, it takes the strategies of emplotment far, too far perhaps, beyond what is acceptable in a historical novel. The murder illustrates that history has been turned into fiction and that it has adapted to a myth that is in a way truer than history, ending – as Eva-Marie Kröller points out – 'with a death mythologically more fitting than [Vancouver's] historical end: like Narcissus and Ahab, Vancouver drowns in the sea that he tried to make the reflection of his own self.'[43]

The mythologization that comes with Bowering's emplotment of Vancouver's story is also obvious in another deviation from factual history. While Vancouver's *Discovery* was in fact only a namesake of Cook's *Discovery* launched as late as 1789, Bowering suggests that it was the same ship that 'thirteen years earlier ... had appeared at Nootka, under the command of the as yet uneaten Captain James Cook' (19). Such a change of the facts serves to emphasize the father-son relation that Bowering constructs between Vancouver and his mentor, and for which there is certain evidence such as the real Vancouver's unwillingness to criticize and revise Cook's text even when he knows it to be wrong. Edward Lobb comments on the 'anxiety of influence' on the part of Vancouver and links it with Vancouver's contemplation of actual 'cannibalism after recovering Cook's body' (126), which is reflected by Bowering's literary cannibalism of 'earlier writers through quotation and allusion,'[44] what I have called parody.

Bowering's 'literary cannibalism' comes to the fore in his rewriting of the historical exploration reports emplotted by Vancouver and Menzies. The strategy of emplotment is at work not only in the historical exploration reports but also in a latter-day secondary version of history such as *Burning Water*. The George Bowering within the novel claims that for him it is a 'strange *fancy* that history is given' (9), whereas he knows that it is a 'strange *fact* that history is taken.' Here, however, the process of emplotment is quite far-reaching: in MacLulich's terms, Vancouver's death turns the story that would have been an *odyssey* into an *ordeal*, or – in White's terminology – from a romance into a tragedy. This generic change should be read as a parody in the sense employed in this study, as repetition with a difference, or rather with a vengeance, as a strategy – or a mode – which makes use of old texts by integrating them into a new one. The old direction and intention of the parodied text are then subsumed under the new perspective of the parodying text. Whereas MacLulich may have been right in claiming that 'explorers are ... relatively unsophisticated storytellers, who tend to emplot their stories in a simple manner,'[45] we certainly cannot say this about the twentieth-century critic, novelist, and poet George Bowering or his persona within the text.

Within the novel, Quadra's role foreshadows Bowering's as an author. Bowering finds himself in an awkward role: he is writing a postcolonial novel from the point of view of the colonized Canadians, but at the same time he has to realize that he is a descendant of the white colonizers, whereas the indigenous people play nothing more than the role of Shakespearean fools. Quadra himself, who was born in Peru, verbalizes this problem in the novel: 'I am a European only by virtue of the stories and traditions I always heard from my parents and their friends' (28).

To say that the Canadian writer Bowering kills off the British colonizer and explorer Vancouver in order to make the story and history of Canadian exploration his own may be taking the interpretation of *Burning Water* as parody and self-appropriation quite far, but such would be postmodern and postcolonial parody as repetition or rewriting with a vengeance *par excellence*. We have to admit, though, that it is the enlightened colonizer Menzies rather than the colonized Indians who takes history into his own hands and kills Vancouver. And Bowering and his audience are not exactly representatives of the autochthonous Canadian population.

The preceding pages have clearly shown that parodic techniques are practically omnipresent in *Burning Water*, as they had been in *A Short Sad Book*. Although the novel abounds with linguistic puns and parodic literary allusions that at first sight do not seem to amount to more than clever games that Bowering plays with his readers, the metafictional (or rather, metahistorical) musings that are included in the two novels show there is more to Bowering's deconstructionist stance than irresponsive and irresponsible game-playing, that at the very least 'stereotypes are the subject of a parodic re-evaluation, which makes readers realize that what they hold to be true, or realistic, is very often part of a set of conventions which literature (and historiography) has engraved in our thought system.'[46]

The aspect of game-playing, though, should not be neglected in a postmodern text written by an author of Bowering's persuasion. In a recent discussion with Robert Kroetsch, he admits to playing such a game of hide-and-seek with his audience. His writing from the margin of a former empire is marginal even in Canada: Alan Twigg summarizes Bowering's point of view as follows: 'He has a new theory: Albertans like his friend Robert Kroetsch reject history and make myth. Quebecois writers reject history and then make their own. But in B.C., where a boy could grow up not knowing the street names, history is fair game to be explored and re-invented.'[47] Bowering is not the only writer from British Columbia to have reinvented history, as Jack Hodgins's title *The Invention of the World* suggests. But besides being reinvented, history is also fair game to be parodied, such a parody often resulting in a deconstruction rather than a reconstruction of the imperial master narrative, whether this imperial master narrative be of a historical, non-fictional quality – such as Vancouver's writing – or of a more lyrical quality – such as Coleridge's *Ancient Mariner*.

The writing of history and historical fiction in a formerly colonized country such as Canada has to come to grips with the typical problems of what Linda Hutcheon calls historiographic metafiction and what I have called metahistorical parody. Although I refer to *Burning Water* as a historical novel, I am well aware that it is not a typical novel of the Walter Scott / James Fenimore Cooper tradition that leads up to George Lukács's realist historical novel. Bowering's novel – as well as Findley's studied above – is rather an example of what Hans Vilmar Geppert calls the 'other' historical novel: it puts emphasis on the built-in 'Hiatus von Fiktion und Historie,' the 'hiatus' between the fictional act of re-creating the past and the past itself.[48]

Burning Water has to share some of the criticism that other novels profiting from the narrative possibilities of this hiatus opening up have attracted. T.D. MacLulich's bitter comment on the ludism of postmodernists such as Bowering that 'may not announce the health of a national tradition, but may predict its death, crushed by the weight of excessive self-consciousness' is certainly an over-reaction arising from the fact that 'his often whimsical rewriting of history never did sit well with those trying to formulate and ennoble the Canadian national identity.' And Terry Goldie may go quite far in the other direction when he calls the novel 'a text which makes a significant attempt to be sensitive to the indigenous culture.' But, however ironic Chris Scott's statement about *Burning Water* may have been ('Historical novel this ain't, real fiction it is, and how')[49] and whatever Bowering may have said in interviews about his political commitment, his strength and motivation lie in the admirable structural acrobatics of parody rather than in the political arguments that are the intention behind these parodies.

5 Atwood: Parodies from a Feminist Point of View

'What I'm going to tell you now,' he said, 'may sound incredible. But then, when you're not accustomed to history, most facts about the past *do* sound incredible.' *Aldous Huxley*

All history was a palimpsest, scraped clean and reinscribed exactly as often as was necessary. *George Orwell*[1]

Margaret Atwood is doubtless the suitable contemporary Canadian novelist with whom to close this study. Not only is she the best-known Canadian writer – at home in Canada as well as abroad – but as a woman writer in a world that is still generally seen to be dominated by men she also becomes doubly representative of parodic strategies in contemporary literature, of using and undermining dominant discourses and 'inherited fictional forms.' Coral Ann Howells draws attention to this double bind when she points out the affinities existing between, on the one hand, 'women's experience of the power politics of gender and their problematic relation to patriarchal traditions of authority' and, on the other hand, 'Canada's attitude to the cultural imperialism of the United States as well as its ambivalence towards its European inheritance.' Parody here works on the level of gender as well as nation; as Lorna Irvine puts it,

> Although Canadian writers in general often illustrate adventure and escape differently from American writers, women writers more consistently than male writers situate and celebrate a maternal domain that presents an alternative structuring to that of patriarchal systems. As a result, within already established patterns of colonization, or at least of economic and political domination, women writers find that subversive language powerfully connects their cultural and psychological situations, their positions as Canadians and women.[2]

Patricia Waugh points out to what extent the works of contemporary women writers such as Margaret Atwood differ from the present male-oriented postmodern kind of writing which in Canada is dominated by writers such as George Bowering, the subject of the preceding chapter. Canadian women authors share with the male postmodernists their preference for the popular, 'rejecting the elitist and purely formalist celebration of modernism.' But, 'at the moment when postmodernism is forging its identity through articulating the exhaustion of the existential belief in self-presence and self-fulfilment and through the dispersal of the universal subject of liberalism, *feminism* (ostensibly, at any rate) is assembling *its* cultural identity in what appears to be the opposite direction.' Feminist or feminine writers go in this opposite direction of creating a different but still coherent cosmology by using techniques such as consciousness-raising, 'aimed precisely at the forging of an individual and collective sense of identity.' In this sense they clearly deviate from 'male' types of postmodern writing such as Bowering's. For this reason, a statement such as Linda Hutcheon's that 'Atwood's fiction is ... the epitome of this postmodern contradiction'[3] is debatable and will be discussed at the end of this chapter.

If we look for the *narrative* strategies of women's 'alternative structuring to that of patriarchal systems,' even a short and mostly thematically oriented introduction to Atwood's work such as Barbara Hill Rigney's points to the important role that parody plays in Atwood's novels, and it hints at the special meaning that parody has in this context: 'All of Atwood's works are, in some sense, parodies, critical of any ideology or literary style which has "pretensions to profundity." But her concerns, as we know most particularly from *True Stories, Bodily Harm*, and *The Handmaid's Tale*, go deeper than mere parody can convey.' 'Mere parody' is probably supposed to mean parody as it has been traditionally defined as a humorous and playful version of earlier texts, just as it has – at a superficial reading – been used by Bowering. And this is the way Atwood herself has defined it in an essay on Canadian humour, in which she sees parody as 'habitually work[ing] in a double-edged way: by trivializing a specific work or style whose original has pretensions of profundity, it allows the audience an escape from the marginal and mysterious in "art." '[4]

If we abstract from parody's humorous features and redefine it in the way suggested by Hutcheon and others in the first part of this study, we arrive at a parodic art form that can 'go deeper than mere parody,' that 'subverts and revises certain conventions of the novel.' Such a view of parody would also take into account what Frank Davey describes as translation from one discourse into another, of 'instances in recent Canadian writing where previously inscribed strategies are resisted or where inherited literary texts or practices are transformed and translated.' This redefinition would then also include Coral Ann Howells's view of Atwood exploring the 'implications for women's writing as dissent from existing structures of authority.'[5]

In her essay 'Telling It Over Again: Atwood's Art of Parody,' Barbara Godard gives a good introduction not only to Atwood's poetry but also to contemporary theories of parody (focusing on Linda Hutcheon's approach). She shows to what extent parody in the sense used in this study has always been important in Atwood's poetry, starting even before her first published volume, *Double Persephone*. Mentioning Atwood's novels and the tendency of her protagonists to 'cure themselves of a habit of taking or borrowing from other artists/writers by exposing the distortion of such derivation or copying,' Godard states that 'Atwood's fiction is grounded in paradox, however. While the embedded narratives denounce all imitation, the text is composed through such superposition of ready-made narratives. The purported reductiveness of the copy, suggested in the embedded text, is counterbalanced by the expansiveness of the synthesis in the new text. Moreover, discrimination of originality depends on the reader's thorough knowledge of and detection of copied forms, paradoxically valorised.'[6]

Bodily Harm and *The Handmaid's Tale*, the two novels among the Atwood titles that Rigney mentioned earlier on, fit ideally into the framework of this study, not only because they are parodic in the sense of the word used here, but also because in them Atwood comes closest to, and at the same time extends, the realm of what one can refer to as historical novels. In the earlier *Lady Oracle*, Margaret Atwood had already made use of parodic strategies when she shaped standard and clichéd forms of literary mass products such as cheap romances into an original new form of writing, but I would agree with Coral Ann Howells that '*Bodily Harm* and *The Handmaid's Tale* show Atwood in her most radical light, for here not only is she rewriting traditional literary genres like gothic romance and the utopias of science fiction but she is also attempting to revise the categories of "Canadian" and "female" through which her own identity is constituted.'[7] In addition to this, the two texts are 'profoundly political' novels that 'represent the confrontation with power and its universal forms: dictatorship, tyranny, torture and the reality of violence.' In a strictly traditional sense, of course, neither book can be called a 'historical' novel because one is set in the present and the other one in the future. Still, they belong to a group of novels that 'may be read as revisions of history told from a marginalized feminine perspective.'[8]

Bodily Harm fits into this category for yet another reason: it shows us two societies, Canadian and Caribbean, which exist at two different stages of their political development, and Rennie, who has come to the Caribbean in order to do a travel piece, is a time traveller as much as she is a tourist. To quote Ezra Pound on the coexistence of different phases of history at the same time, 'all ages are contemporaneous. It is B.C., let us say, in Morocco. The Middle Ages are in Russia. The future stirs already in the minds of the few.'[9] The political corruption of the Caribbean, with power elites such as the corrupt dictator Ellis and his supporters clinging to their positions, might be interpreted as a repetition of the nineteenth-century Canadian situation. And the novel may even be read as historically prophetic in the sense that from the island of St Antoine 'when it is not so hazy you can see Grenada,'[10] where – as we are told – 'the Cubans are building a large airport' (135). The omnipresent CIA agents in *Bodily Harm* – there 'to nip history in the bud' (135) – uncannily prove to have been precursors of President Reagan's later military invasion of Grenada.

The Handmaid's Tale, a dystopia about late twentieth-century America, gives us the 'tale' as it has been reconstructed and is discussed by historians at a conference in the late twenty-second century. Seen from the perspective of the conference in 2195, the tale is a historical report, and the discussion of its veracity as well as the handmaid's remarks on her own version – or rather versions – of the past focus on some of the main problems of writing historical texts, whether they be novelistic or factual.

Rennie Wilford, the protagonist of *Bodily Harm*, travels to what she expects to be a paradisal Caribbean group of islands in order to escape from the threats of the Toronto of the 1980s. Suffering from breast cancer, she has undergone a partial mastectomy, but not only her body is threatened by the intrusion of evil: an unknown person has left a rope in her apartment, hinting that there is more and more immediate bodily harm waiting for her. Rennie, who earns her living as a journalist writing for Toronto lifestyle magazines, which are in themselves rather bland and literarily unsophisticated reflections of historical developments, decides to leave behind these threats as well as a somewhat disorderly love life in order to enjoy the fun and the sun of the Caribbean. The islands of St Agathe and St Antoine do in fact offer her an escape from Toronto lifestyles, but they also give her a lot more than she has bargained for; they confront her with a different historical situation, in which the textual (journalistic) grids through which she had been able to perceive the world in Canada – and to function in it

– prove useless. The register and tone of lifestyle articles are inappropriate in the 'tropical trauma'[11] of a society dominated by utmost poverty and political upheaval: the islands have just won their independence from Britain and are heading for their first elections. Rennie's attempts at integrating her experience into the journalistic style she normally uses sound like inadvertent parodies, and they serve a clear parodic (and didactic) purpose on the part of Atwood the implied author.

But not only single elements of story and style are parodic; parody works here on a generic level too. One may agree with Frank Davey that *Bodily Harm* is one of Atwood's four female comedies, but then one has to make allowances for the ending of such a novel as *Bodily Harm*, which does not conform to what one expects from a comedy. Atwood's repetition of the traditional genre of comedy is a repetition with a difference: the 'inherited patriarchal narrative pattern,' in other words 'the comic pattern itself,' is inverted and parodied. Davey states about the main characters of Atwood's novels that 'all of these women feel trapped by the static patterns of their art and attempt in some way to challenge or destroy these patterns.' In the case of *Bodily Harm*, 'Rennie becomes increasingly aware of the ironic disparity between her journalistic catchwords and the actual events she encounters ...'[12] She is finally able to overcome this rift, though, through active involvement.

As mentioned, the most obvious part in which *Bodily Harm* deviates from or parodies the comedic pattern is the ending of the book. While some critics (rather naïvely, one might argue) read the final section, the beginning of which is written in the future tense, as a clear indication that Rennie will be able to return safely to Canada, others would agree with Davey's reading that 'the novel concludes with two rescue fantasies ... which Rennie composes amid the increasing horror of a political prison.' Atwood herself does not commit herself to more than the statement that the outcome of the novel is open to question. Still, there is of course a positive aspect that might justify our calling *Bodily Harm* a comedy even in a traditional sense. In what Elaine Tuttle Hansen calls a 'moment of "epiphany," ' Rennie arrives at a wholesome insight, reaches an inner state of greater political maturity. According to Rowland Smith, 'she changes in perception, in understanding rather than by any change of option or action,' so that we are unable to say whether this inner growth is enough to save her from the Caribbean dungeon. This is more or less also the point of view Sharon Wilson takes: 'Whether or not she literally returns to Canada (a point Atwood chooses to leave unresolved), symbolically her body ultimately in-

cludes all women, all victims and oppressors, all human beings, all.'
While, as Davey argues, in traditional 'male' comedy the characters
are restored to the old order, 'Atwood's concern with metamorphosis
alters the comic pattern greatly. The individual is restored ... not to
order but to growth. The traditional comic pattern is in a sense over-
turned; order becomes equated with dehumanizing systematics, with
ill-health, "disorder"; traditional disorder becomes organic process.'[13]

Hansen interprets Rennie's narrative as 'a kind of traditional ther-
apeutic model, a talking out of memories of personal trauma.' The
novel starts with the one-sentence paragraph 'This is how I got here,
says Rennie' (11). The two words *says Rennie* characterize the rest of
this first section of the first part of the novel as a long portion of direct
speech rather than a first-person narrative, and they also set a pattern
for four of the novel's six parts (part 2: 'One of the first things I can
remember, says Rennie ...' [53]; part 3: 'My father came home every
Christmas, says Rennie' [109]; part 6: ' "I thought it was dumb," says
Lora' [265]).[14]

In itself, the first sentence of the novel sounds almost like a parodic
answer to Northrop Frye's famous question 'Where is here?' which –
according to Lorna Irvine – 'seems designed to alert the reader to the
novel's interest in Canadian nationalism and to certain of its political
intentions.' Here we are dealing with another, as the Caribbean pol-
itician Dr Minnow would call her, 'sweet Canadian,' asking the archetypal Canadian question of cultural identity. Her whereabouts are
probably the dungeons of the former colonial fort and now postcolonial
prison, which used to be called Fort George and has now (parodically?)
been named Fort Industry. She has come a far way from her original
plan to abstain from any political topics and to do 'a good Fun in the
Sun' (16) piece for a men's magazine called *Visor*. She, who is 'all in
favour of protection against disease' and has 'contacts' rather than
'friends' (16), is normally able to shift her narrative or journalistic
perspective according to the orientation of the magazines for which
she is writing (female-oriented: *Pandora*; male-oriented: *Visor* or *Cru-
soe*). She 'packages' or 'frames' the material about which she is writing
rather than really touching it or being touched by it. In Sharon R.
Wilson's words, Rennie is 'a character who specializes in packaging
experience (this time including disaster, torture, and revolution) for
popular consumption.'[15]

So far, the stories Rennie writes about Toronto life have provided
her with metaphors sufficient for most of the situations of everyday
life in Canada. Once she has gone abroad, she tries to integrate foreign

experience into the ready-made Canadian frames; even the dismal state of the Caribbean airline industry can be read as a rewrite of an essay on Toronto cuisine:

> St. Antoine isn't a rich country, they probably buy their planes fourth-hand from other countries, then stick them together with Band-Aids and string until they fall apart irreparably. It's like the fat trade in restaurants. Rennie knows a lot about the fat trade in restaurants: the good ones selling their used fat to the second-rate ones, and so on down the line until the fat reaches the chipworks of cheap hamburger stands. Rennie's piece on the fat trade was called, 'By Their Fats Ye Shall Know Them.' (22)

But the reality through which she lives does not follow the standard plots she knows and rewrites into so many more articles. Neither does rather obvious biblical parody prove useful in this case: there are no Canadian tropes that would be able to deal with the political development in the tropics.

The only story elements that Rennie still *is* able to revise and manipulate relate to the Toronto events that have made her flee from Canada after her mastectomy: in her (oral?) retelling Rennie keeps the story of her relationship with her Jewish boyfriend Jake separate from her version of the scary incident during which an intruder left a coil of rope on her bed. But, although Roberta Rubenstein points out that the 'faceless stranger' in Rennie's mind 'is not Jake, not Daniel, not Paul,'[16] the parallels between the rape fantasies that Jake pretends to be acting out when making love to her ('Pretend I just came through the window. Pretend you're being raped' [117]) and the actual intrusion of a possible sexual offender are obvious. To the readers who know that the intruder who left the coil of rope on her bed came through the bathroom window, Rennie's description of some of Jake's surprises must sound familiar: 'Sometimes he would climb up the fire escape and in through the window instead of coming through the door, he'd send her ungrammatical and obscene letters composed of words snipped from newspapers, purporting to be from crazy men, he'd hide in closets and spring out at her, pretending to be a lurker' (27).

Another instance of Rennie's 'parodic' use of 'old' material in her writing – this time from her earlier writing done for one of the Toronto lifestyle magazines and working on the level of contents rather than form – is her 'piece about drain-chain jewellery' (23). In the same way that Rennie uses old and well-used forms of writing in order to come to terms with a new and unusual situation, she tried to instil newness into jaded Toronto lifestyles by inventing new uses for old and well-known appliances. This use of parody may be of importance for the interpretation of the ending of the novel; here we are dealing with a special case of 'prophetic' parody: '... sometimes Rennie liked to write pieces about trends that didn't really exist, to see if she could make them exist by writing about them. Six to one she'd see at least ten women with bathplug chains looped around their necks two weeks after the piece came out' (25). If we interpret the ending of the novel in the same way, there is a six-to-one chance of Rennie surviving the ordeal in Fort Industry, but no guaranteed positive answer to Ildikó de Papp Carrington's question 'Can she make her freedom exist in the future by imagining it in the present?'[17]

All the same, Rennie does use her acquired 'lifestyles' style in order to try to make sense of the new situation in which she finds herself: 'Rennie begins to compose, from habit and to pass the time, though she does not think the Sunset Inn will find its way into her piece: *The décor is nondescript, resembling nothing so much as an English provincial hotel, with flowered wallpaper and a few prints of hunting and shooting*' (42). But Rennie is not the only producer of parodies in the novel. Having got used to thinking along parodic patterns, she also perceives Caribbean versions of supposedly traditional Western legends, such as the story of the patronymic saint of the island, St Anthony, as somewhat parodic: a sign that parody can also fulfil an educational role in international and intercultural relations through the shock of recognition that it brings forth in ethnocentrically educated readers: 'It's St. Anthony, being tempted in the desert; only the desert is bursting with tropical vegetation, vivid succulent red flowers, smooth fat leaves bulging with sap, brightly coloured birds with huge beaks and yellow eyes, and St. Anthony is black. The demons are noticeably paler, and most of them are female' (70). Also, as far as the role of women is concerned, First and Third World are not that different, unfortunately.

Dorothy Jones comments on the use of the names of Christian saints in Atwood's Caribbean toponymy, and in addition to the Egyptian saint Anthony Abbot, her reference to St Agatha, after whom St Antoine's sister island is named, is of importance here because St Agatha 'was a virgin martyr who had her breasts cut off with shears because she refused to accept the advances of Quintanus, consul of Sicily ...'[18] Jones's comments prove that Atwood the author uses parodic methods in the naming of the locale of her novel, parodic methods, though, which are hardly obvious to the casual and even the academic reader. I doubt very much that Rennie would be aware of them.

Rennie is a writer (and reader) whose point of view is soundly located in a clearly defined ethnic environment, her home town of Griswold in the heartland of the Southwestern Ontario gothic tradition, but in Toronto she has learned already that her own points of view have to be accommodated, that her texts have to be edited, in order to fit completely the urbane style of the metropolis: 'Rennie sits by the window, staring at her notebook, in which she's managed to write four words: *Fun in the Sunspots*. But why worry? The editors always change her titles anyway' (123). But, while in Canada one finally settles for one version, Paul, the drug-dealing American, instructs Rennie that 'in this place you get at least three versions of everything, and if you're lucky one of them is true. That's if you're lucky' (150). Rennie herself is still too clumsy to be able to function completely in this environment. 'There are a lot of things here that Rennie has no names for' (194). After she has been shown that one perspective she has adopted is wrong, she switches around completely, without being able to adapt to small differences. Once she has been told by Paul that the men she took for dentists from Wisconsin are really Swedes (148), all tourists look Swedish to her (151). Finally, reality becomes too strange to be assimilable into any of her own genres of writing: 'This, thinks Rennie, is an exceptionally tacky movie. What next, what now? It's not even a good lunchtime story ...' (159). Her affair with Paul, however, fits well into the world of Dell mysteries: 'She knows she's fallen right into the biggest cliché in the book, a no-hooks, no-strings vacation romance with a mysterious stranger' (222).

Atwood's novel itself, although it may well be accused of being a pot-boiler, escapes from being one of the biggest clichés of the book-market by denying us the certainty of the happy ending every reader must have been waiting for. Even if the ending exists only in Rennie's mind, 'for the first time in her life, she can't think of a title' (301). The last paragraph of the novel sounds contradictory: 'She will never be rescued. She has already been rescued. She is not exempt. Instead she is lucky, suddenly, finally, she's overflowing with luck, it's this luck holding her up' (301). The actual rescue alluded to in this paragraph – 'She has already been rescued' – may well be the restoration of her contact with the rest of humanity, here represented by Lora, a woman Rennie would have shunned in Toronto. We witness the collapse of the barriers that she had erected for fear of being reinfected with the cancerous cells present everywhere in her environment. She is restored to a full life, however long it may last.

This new perspective on life also provides her, of course, with a new (parodic) perspective on the events told. It may not be completely coherent – at least Rowland Smith denies Rennie the ability 'of making any all-encompassing gesture at the end of the novel'[19] – but it restores her life to a oneness and wholeness that it had not had any longer in the outer-dominated and glitzy society of urbane Toronto. A comedy it is – but a comedy the positive ending of which is the healing of the rift in Rennie's personality, not necessarily a happy ending to the story in which she has become involved. Through personal and bodily involvement, she arrives at the stage of direct participation in her fellow humans' lives. Ironically, it is through parody that a mind dominated by atrophied parodies (in the traditional sense) is restored to mental health.

It is through parody, as well, in the original sense of talking alongside the original text while changing its meaning, that the clichéd style of lifestyle magazines can still serve the purpose of furthering the political goals of feminism. Parody as textual appropriation here means, on the one hand, appropriation of the stylistic features and narrative structures of a text by a new text; and, on the other hand, the appropriation of the old text's 'momentum' as a recognized and accepted/acceptable one by the new text, which proceeds to undermine the old message contained in clichés and standardized, would-be value-free textual forms.

Written four years later than *Bodily Harm*, *The Handmaid's Tale* is Margaret Atwood's first novel to be set in the future. But even if it breaks new ground for her personally, the novel can and should of course also be read as part of the Atwood canon: Atwood's reaction against her own former styles of writing as well as her response to accepted traditions and genres of utopian or dystopian literature. Arguing from a more thematic point of view, Roberta Rubenstein situates *The Handmaid's Tale* within Atwood's work by stating that 'she stunningly extends, re-casts, and inverts two of the most persistent clusters of theme and imagery that originate in her earlier concern with survival: *nature* and *nurture.*' This becomes possible by replacing the male hero of traditional anti-utopia with a heroine.[20]

From a structural perspective, *The Handmaid's Tale* confronts the reader with two different time frames, both of which are situated in the future. The main story, the handmaid's tale within the novel, is told in the style of a private journal which is set in the near future, in the late twentieth century, in the region that is now still known as New England. Here, in the heartland of American Puritanism, lie the roots of Atwood's family,[21] and here she herself pursued her graduate studies in English at Harvard, where she was influenced by leading scholars of Puritanism such as Perry Miller. The outer frame of the novel, into which the tale proper is fit, is set more than two hundred years away in the future. Once again, the setting is a university environment, not in the former United States, but in the northern reaches of the North American continent, what is now still known as Canada. This outer 'frame' of the novel, which will be dealt with later, consists of the comments that a twenty-second-century historian – Professor Pieixoto – has to make on the handmaid's tale, which he has transcribed and edited.

The inner frame of the novel, the tale proper, presents a frightening kind of parody as 'repetition with a difference' in the political use to which biblical precedent can be put in a totalitarian state. After a civil war, the Northeast of the former United States has been taken over by right-wing Christian fundamentalists who govern what they call the Republic of Gilead according to the Word, claiming to follow biblical law literally. David Cowart rightly points out a hint on Atwood's part 'that the Republic of Gilead exists at the same period as the regime of Iran's Ayatollah Khomeini.' A totalitarian and patriarchal system has been imposed in this region, which is oddly enough named after a somewhat marginal part of Palestine, from which at one time all the Israelite population had been carried away by the Assyrians so that 'from that time on it was no longer part of the kingdom,'[22] and the most notable reference to which is the question 'Is there no balm in Gilead? Is there no physician here?' (Jer. 8.22).

The universities of Gilead are no longer places of higher learning that might bring forth such a physician; they have largely been turned into the headquarters – now shielded behind 'the Wall' – of a state agency supervising the population, the Eyes. Instead of being places of multi-voiced discussion, the universities have become the centre of political synchronization and religious monologism typical of many fanatically minded theocratic regimes.

The single role left to women in this system seems to be that of serving as breeding machines. Nevertheless, this task has become a major one, as the general pollution of the environment, enhanced by radioactive fallout from earthquakes in the San Andreas Fault area as well as from military encounters, has had disastrous effects on the human fertility rate and the gene pool of this society, so that fertile women – the fertility of men is never questioned in this patriarchal society – have become a national resource on whom the survival of the nation depends. Although they are despised, these women are also needed: by biblical precedent (the maid Bilhah replacing Rachel in Genesis 30.1–3), women who have proved their fertility, so-called handmaids, replace the 'infertile' wives of the ruling-class males in the sexual act, though without being rewarded by mention in the history books or even in family albums.[23]

The narrative that Atwood uses for her depiction of the plight of Gileadean women in general – and of the one handmaid only referred to by her patronymic, Offred, in particular – relies on – or parodies – several models, most of which have already been identified in various secondary sources. Critics such as Frank Davey, for example, mention the Bible and novels such as Zamiatin's *We*, Orwell's *Nineteen Eighty-Four* and Huxley's *Brave New World*, which will be discussed in more detail later on. To these obvious models of *The Handmaid's Tale*, Michèle Lacombe adds a feminist perspective; analysing Offred's language, she claims that 'her story has more in common with *Mrs. Dalloway* and *The Bell Jar* than with *1984*, and that the confessional mode of the spiritual autobiography is as relevant as science fiction to a proper understanding of her discourse: direct allusions range from Virginia Woolf's "A Room of One's Own" to Sylvia Plath's poetry.'[24]

Lacombe's point of view is certainly valid as far as Atwood's attention to female nuances of language-use and to the sense of female entrapment in novels such as *The Bell Jar* is concerned, but as for elements of plot and structure, the female reaction to the above-named male models is the more interesting aspect in the context of this study. It is true that what formerly was Harvard University and its library is now as unattainable for women as the Oxbridge library to which Virginia Woolf's persona was not admitted in *A Room of One's Own*, but the suppression of women – especially of the handmaids – seems to be of quite a different quality in Atwood's story than it was in Woolf's.[25]

The structure of the Gileadean state system and the terminology referring to its members can be traced back to those of the United State in Eugene Zamiatin's *We*. Some plot elements – Linda Hutcheon lists 'the police state; the secret agents; the subversion of authority by love; the escape [?]; the state-regulated sexuality'[26] – are equally derived from Zamiatin's work. In the diary notes of both *We* and *The Handmaid's Tale*, which establish another formal correspondence between the two novels, the societies which claim to have restored, or to be on their way towards restoring, an Edenic state seem to be able to suppress atavistic tendencies among their population as well as threats from outside.

Zamiatin's vision is even somewhat bleaker than Atwood's own: his protagonist, D–503, would wonder at the inefficiency of the regulation of daily life in Gilead, which does not yet run smoothly on the basis of Multiplication Tables. He who wonders whether it is 'not absurd that their State (they called it State!) left sexual life absolutely without control?' when he muses about earlier stages of his own society would probably find the Gileadean attempts at overcoming the birth deficit ridiculously unrefined. When his revolutionary urge is erased from his brain by means of a clinical operation – a technique not yet available in Gilead – he ends up as a good Number again who cannot make any sense of the earlier aspirations set down in his diary:

> Is it possible that I, D–503, really wrote these – pages? Is it possible that I ever felt, or imagined I felt, all this?
>
> The handwriting is mine. And what follows is all in my handwriting. Fortunately, only the handwriting. No more delirium, no absurd metaphors, no feelings – only facts.[27]

Another model clearly used as a foil to be parodied in *The Handmaid's Tale* – at least on the level of contents – is Aldous Huxley's *Brave New World*, written about a decade after Zamiatin's *We*. Set in a future far beyond that of Offred's Gilead, the novel depicts a society that no longer depends on the re-education of human beings born without its blessings – unless it be in the unlikely case of someone like John, Mr Savage, born and raised on a New Mexican Reservation. Gileadean society does not have such reservations, only some colonies where undesirable individuals are sent to risk and lose their lives while cleaning up nuclear waste. Unfortunately, at the end of the twentieth century, relatively primitive Gileadean society had not yet developed for this purpose what the scientists of Huxley's World State were to create later: chemical workers 'trained in the toleration of lead, caustic soda, tar, chlorine.'[28] The creation of such resistant workers enabled the authorities to be more humane in their dealings with dissidents and to exile them to less deadly environments, such as the Falkland Islands.

In the same way that Offred's Commander in *The Handmaid's Tale*, possibly a leading figure in Gileadean society, has illicit reading material hidden away in his private rooms, in Huxley's World State 'there were those strange rumours of old forbidden books hidden in a safe in the Controller's study. Bibles, poetry – Ford knew what.' These rumours are substantiated when John discusses Shakespeare with the Controller, Mustapha Mond.[29] Here, in an atheist state, the Bibles are of course hidden away for different reasons than they were in Gilead, which is ruled according to a unique reading of the Bible that might easily be shown to be faulty, if any member of the suppressed castes got hold of the real text. Promiscuity is the generally accepted and approved standard of sexual relationships in the Brave New World and does not have to be justified by reliance on biblical texts.

What in *Brave New World* has become the refined ceremony of Community Sings with their final orgy-porgies is still much cruder and more brutal in the Salvagings of Atwood's world, during which people are actually killed. The many parallels between the societies devised by Atwood and Huxley suggest that Gileadean society is in fact partly based on the World State. Gilead thus becomes a parody, or a repetition with a vengeance, of the Brave New World, but as *The Handmaid's Tale* is set something like five hundred years before Huxley's novel, the model that is changed has first to be extrapolated from Huxley's seventh century A.F.

George Orwell's *Nineteen Eighty-Four* is the third important dystopian forerunner that has left its imprint on *The Handmaid's Tale*. Both Orwell's and Atwood's novels belong to a class that – as Huxley had put it in 1958 – describe 'a society controlled almost exclusively by punishment and the fear of punishment.' His own novel, Huxley claimed, had profited from recent insights that punishment is a less effective teaching method than the reinforcement of desirable behaviour, so that 'in the imaginary world of my own fable punishment is infrequent and generally mild.' Writing in the late 1940s, Orwell set his story one year before what was going to be the publication date of Atwood's novel, so that the Canadian reply to his model did not have to be based on backward-oriented extrapolations but on Orwell's own text. Huxley admitted in 1946 that he had not taken into account the progress in research concerning nuclear fission in his writing of *Brave New World*, and a similar point can be made about Orwell's not having predicted the computerization of late-twentieth-century society and especially publishing, which makes Winston Smith's job of 'rectifying' (parodying) old texts in the Ministry of Truth look rather quaint and antiquated to anybody only slightly acquainted with contemporary methods of word processing.[30] Even Gilead, although suffering from a lot of technological misadventures, had started computerizing its library holdings.

Whereas the Community Sings in Huxley's *Brave New World* were an expression of his 'soft' pedagogical strategies in a society composed of genetically and chemically pre-conditioned and mass-produced individuals, the daily Hate ceremonies in *Nineteen Eighty-Four*, which 'it was impossible to avoid joining in,'[31] have quite a lot in common with Atwood's Salvagings; many members of the societies depicted in Atwood's and Orwell's books were brought up, and still remember life, before the respective revolutions, and have to be re-educated in special centres or treated in the Ministry of Love: they 'need' those atavistic ceremonies involving hate and death. The same is true of public hangings in both societies.

Alden R. Turner locates *The Handmaid's Tale* within (or, identifies it as a parody of) an even older tradition that is not generally seen to be part of the utopian or dystopian vein of writing, namely, 'within the American documentary tradition of "fiction 'founded on fact'"' that began with the story of America's history chronicled in seventeenth-century histories, essays, sermons, journals, autobiographies, captivity narratives and topical poetry.'[32] It is from this literature's reliance on typology and the Puritan insistence on literal interpretation of the Bible that Atwood derives most of the underlying metaphors of her novel. But the way she integrates them into her writing deviates clearly from traditional American typology: her antitypes are not those generally expected; they deviate from the model and parody it. Out of the same tradition comes Nathaniel Hawthorne's *The Scarlet Letter*, which Linda Hutcheon sees parodied in Atwood's work: 'Its setting, what we might call its colour-coding, and its frame narrative, which suggests historical verification through documentation, are all present, but are also all made ironic in context: the "Custom-House" genesis (and foreword) of Hawthorne's novel is here inverted into Atwood's epilogue, with its sexist and academic interpretations by male experts; the embodiment of shame (the illegitimate child) becomes the aim of all sex (reproduction by surrogate mothers of sorts).'[33]

From a thematic point of view, parallels between *The Handmaid's Tale* and nineteenth-century narratives dealing with the situation of the American blacks – such as *Uncle Tom's Cabin* – come to the fore. For example, while for the blacks there was an underground railroad to Canada, which was organized by Quakers and led them into freedom, there now is an 'Underground Femaleroad' (258) by means of which women are smuggled out of Gilead. Once again it is 'the heretical sect of Quakers' (93) leading them to freedom in Canada.

As far as biblical material that is parodied or incorporated in *The Handmaid's Tale* is concerned, Atwood seems to be following the example set by William Styron in what critics have referred to as his historical novel or meditation on history, but which Styron – and this is important in this context – also called 'a religious allegory,' *The Confessions of Nat Turner*. Atwood emulates the technique Styron had used to incorporate Nat's unique interpretation of biblical texts into the story in order to motivate his insane acts. In a 1965 interview, given while he was writing *Nat Turner*, Styron remarks upon Nat's marginal (and in the sense of this study, parodic) perspective: '[Nat] realizes that he's been working on rather one note, that he's been getting these messages from God through the prophets to go kill, to annihilate, to slaughter ruthlessly men, women and children ...' But while Styron's character, motivated by his religious fanaticism, had truly believed in the erroneous interpretation of the Bible and of himself being 'an avenging Old Testament angel' before he got 'the message that maybe this wasn't the real message at all,'[34] in Atwood's case, the representatives of Gilead's governing class are fully aware that they parody biblical commandments by repeating them with slight but telling changes. These changes are instituted by leaders who forbid their subjects to read the original texts and thus keep them from realizing – or at least from being able to prove – that they are duped: 'We can be read to from [the Bible], by him, but we cannot read' (98). Thus only the community leaders are fully aware of the parodic status of their messages, whereas the listeners have to treat their words as if they were the Word.

As in *The Confessions of Nat Turner*, old religious discourse, whether it be the Miltonic 'They also serve who only stand and wait' (28) or the Puritans' version of biblical parables, is used parodically in new contexts: 'She also said, Not all of you will make it through. Some of you will fall on dry ground or thorns. Some of you are shallow-rooted ... She said, Think of yourselves as seeds ...' (28). While Styron's Nat Turner himself misinterprets the biblical message, Atwood's handmaids are aware – at least at the beginning – of the fact that the biblical texts read to them, such as the Sermon on the Mount, have been tampered with:

> If you have a lot of things, said Aunt Lydia, you get too attached to this material world and you forget about spiritual values. You must cultivate poverty of spirit. Blessed are the meek. She didn't go on to say anything about inheriting the earth. (74)

> For lunch it was the Beatitudes. Blessed be this, blessed be that. They played it from a disc, the voice was a man's. *Blessed be the poor in*

spirit, for theirs is the kingdom of heaven. Blessed are the merciful.
Blessed are the meek. Blessed are the silent. I knew they made that up, I
knew it was wrong, and they left things out too, but there was no
way of checking. (99–100)

There is no way of checking the most overtly sexist biblical parody
either. St Paul may have to answer for a lot of male-centred aspects
of Christianity, but he cannot be held responsible for the following
parody 'appropriating a suddenly useful bromide from Marx and Bak-
unin':35 '*From each*, says the slogan, *according to her ability; to each*
according to his needs ... It was from the Bible, or so they said. St. Paul
again, in Acts' (127). The ultimate parody of religious texts is reached
in the Soul Scrolls, phone-ordered printouts of prayers that are shred-
ded and recycled into new paper immediately after having been read
out by 'toneless metallic voices' (176).

Whereas in *Nat Turner* it had been mostly textual fragments from
the Bible that were mis- or reinterpreted by Nat, here old terms and
names are kept over from biblical or historical sources – so that they
often come to mean the opposite of what they used to signify. On the
one hand, the biblical semiology that applied in prelapsarian times is
resurrected: a name has a close relationship to the thing or person to
which it corresponds; a sign – such as a shopping token – is the iconic
representation of the thing it represents: 'You can see the place, under
the lily, where the lettering was painted out, when they decided that
even the names of shops were too much temptation for us. Now places
are known by their signs alone' (35). Shopping thus becomes easier,
although sometimes the symbols standing for merchandise are quite
arbitrary depictions. Still, they are not as arbitrary as the graphemes
of written language had been: 'I take the tokens from Rita's outstretched
hand. They have pictures on them, of the things they can be exchanged
for: twelve eggs, a piece of cheese, a brown thing that's supposed to
be a steak' (21).

On the other hand, Gileadean semiology often deviates from the
biblical model, so that things and signs do not really go together any
more. The result is often a 'palimpsest' of meanings and connotations
which may arise from material necessities, such as the army-issue blan-
kets in the Red (or Rachel and Leah) Centre 'that still said U.S.' (13).
On another level, the recycling of old material also finds its expression
in everyday furnishings and has lost the positive appeal it had in the
earlier context of Buckler's *The Mountain and the Valley*: 'There's a rug
on the floor, oval, of braided rags. This is the kind of touch they like:

folk art, archaic, made by women, in their spare time, from things that have no further use. A return to traditional values. Waste not want not. I am not being wasted. Why do I want?' (17). The urge to reuse old materials seems to have become manic: Offred sometimes thinks 'that these scarves aren't sent to the Angels at all, but unravelled and turned back into balls of yarn, to be knitted again in their turn' (23).

Whereas the general use of the name *Martha* for household employees is still more or less based on biblical precedent, and whereas the naming of the different types of automobiles as *Whirlwind, Chariot,* or *Behemoth* (27) may be justifiable, the biblical model of naming that establishes a one-to-one relationship between things and signs is perverted in the handmaids' training centre when brutal guards are referred to as *Angels* (14) or when sadistic supervisors armed with 'electric cattle prods' (17) are called *Aunts*. Michèle Lacombe refers to this parody of biblical semiotics when she writes that any analysis of the novel that does more than scratch its surface 'must read its plot as the story of non/signification, of the breakdown of normal relations between signifier and signified.'[36] This breakdown of 'normal relations' does not lead, however, to a postmodern situation of totally arbitrary relationships, but rather to one in which new relations are parodically imposed. There is a precedent for this kind of naming in Zamiatin's *We,* where the totally and totalitarianly materialistic society of the United State has adopted Christian metaphors in referring to the unanimously (or not so unanimously) elected *Well-Doer* and his spies, the *Guardians* or *Guardian Angels*. The handmaids, who before the revolution had had names identifying them as individuals in their own right, 'Alma. Janine. Dolores. Moira. June' (14), are now referred to as property of the respective male whose child they are supposed to bear.

This parodic use of frames – the technique of including old words, terms, names, and elements of discourse within new contexts – also has its counterpart in the action of *The Handmaid's Tale*: on the one hand, even when she is giving birth, a handmaid is 'framed' by the Wife: 'She scrambles onto the Birthing Stool, sits on the seat behind and above Janine, so that Janine is framed by her ...' (135). On the other hand, the handmaid herself has to wear 'white wings framing my face' (19), which keep her from getting a full view of her surroundings. Here the things excluded from the frame are more important than those included in it. The handmaid's image becomes 'a parody of something, some fairytale figure in a red cloak ...' (19).[37]

One of the few possibilities of regaining a fuller view of her surroundings is once again the experience of an epiphany: a single, almost unconnected, everyday utensil seen through the tunnel of vision left open by the wings – such as a dishtowel – can lead to an epiphanic insight that momentarily liberates Offred from her narrow existence, although here it is clearly a personal experience that does not have the social implications that Rennie's epiphany in *Bodily Harm* had: 'Dishtowels are the same as they always were. Sometimes these flashes of normality come at me from the side, like ambushes. The ordinary, the usual, a reminder, like a kick. I see the dishtowel, out of context, and I catch my breath. For some, in some ways, things haven't changed that much' (58).

Offred's story of her existence as a handmaid is, of course, an emplotment, in which – because of the historical distance between the events themselves and the time when she recorded them and also because of the revisions she may have introduced for personal reasons – she presents her own version of the past: a heroic undertaking in the shadow of an overwhelming right-wing regime. While frames have so far been seen as methods of parodically integrating older texts into new ones, or of excluding certain elements from an audience's field of vision, Offred also points out the importance of frames in the reconstruction of her story: 'What I need is perspective. The illusion of depth, created by a frame, the arrangement of shapes on a flat surface' (153).

Offred – if we are willing to grant the Offred reconstructed by Pieixoto any authentic voice of her own, and if we are not, this would mean that the professor's tale harbours a built-in self-deconstructing device – had already been aware of the problematics of telling a story in hindsight, of the parodic strategies that one makes use of more or less involuntarily, especially when one has to admit that 'I don't want to be telling this story' (237). Quite early in the novel she remarks:

> I would like to believe this is a story I'm telling. I need to believe it.
> I must believe it. Those who can believe that such stories are only
> stories have a better chance.
>   If it's a story I'm telling, then I have control over the ending.
> Then there will be an ending, to the story, and real life will come after
> it. (49)

In some ways she does have control over the story, if not over her own life. Her telling of her own story undergoes changes and revisions in the act of telling: every now and then she has to correct herself, to revise (114) what she had said earlier on. So when she claims that on the days when one of the handmaids is supposed to give birth 'we can do anything we want,' she adds immediately, 'I revise that: within limits' (121–2; see also 273–5). She begins one chapter with the words 'I wish this story were different' (279) and then goes on defining an as yet non-existing audience (which includes, but also goes beyond, her vanished husband, Luke):[38] 'I tell, therefore you are' (279). Human beings of her time can no longer afford to claim a Cartesian *Cogito ergo sum* as the basis of their existence; instead, they have to settle for creating in their stories a society worth living in. Nevertheless, Offred's situation of having to create her own audience is of course that of every writer setting out to compose a story.

At the beginning of chapter 23, Offred openly admits that her text is an act of historical recollection: 'This is a reconstruction. All of it is a reconstruction. It's a reconstruction now, in my head, as I lie flat on my single bed rehearsing what I should or shouldn't have said, what I should or shouldn't have done, how I should have played it. If I ever get out of here –' (144; see also 150). The chronological location of such a 'metafictional' commentary is somewhat ambiguous as it might refer to her act of ordering her thoughts and reminiscences after having attended the Birth-Day and while she is still at her Commander's home, or it might be a commentary on the telling of her story while she is in hiding in Bangor, Maine, as the historians suppose she must have been. One of the following paragraphs seems to support the first inter- pretation: 'When I get out of here, if I'm ever able to set this down, in any form, even in the form of one voice to another, it will be a reconstruction then too, at yet another remove. It's impossible to say a thing exactly the way it was ...' (144). Be that as it may, after being spoken into the tape recorder and having been listened to and written down again, the text now is removed several times over, and Offred seems to have foreseen the type of historian by whom she was going to be read in the future: 'But if you happen to be a man, sometime in the future, and you've made it this far, please remember: you will never be subjected to the temptation of feeling you must forgive, a man, as a woman' (144).

Whereas in *Bodily Harm* it was evident from the beginning that there is a third-person narrator, even if some sections of the novel appear to be first-person narratives, it is only in the appendix, the 'Historical Notes on *The Handmaid's Tale*,' that we discover the novel is not really or not only a first-person narrative – at least not a first-person narrative in which the narrator can be assumed to be reliable. We learn that the tale has gone through the hands of historians, Professors Wade and Pieixoto from Cambridge, England, who tried to patch together and

reconstruct a coherent story from two-hundred-year-old tape record-
ings, 'approximately thirty tape cassettes' (313), in fact, which represent
an odd form of 'oral history.' The 'Historical Notes' claim to be the
transcript of the proceedings of a symposium on Gileadean studies
held in 2195 at the University of Denay, Nunavit, a place that by its
name also suggests a northern, even arctic, North American (i.e., Canadian) environment. This impression is reinforced by the supposedly
Indian or Inuit names of the local academics – such as Professors Mary-
ann Crescent Moon and Johnny Running Dog (311).[39]

The speaker, the above-mentioned Professor James Darcy Pieixoto,
whose talk on 'Problems of Authentication in Reference to *The Handmaid's Tale*' (312) makes up most of the proceedings, does not seem
to have learned much from his study of a woman's reaction to a totalitarian patriarchal society. Michèle Lacombe sees him as 'a biased
if not misogynistic historian whose own academic ambitions "frame"
Offred's story.'[40] His mildly chauvinistic puns make readers wonder
whether the changes he undertook in piecing together the tale do not
falsify the text. Of course, he is right – at least judging from the transcripts he (i.e., Atwood) gives us – to conclude about the original recording of the tapes that 'there is a certain reflective quality about the
narrative that would ... rule out synchronicity. It has a whiff of emotion
recollected, if not in tranquillity, at least *post facto*' (315). Professor
Pieixoto's remarks, as well as his colleague's naming of the 'tale' after
Chaucer's *Wife of Bath's Tale*, shed some oblique light on their quali-
fications and their impartiality towards a woman's point of view.

The handmaid's report is thus itself put into perspective through the
framing device of the 'Historical Notes': the 'old' text is integrated into
a new frame or perspective, and the integration of a strongly engaged
feminist text into the would-be scientific (and obviously blatantly chauvinistic) mode of an academic paper leads to a relativization of its urgent
political message. For example, Professor Pieixoto asks his audience to
be 'cautious about passing moral judgement upon the Gileadeans,'
because 'surely we have learned by now that such judgements are of
necessity culture-specific. Also, Gileadean society was under a good
deal of pressure, demographic and otherwise, and was subject to factors
from which we ourselves are happily more free. Our job is not to
censure but to understand. (*Applause*)' (314–15).

This aspect of *The Handmaid's Tale* has been pointed out by Arnold
E. Davidson, whose interpretation of the novel stresses the problems
of history-writing by latter-day intellectuals and problematizes the relationship between text and notes: 'Atwood's epilogue loops back

through the text that precedes it to suggest that the ways in which scholars (present as well as future) assemble the text of the past confirms the present and thereby helps to predict the future, even the horrific future endured by Offred. In short, Atwood does not let intellectuals off the hook ... How we *choose* to construct history partly determines the history we are likely to get.' Davidson's interpretation of historiography ('... the very process of assembling a text [or writing the history of any age from its surviving traces] means *creating* a fiction')[41] is reminiscent of the historiographic theories quoted above (chapter 2), and thus shows to what extent writers such as Atwood (and Findley and Bowering) reflect contemporary theories in their writing. In an uncanny fashion, Davidson's formulation that 'the ways in which scholars assemble the text of the past ... helps [*sic*] to predict the future' refers us back to Rennie's sometimes prophetic gift of writing trends and fads into existence in *Bodily Harm*.

Professor Pieixoto might not agree with such a reading of his scholarly paper, but he gives us a clue to the importance of what I have called a parodic technique in this specimen – as well as in all the other ones – of a historical novel: 'As we know from the study of history, no new system can impose itself upon a previous one without incorporating many of the elements to be found in the latter ...' (317). This method of incorporative parody turns the old New England into the new Gilead; it also uses canonical 'old' texts such as the Bible, Milton's sonnet 'On His Blindness,' *Uncle Tom's Cabin*, *We*, *Brave New World*, *Nineteen Eighty-Four*, and *The Confessions of Nat Turner* as the models that are reformed and parodied in the 'feminist dystopia'[42] of the handmaid's tale, which in its turn is parodied (and reinforced) by being framed by the inane comment of a latter-day male chauvinist professor (a 'narrative situation' which makes every male critic working on the novel, including the present one, feel somewhat uneasy).

Arguing from a largely structuralist point of view, Linda Hutcheon points to the similarities between postmodernist writing and Atwood's feminist texts: like many other contemporary novelists male and female – Hutcheon lists Leonard Cohen, Rudy Wiebe, Timothy Findley, Clark Blaise, Michael Ondaatje, Jack Hodgins, Audrey Thomas, Aritha Van Herk, and Alice Munro – Atwood writes novels which 'are thematically and formally obsessed with the tension between art as kinetic process (its writing and, again, its reading) and the final result – "Art" – as inevitably a fixed and final product.'[43]

The third element in the title Hutcheon chose for her Atwood chapter – 'Process, Product, and Politics: The Postmodernism of Margaret Atwood' – indicates, however, that there is a major difference between playful postmodernism à la Bowering and Atwood's politically committed postmodernism. While the ludic element is a very strong one in Bowering's fiction, so that the political motivation underlying the 're-patriation' of Vancouver's story seems to be of secondary importance, Atwood's use of postmodern strategies obviously has a more urgent political and feminist background. 'Both Atwood's feminist and postmodernist impulses' may 'work to question the very nature of selfhood as it is defined in our culture: that is, as coherent, unified, rational,' as Hutcheon has it,[44] but the combination of feminist political goals and postmodernist structural experiments makes her writing deviate markedly from radical male styles such as Bowering's.

If Margaret Atwood does not write her historical novels in exactly the same manner as the two male authors on whom I concentrated in the earlier parts of this study, this may very well be because of her different (i.e., feminist) way of parodying the more 'traditional' modern and postmodern parodic strategies of male writers such as Timothy Findley and George Bowering. In *Famous Last Words*, Findley has two historically minded soldiers comment upon Hugh Selwyn Mauberley's emplotment of his own experiences. In *Burning Water*, George Bowering intentionally blurs the pronominal distinction between George Vancouver's perspective and his own, writing himself into his novel and drawing attention to this manipulation. Bowering thus collapses the position of author and first-person narrator, making it somewhat difficult for critics to believe in the seriousness of the political message that he claims exists in his works. In *The Handmaid's Tale*, however, it is impossible to locate the revisions that the male historian may have made in transcribing Offred's first-person narrative. While there was a George Bowering in *Burning Water*, Atwood finally resists the temptation to write herself into *The Handmaid's Tale*, but she includes the male historian who does not hesitate to impose his own perspective in the same way that – as we know – Bowering imposes his and that – as Freyberg assumes – Mauberley imposes his. From the outside of her novel, Atwood as the author thus implicitly makes her own comment on male versions of historiography, whether they be modernist or postmodernist: '… instead of presenting an oppositional strategy where the individual courts certain defeat by confronting authority at its strongest point, Atwood's narrative relies on the guerilla tactics of humor, evasion, survival, all devices designed to allow the seeds of destruction within the authoritarian monolith to grow and bear fruit.'[45]

What links Atwood's writing with that of her male colleagues, though, and this is a topic that has come up time and again, is her interest in the process of writing historical novels. As Arnold E. Davidson points out, *The Handmaid's Tale* is 'not just a history of patriarchy but a meta-history, an analysis of how patriarchal imperatives are encoded within the various intellectual methods we bring to bear on history.'[46] Professor Pieixoto complains about Offred's 'unscientific' ways of dealing (or rather not dealing) with what he thinks could have provided basic data of historical research 'had she had a different turn of mind' and 'had she had the instincts of a reporter or a spy' (322). Had she had a different turn of mind, the novel would not have been parodic in the sense it has been shown to be, and it would not have been the foremost example of a special feminist metahistorical parody with which to conclude this study of different types of historical parodies in contemporary English-Canadian literature. Margaret Atwood the author frames James Darcy Pieixoto – and with him many male historians, historiographers, and authors of historical novels, perhaps including some of the novelists discussed in the preceding chapters – by including him within the covers of yet another historical novel.[47]

6 Concluding Remarks: Parody in Canada ... and Beyond

As this study has shown, there is a strong tendency in the English-Canadian historical novels we have examined towards parodic strategies of dealing with preceding texts and models of writing. Parody in the sense used in this study means the taking up of literary structures from these preceding texts and integrating them into a new context or frame by repeating them with a difference and with a purpose. This repetition with a difference serves to accommodate traditional structures to a new textual, social, and national environment. In this situation, the new, Canadian text seems to swallow or frame the old one – mostly English or American – completely, but often features of the old text survive in the new one as well.

Historical novels differ from other novelistic genres in their use of parodic strategies because the textual material they incorporate is often of non-fictional origin. This integration of 'real' elements into the fictional universe then leads to new metafictional, or rather metahistorical, questions about the quality of 'realism' in these novels. The contemporary novelists dealt with in this study react against textual models, on the one hand, by turning them around and integrating them into their own writing, and, on the other, by directing the narrative energy of established genres to new historic situations and contexts.

While the parodic reception and adaptation of earlier texts functions on the level of content as well as structure, and while this study has touched on both these levels, the main interest has not been to identify sources and to indulge in the source hunting typical of traditional philology, but rather to trace the way in which foreign elements are integrated into the framing narrative structure of the new, that is, Canadian text.

In the nineteenth century, with native authors such as Major John Richardson, and also with immigrants such as Susanna Moodie, the strategies of New World imitation and parody of Old World texts were still rather crude. While Susanna Moodie claimed to have made 'a distant land' her own through 'painful experience,'[1] we may wonder whether the writing of her generation is not rather an inadvertent parody of European models. In the same way that her European concepts of the picturesque were only partially able to accommodate the experience of North American nature, her writing often could not really go beyond the inadvertently parodic. Neither can Richardson's *Wacousta*, the first example treated at length in this study, escape the model of a Scottian romance, even if Major Richardson really was a personal acquaintance of Tecumseh and could claim firsthand experience on which to base his 'realistic' account.

The tradition of Richardson's Canadian version of a European revenger's tale still lives on in highly successful historical romances of the commercial kind, but it is not reflected in the novels discussed here – Findley's wars are completely different from Richardson's. The other types of early novels treated in chapter 2, however, find corresponding elements in the contemporary historical novels chosen for this study. Grove's somewhat stilted parody of an expedition report is echoed, as a genre if not in detail, by Bowering's version of George Vancouver's expedition as well as by the twenty-second-century scholars' view of the past – which is our future – in Atwood's dystopia. Buckler's twentieth-century protagonist seems to remain caught in the fruitless imitation of foreign models, but he thus enables his creator to write what may be claimed as a fruitful repetition with a difference, a true parody: David Canaan cannot use the same solipsistic technique that his European model, Marcel, had used in order to overcome historical distance. In its own turn, Buckler's parody cannot escape Bowering's judgment in *A Short Sad Book*, where *The Mountain and the Valley* is included for parodic purposes as a 'pretty good Canadian novel.'

The parodic techniques employed in historical novels have become more sophisticated and more self-confident lately. While in the nineteenth century the parodic strategy was clearly one of emulation, twentieth-century writers feel less inhibited about using foreign texts for their own purposes. If the effects are felt to be crude, as in George Bowering's case, readers can generally assume the writer's intention is to shock, rather than having to make allowances for poor imitations written in a culturally underdeveloped colony.

In addition to their reliance on Canadian models, the contemporary novels discussed in this study respond to various European and American forerunners: Timothy Findley uses autobiographically influenced novels about the Great War, the Bible, modernist poetry, and contemporary biographies; George Bowering integrates romantic ballads as well as eighteenth-century exploration reports and twentieth-century Canadian novels into his own parodic universe; Margaret Atwood bases her parodies on such genres as travel and fashion magazine writing and dystopian as well as typological novels (not to forget the Bible). All these different structural models contribute to the shaping of novels that focus on writing history and writing about history in a country that is not supposed to have much of a history of its own but which gains its unique character from the ways in which it deforms and reforms traditions, texts, or structures brought in from abroad.

But as the definition of parody underlying the whole approach in this study includes a strong dose of purposefulness and intention on the author's part, which in fact differentiates parody from other intertextual modes, we should close with another look at the purposes to which the old texts have been accommodated.

Findley uses his European models in *The Wars* in order to protest against the inhumanity of war, turning his novel into a manifesto of pacifism. His treatment of Fascism and the English throne in *Famous Last Words* can be interpreted as a warning of the lures of totalitarian ideologies and perhaps also as a declaration of Canadian independence and coming of age as a political power on an international scale.

Bowering's position might, on the basis of his personal statements, be seen as that of a Canadian nationalist, but he is also one of the leading Canadian representatives of the international movement of postmodernism, and thus his message is primarily an aesthetic one, deconstructing old mythologies and cosmologies upon which Canadian culture has been based. Although there clearly is a political and historical message in his books – after all, he calls both novels dealt with here historical novels and goes at length into the problematics of writing historical novels – the ludic, disseminating temptation of postmodernism is greater than the will to represent a coherent political position. The text invites the reader to join an ongoing game, rather than engaging him in political discussions or even actions.

The will to represent a coherent political position, to invite political action of the feminist kind, distinguishes Atwood's from the male version of postmodernism. Her feminist message and her Canadian nationalism are all-pervasive in her two novels studied here. *Bodily Harm* shows us a Canadian woman caught not only in an act of personal liberation towards active participation in life but also in a former colony's struggle for its national liberation and identity.

The final historical novel studied, Atwood's *The Handmaid's Tale*, serves as a complex summary of various possibilities of structuring historical novels by means of parodic principles: the inner tale, the handmaid's tale proper, shows us a first-person narrator emplotting her own history in a way similar to Mauberley's (albeit male) retelling of his own story and to Vancouver's writing in his log. Her male commentator is as unreliable as the two types of interpreters personified by Findley's Freyberg and Quinn or as George Bowering, the narrator in *Burning Water*. While *The Handmaid's Tale* is thus a parody in the incorporative sense that lies at the base of this study, the novel can and should also be read as a more traditional parody of male historians – but once again parody in a sense that is not necessarily a very humorous one.

The interpretations gathered in this study might easily be complemented by references to other authors and titles, so that one feels tempted to claim that the prevalence of the parodic model extends to contemporary English-Canadian novels in general, all the more as the restriction to historical novels in this study arose from the need to single out a limited and interesting number of books to be examined, rather than from any theory that would concentrate on historical novels as the only parodic ones. Among contemporary postmodern authors not dealt with in detail here, Robert Kroetsch is certainly one of the leading parodists. While *The Studhorse Man*, which might also be counted among the historical novels, is an exhilarating parody of the *Odyssey*, a novel such as *What the Crow Said* reacts to the influences of Latin American magic realism, and *Alibi* works parodically with the structures of the detective novel while teaching us that 'selection is distortion, and distortion breaks the truth into visibility.'[2] Other writers, most of whose names have already been mentioned in the course of this study, come to mind: Rudy Wiebe's versions of the Mennonites' and the Indians' past; Jack Hodgins's invention of a parodic world; Leon Rooke's canine view of the Shakespearean age; and so on.

Although parody is one way that authors such as Kroetsch, Hodgins, and Wiebe integrate foreign influences into their works, it would be absurd to say that parody as such is a specifically Canadian way of reacting to new developments in world literature. The introductory chapter has shown that parodic strategies have been a staple of literary evolution for thousands of years. Parody is a ubiquitous technique in twentieth-century art forms, as the subtitle of Linda Hutcheon's *Theory of Parody* claims. And examples abound: an American novelist such as

E.L. Doctorow parodically integrates Heinrich von Kleist's German novella *Michael Kohlhaas* into his historical novel *Ragtime*.[3] An author such as the Englishman David Lodge suggests in *The British Museum Is Falling Down* that parody is an entertaining way of approaching and comparing the styles of different writers. His compatriot Julian Barnes (in *Flaubert's Parrot*), the Italian Umberto Eco (in *The Name of the Rose*), or the Austrian Christoph Ransmayr (in *The Last World*) have shown similar intertextual techniques in recent works, although the purposefulness that would qualify their adaptations as parodies or 'repetitions with a vengeance' in the sense used in this study sometimes remains rather mysterious to reviewers.[4] Their often ingenious parodies often seem to lack the special commitment to new and challenging tasks going beyond the purely literary – social, national, international, and feminist – which many of the Canadian parodists have taken up. This commitment thus becomes a salient feature of parody in Canadian fiction.

Notes

Works cited in short form only are listed in the Selected Bibliography.

Chapter 1 Introduction

1 Julian Barnes, *Flaubert's Parrot* (London: Jonathan Cape 1984), 18
2 Samuel Johnson, *A Dictionary of the English Language*, 2 vols. (1755; Hildesheim: Olms 1968)
3 Hutcheon, *A Theory of Parody*, 10
4 See for example Gilbert Highet, *The Anatomy of Satire* (Princeton: Princeton University Press 1962). In an interesting argument, Joseph A. Dane in 'Parody and Satire: A Theoretical Model,' *Genre* 13 (1980), resolves the opposition between the genres of parody and satire by claiming that satire refers to 'things' (content) and parody to 'words' (form). Cf. also Karrer, *Parodie, Travestie, Pastiche*, 41.
5 Thomson, 'Parody/Genre/Ideology,' 96, 97, 100; see also Clive R. Thomson, 'Problèmes théoriques de la parodie,' *Etudes littéraires* 19, no. 1 (1986), 14. In a later essay, Thomson adds Gérard Genette to this third group.
6 For a different solution of the genre/mode problem in the context of Russian Formalism, see Karrer, *Parodie, Travestie, Pastiche*, 189.
7 I owe this Freudian (?) typographical error to Kiremidjian, *A Study of Modern Parody*, 10.
8 Aristotle, *Poetics: A Translation and Commentary for Students of Literature*, trans. Leon Golden (Englewood Cliffs: Prentice-Hall 1968), 5; Genette, *Palimpsestes*, 17. For other early parodists, see Martin, *On Parody*, 2. Aristotle's distinction between high and low genres will have to be discarded in a twentieth-century context, as it suggests 'the categories of another age, of an aesthetic that is much more rigid than ours would appear to be today in its norms' (Hutcheon, *A Theory*, 40).
9 Fred W. Householder, 'Parodia,' *Classical Philology* 39 (1944), 2; Kiremidjian, *A Study*, 2
10 See Wido Hempel, 'Parodie, Travestie und Pastiche: Zur Geschichte von

Wort und Sache,' *Germanisch-Romanische Monatsschrift* n.s. 15 (1965),
152; and Verweyen and Witting, *Die Parodie in der neueren deutschen
Literatur*, 7. For a definition of travesty, see Genette, *Palimpsestes*, 29: 'Le
travestissement burlesque modifie donc le style *sans modifier le sujet*; in-
versement, la "parodie" modifie le sujet *sans modifier le style* ...'

11 Kiremidjian, *A Study*, 17

12 See Rose, *Parody//Meta-Fiction*, 28.

13 See Hermann Koller, 'Die Parodie,' *Glotta* 35 (1956), 22. Another theorist who sees parody – at least in its origins – as non-comical is O.M.
Freidenberg, 'The Origin of Parody,' in *Semiotics and Structuralism: Read-
ings from the Soviet Union*, ed. Henryk Baran (White Plains, NY: International Arts and Sciences Press 1976), 282–3: 'Thus parody is not the
product of someone's individual invention or someone's merry fantasy.
Parody is not imitation, ridicule, or mimicry. Parody is the archaic religious conception of "the second aspect" and "the double," with a total
unity of form and content ... We must draw a boundary between the
lofty religious conception which has engendered the traditional literary
form and the life of that very literary form, which has forgotten its religious origin and has turned to the service of a new content.'

14 Cf. Heide Ziegler's somewhat different distinction between progressive
and regressive parody in contemporary American literature in 'Love's
Labours Won: The Erotics of Contemporary Parody,' in O'Donnell and
Davis, eds., *Intertextuality and Contemporary American Fiction*, 58–71.

15 Kiremidjian, *A Study*, 5–6

16 J.W.H. Atkins, *Literary Criticism in Antiquity: A Sketch of Its Development*,
2 vols. (Gloucester, Mass.: Peter Smith 1961), 1:79, 280

17 Brooks Otis, *Virgil: A Study in Civilized Poetry* (Oxford: Clarendon 1963),
20, 39; and Brooks Otis, *Ovid as an Epic Poet*, 2d ed. (Cambridge: Cambridge University Press 1970), 374

18 Rotermund, *Die Parodie in der modernen deutschen Lyrik*, 10 (my translation)

19 Julius Caesar Scaliger, *Poetices Libri Septem* (1561; Stuttgart: Frommann
1964), 46

20 For non-adversative parodies, see Verweyen and Witting, *Die Parodie*, 9;
and Rotermund, *Die Parodie*, 12. See also Martin, *On Parody*, 15, according to whom the first important work on parody was written by Henry
Stephens in 1573 and 1575. Florio is quoted after Joan Hartwig, *Shakespeare's Analogical Scene: Parody as Structural Syntax* (Lincoln: University
of Nebraska Press 1983), 5.

21 Karrer (*Parodie, Travestie, Pastiche*, 180) sees parodies of this time in the
context of the quarrel of the Ancients and the Moderns.

22 Therese Fischer-Seidel, *Mythenparodie im modernen englischen und ameri-
kanischen Drama: Tradition und Kommunikation bei Tennessee Williams,
Edward Albee, Samuel Beckett und Harold Pinter* (Heidelberg: Winter

1986), 19; Henry Fielding, *'Joseph Andrews' and 'Shamela'* (London: Dent 1983), 47. Johnson is quoted after J.W.H. Atkins, *English Literary Criticism: Seventeenth and Eighteenth Centuries* (London: Methuen 1966), 289.

23 Reuben Brower, *Mirror on Mirror: Translation – Imitation – Parody* (Cambridge, Mass.: Harvard University Press 1974), 89. For the importance of parodic strategies in *Northanger Abbey* and the development of the realist novel in general, see Harry Levin, *The Gates of Horn: A Study of Five French Realists* (New York: Oxford University Press 1963), 47: 'It cannot be an accident that realism, from Rabelais' burlesque of the Arthurian legend to Jane Austen's glances at Fanny Burney and Anne Radcliffe, has so often originated in parody; that the genre of the "parody-novel," as it remained for the Russian formalists to point out, was so fully developed in *Tristram Shandy*; that so many novelists, like Thackeray, have started as parodists, playing the sedulous ape to their seniors.' See also George Levine, *The Realistic Imagination: English Fiction from 'Frankenstein' to 'Lady Chatterley'* (Chicago: University of Chicago Press 1981), 61–80.

24 Abastado, 'Situation de la parodie,' 14

25 Sander L. Gilman, *Nietzschean Parody: An Introduction to Reading Nietzsche* (Bonn: Bouvier 1976), 9, 17. Michel Foucault shows that Nietzsche also saw parody as one of the three uses to which the interpretative historical sense, as opposed to the documentary genealogical sense, gives rise, and he quotes him to the effect that 'perhaps, we can discover a realm where originality is again possible as parodists of history and buffoons of God.' See Michel Foucault, 'Nietzsche, Genealogy, History,' trans. Donald F. Bouchard and Sherry Simon, in *The Foucault Reader*, ed. Paul Rabinow (New York: Pantheon Books 1984), 94. I am indebted to Professor William Spanos, SUNY Binghamton, for this reference.

26 George Kitchin, *A Survey of Burlesque and Parody in English* (1931; New York: Russell and Russell 1967), ix, 247. For Levin, see his *James Joyce: A Critical Introduction*, 2d ed. (London: Faber and Faber 1968), 95: 'Having subverted Homer and Shakespeare to his purposes, he is not anxious to submit to the limitations of lesser writers, but rather to extend his own. When a self-effacing parodist – a Max Beerbohm – takes off a writer, the result is acute criticism. When Joyce is dealing with others, he lacks this insight and precision. His parodies reveal himself ...' See also Harvey Gross, 'Parody, Reminiscence, Critique: Aspects of Modernist Style,' in *Modernism: Challenges and Perspectives*, ed. Monique Chefdor, Ricardo Quinones, and Albert Wachtel (Urbana: University of Illinois Press 1986), 128–45. Another theorist who mentions the progressive function that parody can play is Tuvia Shlonsky, 'Literary Parody: Remarks on Its Method and Function,' in *Actes du Quatrième Congrès de l'Association*

Internationale de Littérature Comparée / Proceedings of the Fourth Congress of the International Comparative Literature Association, ed. François Jost, 2 vols. (The Hague: Mouton 1966), 2:797–801.

27 Abastado, 'Situation de la parodie,' 15

28 Kiremidjian, *A Study,* 15. Although published as late as 1985, Kiremidjian's dissertation was written in 1964.

29 David Baguley, 'Parody and the Realist Novel,' *University of Toronto Quarterly* 55, no. 1 (1985), 95

30 Shklovsky quoted by Victor Erlich, 'Modern Russian Criticism from Andrej Belyj to Andrej Sinjavskij: Trends, Issues, Personalities,' in *Twentieth-Century Russian Literary Criticism,* ed. V. Erlich (New Haven: Yale University Press 1975), 13; Peter Hodgson, 'Viktor Shklovsky and the Formalist Legacy: Imitation/Stylization in Narrative Fiction,' in *Russian Formalism: A Retrospective Glance. A Festschrift in Honor of Victor Erlich,* ed. Robert L. Jackson (New Haven: Yale Center for International and Area Studies 1985), 195. For the Bergson connection, see Karrer, *Parodie, Travestie, Pastiche,* 95.

31 Jurij Tynjanov, 'Dostoevsky and Gogol,' in Erlich, ed., *Twentieth-Century Russian Literary Criticism,* 102–16

32 Karrer, *Parodie, Travestie, Pastiche,* 112 (my translation). For insightful comments on Tynjanov's theories of literary evolution, see Karrer, 95, 106–11; and Jurij Striedter, 'Zur formalistischen Theorie der Prosa und der literarischen Evolution,' in *Texte der russischen Formalisten,* vol. 1, ed. Jurij Striedter (Munich: Fink 1969), xliii. Another theory based on the insight that literature is parodic in essence is Macherey's (see Rose, *Parody//Meta-Fiction,* 102).

   Tynjanov's system offers one possibility of dealing with the problem of reference in parodies: parodies with close connections to the other literary series are related to literary criticism; parodies with close connections to the extra-literary and social series are more critical of society.

33 Bakhtin, *The Dialogic Imagination,* 5

34 Ibid., 47; Bakhtin, *Problems of Dostoevsky's Poetics,* 189. Tzvetan Todorov establishes a hierarchy of Bakhtin's forms of dialogism in *Mikhail Bakhtin: The Dialogical Principle,* from which the following diagram is drawn (70):

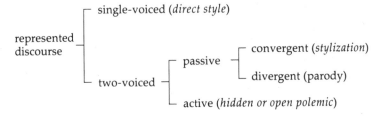

According to Todorov, 'one can finally vary the *degree* of presence of the other's discourse. Bakhtin puts forward a differentiation of three degrees. The first is full presence, or explicit dialogue. At the other end – the third degree – the other's discourse receives no material corroboration and yet is summoned forth: it is because it is held available in the collective memory of a given social group; such is the case of parody, stylization, and another form of summoning forth that Bakhtin calls "variation" ' (73).

35 Bakhtin, *Problems of Dostoevsky's Poetics*, 193–4
36 Bakhtin, *The Dialogic Imagination*, 71
37 Another Russian theory that is based on the work of the Formalists is Jurij Lotman's. Lotman, however, interprets parody as a clearly destructive method and denies the positive values that the Formalists had seen in it. See Jurij M. Lotman, *Die Struktur des künstlerischen Textes* (Frankfurt: Suhrkamp 1973), 438–9.
38 Hutcheon, 'Authorized Transgression: The Paradox of Parody,' in *Le Singe à la porte: Vers une théorie de la parodie*, ed. Groupar (New York: Lang 1984), 15
39 Bakhtin, *Rabelais and His World*, 10, 11
40 Hutcheon, *A Theory*, 76. The Barthes quotation is from *S/Z* (Paris: Seuil 1970), 52.
41 David Roberts, Introduction, *Comic Relations: Studies in the Comic, Satire and Parody*, ed. Pavel Petr, David Roberts, and Philip Thomson (Frankfurt: Peter Lang 1985), 183
42 Margaret Waller, 'An Interview with Julia Kristeva,' in O'Donnell and Davis, eds., *Intertextuality and Contemporary American Fiction*, 281. See also Todorov, *Mikhail Bakhtin*, 60.
43 Leon S. Roudiez, Introduction, *Desire in Language: A Semiotic Approach to Literature and Art*, by Julia Kristeva, ed. Leon S. Roudiez, trans. Thomas Gora, Alice Jardine, and Leon S. Roudiez (New York: Columbia University Press 1980), 15; Kristeva, *Desire in Language*, 66, 69, 71; Laurent Jenny, 'La Stratégie de la forme,' *Poétique* 27 (1976), 260. See also Manfred Pfister, 'Konzepte der Intertextualität,' in *Intertextualität: Formen, Funktionen, anglistische Fallstudien*, ed. Ulrich Broich and Manfred Pfister (Tübingen: Niemeyer 1985), 1–30.
44 Kiremidjian, *A Study*, 26
45 Rose, *Parody//Meta-Fiction*, 63. For a classification of *mises en abyme*, see Linda Hutcheon's summary of Dällenbach's terminology in *Narcissistic Narrative: The Metafictional Paradox* (1980; New York: Methuen 1984), 53–6; and Jean Ricardou, *Le Nouveau Roman* (Paris: Seuil 1978), 47–75. See also Michael Valdez Moses, 'The Sadly Rejoycing Slave: Beckett, Joyce, and Destructive Parody,' *Modern Fiction Studies* 31 (1985), 659–74.
46 Linda Badley, 'The Aesthetics of Postmodern Parody: An Extended Definition,' *Comparatist* 7 (1983), 42. A different view, of postmodern parody

being eclipsed by parody, is held by Fredric Jameson in 'Postmodernism and Consumer Society,' in *Postmodernism and Its Discontents: Theories, Practices*, ed. E. Ann Kaplan (London: Verso 1988): 'Pastiche is ... a neutral practice of ... mimicry, without parody's ulterior motive, without the satirical impulse, without laughter, without that still latent feeling that there exists something *normal* compared to which what is being imitated is rather comic' (16).

47 In his discussion, Karrer (*Parodie, Travestie, Pastiche*, 179–91) compares traditional hierarchies of parodic genres and suggests his own, which sees burlesque as the general term and differentiates the sub-genres according to their main strategies as either parody and travesty (both based on incongruity) or pastiche (based on mechanization). Concerning intentionality, see Deguy, 'Limitation ou illimitation de l'imitation: Remarques sur la parodie'; Anne-Marie Houdebine, 'Parodie et identité,' in Groupar, ed., *Le Singe à la porte*, 57–63; Verweyen and Witting, *Die Parodie*, 57; and Hutcheon, *A Theory*, 22.

48 See Karlheinz Stierle, 'Werk und Intertextualität,' in *Dialog der Texte: Hamburger Kolloquium zur Intertextualität*, ed. Wolf Schmid and Wolf-Dieter Stempel, Wiener Slawistischer Almanach Sonderband 11 (Vienna: Gesellschaft zur Förderung slawistischer Studien 1983), 7–26.

49 Morson, 'Parody, History, and Metaparody,' 67

50 Deguy, 'Limitation ou illimitation,' 2; Hans Kuhn, 'Was parodiert die Parodie?' *Neue Rundschau* 85 (1974), 600–18; Jurij Tynjanov, 'Dostoevskij und Gogol' (Zur Theorie der Parodie),' in *Texte der russischen Formalisten*, vol 1., ed. Jurij Striedter (Munich: Fink 1969), 335; see also Thomson, 'Parody/Genre/Ideology,' 97.

51 Jean-Jacques Hamm, 'Présentation,' *Etudes littéraires* 19, no. 1 (1986), 11

52 Wall, 'Vers une notion de la colle parodique,' 22. See also earlier mentions of the same phenomenon summarized by Karrer, *Parodie, Travestie, Pastiche*, 169.

53 See David Lodge, *Small World: An Academic Romance* (1984; Harmondsworth: Penguin 1985), 51.

54 Rose, *Parody//Meta-Fiction*, 107

55 Harold Bloom, *The Anxiety of Influence: A Theory of Poetry* (New York: Oxford University Press 1973), 14, 34

56 Wall, 'Vers une notion,' 23. See Karrer, *Parodie, Travestie, Pastiche*, 83.

57 Rotermund, *Die Parodie*, 9 (my translation)

58 Verweyen and Witting, *Die Parodie*, 210 (my translation)

59 Rose, *Parody//Meta-Fiction*, 35

60 Hutcheon, *A Theory*, 6, 44, 8, 10, 24

61 Ibid., 16

62 Rose, *Parody//Meta-Fiction*, 113, 44

63 John A. Yunck, 'The Two Faces of Parody,' *Iowa English Yearbook* 8 (1963), 32

64 Hutcheon, *A Theory*, 55, 52, 54, and her earlier essay 'Ironie, satire, par-

odie: Une approche pragmatique de l'ironie,' *Poétique* 46 (1981), 130–55
65 Linda Hutcheon, *Splitting Images: Contemporary Canadian Ironies*
(Toronto: Oxford University Press 1991), 146

Chapter 2 Parodies of History

1 On the relationship between Québécois and French literature, see Patrick
Imbert, *Roman québécois contemporain et clichés* (Ottawa: Editions de
l'Université d'Ottawa 1983), 10: 'La littérature québécoise, jusqu'à ces
dernières années, ne pouvait donc se poser qu'en s'opposant. Elle naît
en réaction à une valorisation omniprésente qui glorifie les grandes lit-
tératures, celles d'origine française ou européenne. Ce sont celles-ci qu'il
faut atteindre de plein fouet avant que les discours d'ici puissent s'im-
poser.' On the German-Austrian situation, see Leslie Bodi, 'Comic Ambivalence as an Identity Marker: The Austrian Model,' in *Comic
Relations: Studies in the Comic, Satire and Parody*, ed. Pavel Petr, David
Roberts, and Philip Thomson (Frankfurt: Peter Lang 1985), 67–77. Concerning Severo Sarduy, see his 'The Baroque and the Neo-Baroque,' *Des-
cant* 55 (1986–7), 133–60; on Franco, see Mary Louise Pratt, 'Margin
Release: Canadian and Latin American Literature in the Context of De-
pendency,' in Balakian and Wilhelm, eds., *Prodeedings ...*, 3:250.
2 Irvine, *Sub/version*, 10
3 Hutcheon, *A Theory of Parody*, 24
4 George Woodcock, 'The Meeting of the Muses: Recent Canadian Fiction
and the Historical Viewpoint,' *Canadian Historical Review* 60, no. 2
(1979), 141; Marshall, 'Re-visioning: Comedy and History in the Canadian Novel,' 56; Hutcheon, *A Poetics of Postmodernism: History, Theory,
Fiction*; Berger, *The Writing of Canadian History*, 2; Tiffin, 'Commonwealth Literature: Comparison and Judgement,' 32; Duffy, *Sounding the
Iceberg*, 54. Duffy unfortunately distances himself from any attempts at
integrating his findings into a theoretical framework.
5 Although I am aware that 'most critics see the romance as a contrasting
stream of fiction from the novel' (Margot Northey, *The Haunted Wilderness: The Gothic and Grotesque in Canadian Fiction* [Toronto: University of
Toronto Press 1976], 13), I will treat both under the same heading, seeing
the romance as a type of novel. As Northey points out, 'many historical
romances emphasized historical details for their own sake, treating the
externals as real objects and occurrences. In this respect they moved
closer to the novel' (14). The first two chapters of Kenneth Hugh Mc-
Lean's PHD dissertation, 'The Treatment of History in Canadian Fiction'
(York University, 1980), show how historical data are emplotted so as to
correspond to the genres of 'white romance' or 'black romance.' For
Scott's influence on Canadian texts, see Bogaards, 'Sir Walter Scott's Influence on Nineteenth Century Canadian Historians and Historical Novelists,' 443–54. For a discussion of Lukács's ideological position, see

Foley, *Telling the Truth*.

6 Cowart, *History and the Contemporary Novel*, 1

7 Foley, *Telling the Truth*, 25, 195–200; 'From *U.S.A.* to *Ragtime*: Notes on the Forms of Historical Consciousness in Modern Fiction,' 101. It is true that Foley mentions theorists of *surfiction* and *fabulation* in her preface, but the bulk of *Telling the Truth* does not take into consideration many contemporary texts 'whose solipsism I found generally irritating and barren' (15).

8 Murray Baumgarten, 'The Historical Novel: Some Postulates,' *Clio* 4, no. 2 (1975), 182

9 Cowart, *History and the Contemporary Novel*, 6

10 Leon Braudy, *Narrative Form in History and Fiction: Hume, Fielding, and Gibbon* (Princeton: Princeton University Press 1970)

11 R.G. Collingwood, 'History as Re-enactment of Past Experience,' in *Theories of History*, ed. Patrick Gardiner (n.p.: The Free Press of Glencoe 1959), 253 (see Barbara Foley's chapter on 'Relativism and Determinism in Modernist Historiography'); Fleishman, *The English Historical Novel*, xv; Bernard Bergonzi, 'Fictions of History,' in *The Contemporary English Novel*, ed. Malcolm Bradbury and David Palmer, Stratford-upon-Avon Studies 18 (London: Edward Arnold 1979), 43; Ricoeur, *Temps et récit*, 1:131–313

12 Frye, 'New Directions from Old,' 53–4. See also LaCapra, *History and Criticism*, 19–20, who states that ' "documents" are themselves texts that "process" or rework "reality" and require a critical reading that goes beyond traditional philological forms of *Quellenkritik*.'

13 White, 'The Historical Text as Literary Artifact,' 42. For a critique of his approach, see for example LaCapra, *History and Criticism*, especially 34–5.

14 Linda Hutcheon, 'History and/as Intertext,' in Moss, ed., *Future Indicative: Literary Theory and Canadian Literature*, 177. See also her recent essay 'Historiographic Metafiction: Parody and the Intertextuality of History,' in O'Donnell and Davis, eds., *Intertextuality and Contemporary American Fiction*, 3–32; and E.L. Doctorow, 'False Documents,' *American Review* 26 (1977), 215–32. Barbara Foley also states at the beginning of *Telling the Truth* that 'finally, I wish to ground my discussion of the documentary novel in a theory of mimesis that dispels conclusively the notion that fictional works do not assert their propositional contents' (43).

15 Hutcheon, *A Poetics*, 16; Foley, *Telling the Truth*, 14

16 White, 'The Historical Text as Literary Artifact,' 47

17 White, *Tropics of Discourse*, 70; *The Content of the Form*, ix

18 Margaret Rose, ' "The Second Time as Farce": A Brief Survey of the Concept of History Understood as Fiction and Farce,' in *Literature and History*, ed. Leonard Schulze and Walter Wetzels (Lanham: University Press of America 1983), 33

19 LaCapra, *History and Criticism*, 36; see also his *History, Politics, and the Novel*.

20 T.D. MacLulich, 'Hearne, Cook, and the Exploration Narrative,' *English Studies in Canada* 5 (1979), 189; 'Canadian Exploration as Literature,' *Canadian Literature* 81 (1979), 74. For literary influences on the composition of Hearne's report, see also I.S. MacLaren, 'Samuel Hearne and the Landscapes of Discovery,' *Canadian Literature* 103 (1984), 27–40.

21 See Berger, *The Writing of Canadian History*, 208–37.

22 George Woodcock, 'History to the Defeated: Notes on Some Novels by Timothy Findley,' in *Present Tense*, ed. John Moss, The Canadian Novel 4 (Toronto: NC Press 1985), 17

23 See, for example, the different traditions of historiography and fiction that T.D. MacLulich identifies in 'Reading the Land: The Wilderness Tradition in Canadian Letters,' *Journal of Canadian Studies* 20, no. 2 (1985), 40–1. J. Wilson Clark, in 'Distortions of Canadian History in Criticism,' *Literature and Ideology* 9 (1971), 45–50, and 'Two Lines in Canadian Literary History,' *Literature and Ideology* 15 (1973), 27–36, distinguishes between two totally different and incompatible schools of Canadian historiography that find their counterparts in literary criticism: pro-imperialist mythical history versus anti-imperialist class history.

24 Marshall, 'Re-visioning,' 57

25 Tiffin, 'Post-Colonial Literatures and Counter-Discourse,' 17, 18

26 Hutcheon, *The Canadian Postmodern*, 21

27 Cowart, *History and the Contemporary Novel*, 8–9

28 Logan, 'Re-Views of the Literary History of Canada,' 126 (see also Thomas Guthrie Marquis, 'English-Canadian Literature,' 535: 'In 1832 the publication of *Wacousta*, by Major John Richardson, marked the true beginning of Canadian fiction.'); Richardson, *Wacousta; or, The Prophecy: A Tale of the Canadas*, ed. Douglas Cronk, xxxiii; Robin Mathews, 'John Richardson: The Wacousta Factor,' in *Canadian Literature: Surrender or Revolution* (Toronto: Steel Rail Publishing 1978), 13; McGregor, *The Wacousta Syndrome*. The quotation on Scott is from Eva-Marie Kröller, 'Walter Scott in America, English Canada, and Québec: A Comparison,' *Canadian Review of Comparative Literature* 7 (1980), 45.

29 Sir Walter Scott, General Preface, *Waverley*, Everyman's Library (London: Dent 1982), 18; Bogaards, 'Sir Walter Scott's Influence,' 446; see also William Renwick Ridell, *John Richardson* (Toronto: Ryerson n.d. [1926?]), 46, who claims that Richardson's speakers 'all have a stilted, artificial style unlike anything that is ever heard in actual life, but not unlike that of ... most of Sir Walter Scott's characters, except the most lowly.'

30 Carl F. Klinck, Introduction, *Wacousta; or, The Prophecy*, by Major John Richardson (Toronto: McClelland and Stewart 1967), xi; Dennis Duffy, 'John Richardson (1796–1852),' in *Canadian Writers and Their Works*, Fiction Series, Vol. 1, ed. Robert Lecker, Jack David, and Ellen Quigley

(Downsview, Ont.: ECW Press 1983), 118

31 Carole Gerson, *A Purer Taste: The Writing and Reading of Fiction in English in Nineteenth-Century Canada* (Toronto: University of Toronto Press 1989), 86

32 Jay Macpherson, 'Reading and Convention in Richardson: Some Notes,' in Ross, ed., *Recovering Canada's First Novelist*, 79. The other two types are 'the inset story, the set-back little picture framed by the whole narrative' (79) and 'backward narrative' (80). See also I.S. MacLaren's identification of parallels between *Wacousta* and Scott's *The Lady of the Lake* in 'Wacousta and the Gothic Tradition,' in ibid., 49–62.

33 Goldie, *Fear and Temptation*, 27

34 Beasley, *The Canadian Don Quixote*, 59 (the reference is to the preface of the second edition of *Wacousta*); Horning is quoted in *Major John Richardson: A Selection of Reviews and Criticism*, ed. Carl Ballstadt (Montreal: Lawrence M. Lande Foundation 1972), 44–5. As Ray Palmer Baker remarks in *A History of English-Canadian Literature to the Confederation*, 'that Cooper ... appears as the godfather of Canadian fiction is a happy instance of the power of art to transcend the barriers of national prejudice' (also quoted after Ballstadt, ed., *Major John Richardson*, 23).

35 Beasley (*The Canadian Don Quixote*, 64) bases his argument on Logan ('Re-views of the Literary History of Canada,' 127–8), who not only rejects any theories 'that Richardson was a mere imitator of Cooper,' but even claims that 'Richardson, if not a better plot-maker than Cooper, is the superior craftsman and stylist, a fact which is proof presumptive that the Canadian ro-romancer [*sic*] developed independently his own mechanics of literary composition.' Marquis ('English-Canadian Literature,' 537) claims that 'Richardson's Indians are his own and are in many ways more natural than Cooper's "noble red men," ' and Leslie Monkman lauds *Wacousta*'s 'refusal to cast either white man or red man as comfortable hero in the quest for ancestry' ('Visions and Revisions: Contemporary Writers and Exploration Accounts of Indigenous Peoples,' in *The Native in Literature*, ed. Thomas King, Cheryl Calver, and Helen Hoy [Toronto: ECW Press 1987], 81). Carl Ballstadt (*Major John Richardson*, 9) remarks that 'even though historical materials are basic to Richardson's fiction, these are shaped to reveal a myth of European adjustment to North America ...,' and Michael Hurley ('*Wacousta*: The Borders of Nightmare,' in *Beginnings*, ed. John Moss, The Canadian Novel 2 [Toronto: NC Press 1980], 66) adds: 'Besides constituting the two poles of the Canadian psyche, the De Haldimar/Morton/Wacousta relationship, conforms to a recurrent romantic convention which reflects the border dichotomy between civilization and wilderness.' Still, none of the characters mentioned is an Indian.

36 T.D. MacLulich, 'Our Place on the Map: The Canadian Tradition in Fiction,' *University of Toronto Quarterly* 52, no. 2 (1982–3), 193

37 Marcia B. Kline, *Beyond the Land Itself: Views of Nature in Canada and the*

United States (Cambridge, Mass.: Harvard University Press 1970), 26

38 MacLulich, *Between Europe and America,* 10–11

39 MacLulich, *Between Europe and America,* 46; George Woodcock, Introduction, *Canadian Writers and Their Works,* Fiction Series, Vol. 1, 7; McLean, 'The Treatment of History in Canadian Fiction,' 135, 139

40 Norman S. Grabo, Introduction, *Edgar Huntly; or, Memoirs of a Sleep-Walker* (New York: Viking Penguin 1988), xiii

41 Quoted after Alfred Weber, 'Charles Brockden Browns Theorie der Geschichtsschreibung und des Romans,' in *Geschichte und Fiktion: Amerikanische Prosa im 19. Jahrhundert,* ed. Alfred Weber and Hartmut Grandel (Göttingen: Vandenhoeck und Ruprecht 1972), 24

42 Lukács, *The Historical Novel,* 42, 64. Lukács's term *Gentilgesellschaft,* denoting a prehistoric form of society, is here translated as *gentile society.*

43 Douglas Cronk, 'The Americanization of *Wacousta,*' in Ross, ed., *Recovering Canada's First Novelist,* 36

44 Frederick Philip Grove, 'Retroaction / Of the Interpretation of History,' in 'An Edition of Selected Unpublished Essays and Lectures by Frederick Philip Grove Bearing on His Theory of Art,' ed. Henry Makow (PHD diss., University of Toronto, 1982), 143

45 Desmond Pacey, *Creative Writing in Canada: A Short History of English-Canadian Literature* (1961; Westport, Conn.: Greenwood Press 1976), 206. For comments on Grove's aestheticism, see Walter Pache, 'Frederick Philip Grove: Comparative Perspectives,' in *A Stranger in My Time: Essays by and about Frederick Philip Grove,* ed. Paul Hjartarson (Edmonton: NeWest Press 1986), 11–20; and David Williams, 'Oscar Wilde and a Swede from Nebraska: Masks of Autobiography in *Settlers of the Marsh* and *In Search of Myself,*' in *Canada and the Nordic Countries: Proceedings from the Second International Conference of the Nordic Association for Canadian Studies, University of Lund, 1987,* ed. Jorn Carlsen and Bengt Streijffert (Lund: Lund University Press 1988), 365–75.

46 'Retroaction / Of the Interpretation of History,' 134–5, 142

47 Ibid., 128

48 Frederick Philip Grove, *In Search of Myself* (1946; Toronto: McClelland and Stewart 1974), 426

49 Ibid., 359; 'Retroaction,' 130. For Phelps's comment and Wheeler as a model, see Douglas Spettigue, Editor's Introduction, *Consider Her Ways,* viii, x.

50 Birk Sproxton, 'Grove's Unpublished *MAN* and It's [*sic*] Relation to *The Master of the Mill,*' in *The Grove Symposium,* ed. John Nause (Ottawa: University of Ottawa Press 1974), 36. Sproxton also provides a readily available reprint of the novel's table of contents.

51 Margaret Stobie, *Frederick Philip Grove* (New York: Twayne 1973), 162

52 Spettigue, Editor's Introduction, *Consider Her Ways,* xii

53 Grove, *Consider Her Ways*, 4. Further references to this work appear in the text.

54 Ronald Sutherland, *Frederick Philip Grove* (Toronto: McClelland and Stewart 1969), 34

55 Swift, *Gulliver's Travels*, 29, 108

56 Jonathan Swift, *Correspondence*, ed. Harold Williams, 5 vols. (Oxford: Clarendon 1963), 3:103. Greve quotes this excerpt in 'Einleitung,' *Prosaschriften*, by Jonathan Swift, ed. and introd. Felix Paul Greve, 4 vols. (Berlin: Reiß 1909–10), 4:23. For the Swift connection, see also Douglas Spettigue, *FPG: The European Years* (Ottawa: Oberon 1973), 210.

57 For the letter, see Swift, *Gulliver's Travels*, iv. For Wawa-quee's insight, see Grove, 'Man,' 89.

58 Kroetsch, *The Lovely Treachery of Words*, 109

59 Marshall, 'Re-visioning,' 60

60 Beja, *Epiphany in the Modern Novel*, 18, 15

61 Proust, *A la recherche du temps perdu*, 3:899; *Remembrance of Things Past*, 2:1015–16. Further references to both works appear in the text, following the titles *Recherche* or *Remembrance*.

62 '... bygone days, times past, which had always balked the efforts of my memory and my intelligence' (*Remembrance*, 2:995)

63 Hans Robert Jauß, *Zeit und Erinnerung in Marcel Proust's 'A la recherche du temps perdu'* (Heidelberg: Winter 1955), 190–1 (my translation)

64 Siegfried Kracauer, 'Time and History,' *History and Theory* [Beiheft] 6 (1966), 75

65 J.M. Kertzer, 'The Past Recaptured,' *Canadian Literature* 65 (1975), 84

66 Buckler, *The Mountain and the Valley*, 195. Further references to this work appear in the text.

67 Cf. Williams, *Confessional Fictions*, 159, for a different interpretation of the preceding quotation as 'a Gantian vision of time frozen into space.'

68 Kertzer, 'The Past Recaptured,' 75

69 A.T. Seaman, 'Visions of Fulfilment in Ernest Buckler and Charles Bruce,' *Essays on Canadian Writing* 31 (1985), 170

70 Douglas Barbour, 'David Canaan: The Failing Heart,' *Studies in Canadian Literature* 1 (1976), 74, 65, 74; Buckler is quoted after Alan R. Young, 'The Genesis of Ernest Buckler's *The Mountain and the Valley*,' *Journal of Canadian Fiction* 16 (1976), 94. See also Alan R. Young, *Ernest Buckler* (Toronto: McClelland and Stewart 1976), 36.

71 Ernest Buckler, 'My First Novel,' in *Ernest Buckler*, ed. Gregory M. Cook (Toronto: McGraw-Hill Ryerson 1972), 23–4

72 Beja, *Epiphany*, 179. See also Wolfe's rejection of the Joycean model, which 'strongly influenced' his own early work ('Writing and Living,' in *The Autobiography of an American Novelist: Thomas Wolfe*, ed. Leslie Field [Cambridge, Mass.: Harvard University Press 1983], 121). For a penetrating analysis of *The Mountain and the Valley* as a parody of Wolfe's *Look Homeward, Angel* and 'a highly sceptical mode of parody to expose the

pitfalls of American transcendentalism for Canadian artists and audiences,' see Williams, *Confessional Fictions*, 4 and 147–73.
73 Williams, *Confessional Fictions*, 151

Chapter 3 Timothy Findley's Metafictional Histories

1 Vauthier, 'The Dubious Battle of Story-Telling: Narrative Strategies in Timothy Findley's *The Wars*,' 14
2 Kroetsch, *The Lovely Treachery of Words*, 23; Peter Klovan, ' "Bright and Good": Findley's *The Wars*,' *Canadian Literature* 91 (1981), 58. See also Diana Brydon, 'A Devotion to Fragility: Timothy Findley's *The Wars*,' *World Literature Written in English* 26, no. 1 (1986), 75–84, and her ' "It could not be told": Making Meaning in Timothy Findley's *The Wars*,' *Journal of Commonwealth Literature* 21, no. 1 (1986), 62–79; and Bruce Pirie, 'The Dragon in the Fog: "Displaced Mythology" in *The Wars*,' *Canadian Literature* 91 (1981), 70–9.
3 Findley, *The Wars*, 10; Kroetsch, *The Lovely Treachery of Words*, 23; Fussell, *The Great War and Modern Memory*, 21. Further references to *The Wars* appear in the text.
4 Foucault, *L'Archéologie du savoir*, 170. Although for economy's sake, I use the pronoun *he* in order to refer to the narrator, one has to keep in mind that Findley does not specify whether we are dealing with a male or female narrator.
5 Robert Kroetsch in Shirley Neuman and Robert Wilson, *Labyrinths of Voice: Conversations with Robert Kroetsch* (Edmonton: NeWest Press 1982), 118
6 Laurie Ricou, 'Obscured by Violence: Timothy Findley's *The Wars*,' in *Actes du colloque sur la violence dans le roman canadien depuis 1960 / Papers from the Conference on Violence in the Canadian Novel since 1960* ([St John's:] Memorial University of Newfoundland Printing Services n.d.), 134
7 Fussell, *The Great War and Modern Memory*, 115, ix
8 John F. Hulcoop, ' "Look! Listen! Mark my words!": Paying Attention to Timothy Findley's Fictions,' *Canadian Literature* 91 (1981), 22–47
9 See Fussell, *The Great War and Modern Memory*, 88–9.
10 York, *The Other Side of Dailiness*, 78
11 Fussell, *The Great War and Modern Memory*, 231. The close relationship between men and animals comes to the fore in the title of the German translation of *The Wars: Der Krieg und die Kröte* (War and the Toad).
12 Fussell, *The Great War and Modern Memory*, 21, 183
13 While Lorraine York claims in *Introducing Timothy Findley's 'The Wars'* (Toronto: ECW Press 1990) that the Clausewitz passage likening war to a minuet 'does not really appear in the works at all' (72), the whole long quotation that Levitt reads out is a direct translation from Carl von Clausewitz's *Vom Kriege* (Berlin: Behr; Leipzig: Feddersen 1933), finish-

ing with the statement that 'Der ganze Krieg wird in einem ernsten, förmlichen Menuettschritt geführt werden' (256).

14 See Howells, ' "History as she is never writ": *The Wars* and *Famous Last Words*,' as well as York, *Introducing Timothy Findley's 'The Wars'*, 20, 35.

15 See Ricou, 'Never Cry Wolfe: Benjamin West's *The Death of Wolfe* in *Prochain Episode* and *The Diviners*,' who also mentions the occurrence of the picture in *The Wars* (184). Most of the relevant text is first-person narrative, as if Robert were addressing the researcher from inside the photograph.

16 Simone Vauthier, 'Photo-Roman: *The Wars* de Timothy Findley,' *Etudes canadiennes / Canadian Studies* 14 (1983), 114

17 Fussell, *The Great War and Modern Memory*, 299

18 An explanation of the horses' behaviour is given in one of Findley's admitted 'sources,' Raymond Massey's *When I Was Young* (Toronto: McClelland and Stewart 1976): 'The horse's instinctive refusal of safety in the face of fire is inexplicable. All other animals flee from danger. It is as though the horse alone among mammals is determined to perish by fire' (84).

19 Whereas Eva-Marie Kröller ('The Exploding Frame: Uses of Photography in Timothy Findley's *The Wars*,' *Revue d'études canadiennes / Journal of Canadian Studies* 16, nos. 3–4 [1981], 74) suspects Fagan to be nothing but a resident of 'Findleyland,' Simone Vauthier ('The Dubious Battle,' 38) states that 'there is no such author.' I made a fascinating discovery studying an early manuscript of *The Wars* in the National Archives, because there Nicholas Fagan's name appears on the title page, and a note explains that it is the pseudonym of the brother of a Canadian author (National Archives, Ottawa, Findley Papers, vol. 16, 'The Wars,' MS).

20 Vauthier, 'The Dubious Battle,' 16, 26, 27

21 Ibid., 15; Findley Papers, vol. 17, 'The Wars,' MS

22 M.L. McKenzie, 'Memories of the Great War: Graves, Sassoon, and Findley,' *University of Toronto Quarterly* 55, no. 4 (1986), 397, 400, 403, 407

23 Fussell, *The Great War and Modern Memory*, 321

24 Vauthier, 'The Dubious Battle,' 15

25 See Eliot, 'Ulysses, Order, and Myth': 'Instead of narrative method, we may now use the mythical method. It is, I seriously believe, a step toward making the modern world possible for art ...' (178).

26 Fussell, *The Great War and Modern Memory*, 23. See also page 106 for 'Hugh Selwyn Mauberley's "consciousness disjunct," a psychological phenomenon perceivable in 1920 as never before.'

27 Vauthier, 'The Dubious Battle,' 15

28 Ibid., 12

29 Hulcoop, 'The Will to Be,' rev. of *Famous Last Words*, 118

30 Marie Vautier, 'Fiction, Historiography, and Myth: Jacques Godbout's *Les Têtes à Papineau* and Rudy Wiebe's *The Scorched-Wood People*,' *Canadian Literature* 110 (1986), 66

31 Howells, ' "History as she is never writ," ' 49

32 Walter Schellenberg, *Aufzeichnungen* (1956; Wiesbaden: Limes Verlag 1979); see the Selected Bibliography for the other works mentioned.

33 Higham, *The Duchess of Windsor: The Secret Life*, 140. See Donaldson, *Edward VIII*, 191, and the whole of her chapter 'The King and Nazi Germany' (191–206), for statements of this kind published before *Famous Last Words*.

34 *The Heart Has Its Reasons*, 355

35 Higham (*The Duchess of Windsor*, 49) refers to recently declassified information which indicates that Wallis may even have been spying on British naval officers when she was in China.

36 On the Oakes murder, see Goldie, 'Timothy Findley: Interview,' 62; and Benson, ' "Whispers of Chaos": *Famous Last Words*,' 601. Findley's solution to the murder was suggested before Charles Higham claimed to have identified Harold Christie, who also figures in the novel, as the murderer. For the real-life model of Lorenzo de Broca, the young Italian poet, see Findley's acknowledgment on the copyright page.

37 Williams, *Confessional Fictions*, 251

38 Findley, *Famous Last Words*, 59. Further references to this work appear in the text.

39 Elizabeth Seddon, 'The Reader as Actor in the Novels of Timothy Findley,' in Moss, ed., *Future Indicative: Literary Theory and Canadian Literature*, 218

40 See also Stephen Scobie's concept of a 'doubling effect ... fundamental to the whole structure of *Famous Last Words*. The narrator is doubled as Mauberley and as the omniscient third-person voice of the framing text' ('Eye-Deep in Hell: Ezra Pound, Timothy Findley, and Hugh Selwyn Mauberley,' 218). This voice has its model in the Book of Daniel (227). For a reading of Mauberley's narrative strategies as a parody of Daniel, see also Shields, ' "The Perfect Voice": Mauberley as Narrator in Timothy Findley's *Famous Last Words*,' 91–2.

41 Williams, *Confessional Fictions*, 252

42 Duffy, 'Let Us Compare Histories: Meaning and Mythology in Findley's *Famous Last Words*,' 191; Shields, ' "The Perfect Voice," ' 87; LaCapra, *History, Politics, and the Novel*, 14. E.F. Shields shows that the 'third-person narratives are neither more nor less historically accurate than the first-person narratives' (86).

43 White, *Tropics of Discourse*, 56; Duffy, 'Let Us Compare Histories,' 192

44 Donaldson, *Edward VIII*, 212

45 Barbara Gabriel, 'Masks and Icons: An Interview with Timothy Findley,' *Canadian Forum* 756 (February 1986), 36

46 See below for an interpretation of these quotations as parodies of Pound's *Hugh Selwyn Mauberley*.

47 See Findley's remark in Bruce Meyer and Brian O'Riordan, 'The Marvel of Reality: An Interview with Timothy Findley,' *Waves* 10, no. 4 (1982),

6. According to Dennis Duffy, Allenby is modelled on Duff Cooper ('Let Us Compare Histories,' 202). E.F. Shields draws parallels between Allenby and Harold Nicolson ('Mauberley's Lies: Fact and Fiction in Timothy Findley's *Famous Last Words*,' 47).

48 '... out of key with his time': Pound, *Hugh Selwyn Mauberley*, 173. For the real Charles Bedaux's far-reaching plans involving the Duke of Windsor and his Nazi sympathies, see Donaldson's reference to the duke's 'long-term political possibilities if he could stage a comeback' (*Edward VIII*, 329). For the duke's own illusions about a comeback, see his *A King's Story*; for example, page 372.

49 See York, *The Other Side of Dailiness*, 88; and Scobie, 'Eye-Deep in Hell,' 215.

50 Donaldson, *Edward VIII*, 187

51 See Donaldson, *Edward VIII*, 362.

52 Donaldson, *Edward VIII*, 371

53 Allen, *The Crown and the Swastika*, 195

54 In the light of recent publications in connection with Hess's death in Berlin, Findley's 'novelistic' version even seems rather tame. See, for example, Hugh Thomas, *Hess: A Tale of Two Murders* (London: Hodder and Stoughton 1988).

55 Benson, ' "Whispers of Chaos," ' 603

56 Goldie, 'Timothy Findley: Interview,' 62; Benson, ' "Whispers of Chaos," ' 601–2; Timothy Findley, 'Alice Drops Her Cigarette on the Floor ... (William Whitehead looking over Timothy Findley's shoulder),' *Canadian Literature* 91 (1981), 16; Johan Aitken, ' "Long Live the Dead": An Interview with Timothy Findley,' *Journal of Canadian Fiction* 33 (1981–2), 81

57 Goldie, 'Timothy Findley: Interview,' 62

58 Scobie, 'Eye-Deep in Hell,' 209, 207; Pound, *Mauberley*, 174

59 Howells, ' "History as she is never writ," ' 52

60 Hulcoop, 'The Will to Be,' 118

61 See, for example, Rosenthal and Gall, *The Modern Poetic Sequence: The Genius of Modern Poetry*, 200, and Witemeyer, *The Poetry of Ezra Pound*, 175.

62 Ezra Pound, *Literary Essays* (1954; New York: New Directions 1968), 75, quoted after Witemeyer, *The Poetry of Ezra Pound*, 3; Witemeyer, *The Poetry of Ezra Pound*, 3; Carpenter, *A Serious Character*, 368

63 Espey, *Ezra Pound's 'Mauberley,'* 16

64 Quoted in Espey, *Ezra Pound's 'Mauberley,'* 49; Berryman, *Circe's Craft*, 135; Pound quoted after Peter Brooker, *A Student's Guide to the Selected Poems of Ezra Pound* (London: Faber and Faber 1979), 188. See also Hugh Kenner, *The Poetry of Ezra Pound* (Millwood, NY: Kraus Reprint Co. 1974).

65 Williams, *Confessional Fictions*, 257

66 Espey, *Ezra Pound's 'Mauberley,'* 82. See Witemeyer, *The Poetry of Ezra*

Pound, 177. Cf. Berryman, *Circe's Craft*, 2, for a different interpretation.
67 Walter Peter, *Studies in the History of the Renaissance* (London 1873),
   vii–ix, quoted after Witemeyer, *The Poetry of Ezra Pound*, 9; Witemeyer,
   The Poetry of Ezra Pound, 9; Berryman, *Circe's Craft*, 71, 80; Carpenter, *A
   Serious Character*, 369
68 Pound, *Mauberley*, 173
69 Pound, *Mauberley*, 175; Howells, ' "History as she is never writ," ' 53
70 Pound, *Mauberley*, 178
71 Pound, *Mauberley*, 182; Rosenthal and Gall, *The Modern Poetic Sequence*,
   201; Howells, ' "History as she is never writ," ' 52–3; Pound, *Mauberley*,
   184; Howells, 'History,' 52; Pound, *Mauberley* 184, 185
72 Carpenter, *A Serious Character*, 153. See also Hugh Kenner, *The Pound
   Ezra* (Berkeley: University of California Press 1971).
73 Espey, *Ezra Pound's 'Mauberley,'* 112
74 Scobie, 'Eye-Deep in Hell,' 210
75 Melmoth, 'The Off-the-Wall Writing on the Wall,' 435. See also Duffy,
   'Let Us Compare Histories': 'Here is where the novel seems so thin, for
   rather than analyzing a ruling class's drift toward Fascism at a time of
   cultural and political crisis, it merely shows it' (199).
76 Melmoth, 'The Off-the-Wall Writing,' 435
77 A similar line of interpretation is taken by E.F. Shields, who states that
   '... Findley does not attempt to use the novel as a substitute for history.
   The fiction is important, enabling him, almost paradoxically, to show
   that, although the difference between fact and fiction is often blurred,
   we must recognize that there is a difference and continue to attempt to
   discern one from the other' ('Mauberley's Lies,' 57). See also her final
   statement in ' "The Perfect Voice" ': 'Accepting the inevitability of a degree of subjectivity and thus of fictionality in our perceptions and our
   evaluations of others, Findley uses fiction to show that the bigger fiction
   is the denial of this subjectivity: the pretence that we can know and
   judge others with godlike objectivity and certainty' (97).
78 See John Barth, 'The Literature of Replenishment: Postmodernist Fiction,' *Atlantic Monthly*, January 1980, 65–71.

Chapter 4 Bowering: Postmodern Parodies

1 Bowering, *A Short Sad Book*, 98. Further references to this work appear in
   the text.
2 Vancouver, *A Voyage of Discovery to the North Pacific Ocean and round
   the World 1791–1795*, 530–1
3 Quoted in Twigg, 'For Batter or Verse,' 10
4 Walter Pache, 'Aspects of Postmodernism in Canada: R. Kroetsch and G.
   Bowering,' in Balakian and Wilhelm, eds., *Proceedings ...*, 3:135 (my emphasis). For Bowering's use of archives, see Smaro Kamboureli, '*Burning
   Water*: Two Stories / One Novel: Narrative as Exploration,' *Island* 10

(1981), 93–4.

5 See Scott, 'A Bum Rap for Poor George Vancouver,' 9.

6 George Bowering, 'A Great Northward Darkness: The Attack on History in Recent Canadian Fiction,' in *Imaginary Hand: Essays by George Bowering* (Edmonton: NeWest Press 1988), 2

7 George Bowering, *Errata* (Red Deer, Alberta: Red Deer College Press 1988), 28

8 For the French original, see Alain Robbe-Grillet, *Pour un nouveau roman* (Paris: Editions de Minuit 1963), 81. I would not agree with Bowering when he often seems to equate realism and modernism in his criticism (cf., for example, Kamboureli, 'A Window onto George Bowering's Fiction of Unrest'). See David Williams's remark in *Confessional Fictions* that 'though a postmodernist such as George Bowering might delight in tarring "modernist realist fiction" with one brush, modernism was hardly a movement which was devoted to the aims of realism' (10). T.D. MacLulich also claims that 'Bowering, Hancock, and Kroetsch habitually equate the techniques of modernist fiction with the techniques of realism' (*Between America and Europe*, 227).

9 Schermbrucker et al., '14 Plums,' 90

10 Kamboureli, 'A Window onto George Bowering's Fiction of Unrest,' 222, 223

11 See Kurt Vonnegut, *Slaughterhouse-Five* (1969; St Albans: Panther 1972), 54.

12 See Bowering's tongue-in-cheek remark that 'of course, I sometimes get accused of using pen names that are not mine. But I can give you one clue – I write under the name of Robin Mathews' (Norris, 'The Efficacy of the Sentence as the Basis of Reality: An Interview with George Bowering,' 19).

13 Norris, 'The Efficacy of the Sentence as the Basis of Reality,' 18

14 Buckler, *The Mountain and the Valley*, 19

15 Hugh MacLennan, *Two Solitudes* (1945; Toronto: Macmillan 1979), 135. See Morson, 'Parody, History, and Metaparody,' 70, for an analysis of word-by-word citation as parody.

16 Schermbrucker et al., '14 Plums,' 101–3. On ludism, see Kamboureli, 'A Window': 'Indeed, ludism is what integrates the disparate elements of *A Short Sad Book* into a surface where they are let be only by means of competing with other elements' (223).

17 The chronology of the chapters of *Burning Water* (references to this work appear in the text) does not follow the actual chronology of Vancouver's travels: at the beginning of chapter 43, for example, 'it was time to call it a summer for the first year on the northern coast' (188). As chapter 1 shows, however, the first summer on the B.C. coast – one wonders if 'Canadian' is equivalent with 'northern' here – had been that of 1792, and the chronology of intervening chapters (although unmarked there) has already proceeded to 1793 (see, for example, chapter 23), at least if

one goes by the dates of the original expedition. Vancouver's own narrative is a special case of an exploration report because it seems to have been written by himself rather than by a ghost-writer, and it is 'a straightforward revision' of his original journal (W. Kaye Lamb, Introduction, *A Voyage*, 229).

As Bowering shows, Vancouver's voyage was not only one of exploration; Vancouver was also to carry out the political task of taking over the Nootka trading station and port from the Spaniards (see Lamb, Introduction, 40).

18 Leslie Monkman, 'Visions and Revisions: Contemporary Writers and Exploration Accounts of Indigenous Peoples,' *The Native in Literature*, ed. Thomas King, Cheryl Calver, and Helen Hoy (Toronto: ECW Press 1987), 89; W.H. New, 'Take your order ...?' *Canadian Literature* 89 (1981), 2; Scott, 'A Bum Rap for Poor George Vancouver,' 9; Anthony S. Brennan, rev. of *Burning Water*, *Fiddlehead* 131 (1982), 87; Kamboureli, '*Burning Water*: Two Stories / One Novel,' 93

19 Berry, 'A Deckchair of Words,' 314; Gary Boire, 'Hear & Their: Editorial,' *Landfall* 159 (1986), 276

20 Berry, 'A Deckchair of Words,' 315; Reginald Berry, 'George Bowering: The Fact of Place on the Canadian West Coast,' *Westerly* 30, no. 4 (1985), 78

21 Visser, 'Historicity in Historical Fiction: *Burning Water* and *The Temptations of Big Bear*,' 98

22 Eva-Marie Kröller, 'Trieste and George Bowering's *Burning Water*,' *Open Letter* 6, no. 8 (1987), 44. Trieste, too, is the setting of part of John Berger's *G.*, which Bowering lists on his acknowledgments page. Bowering quoted after Schermbrucker et al., '14 Plums,' 98

23 Ronald Hatch, 'Narrative Development in the Canadian Historical Novel,' *Canadian Literature* 110 (1986), 95

24 Lobb, 'Imagining History: The Romantic Background of George Bowering's *Burning Water*,' 112, 113

25 Berry, 'A Deckchair of Words,' 317

26 See chapter 3 for the use that Findley makes of the painting in *The Wars*.

27 Vancouver, *A Voyage*, 2:502

28 See George Bowering, 'The Painted Window: Notes on Post-Realist Fiction,' in *The Mask in Place: Essays on Fiction in North America* (Winnipeg: Turnstone 1982), 113–27.

29 John Moss, 'Himmler's Got the King: An Essay on *Badlands* and *Burning Water*,' in *Present Tense*, ed. John Moss (Toronto: NC Press 1985), 255

30 See Lamb, Introduction, *A Voyage*, 5; and Bowering, *Burning Water*, 21.

31 For a more detailed description of Bowering's use of Whorfian theories, see Susan Lynne Knutson, 'Bowering and Melville on Benjamin's Wharf: A Look at Indigenous-English Communication Strategies,' *Essays on Canadian Writing* 38 (1989), 67–80.

32 Hopwood, 'Explorers by Sea: The West Coast,' 62; John Forsyth, 'Biographical Note,' *Menzies' Journal of Vancouver's Voyage*, x

33 Vancouver, *A Voyage*, 2:677

34 For an analysis of further Melvillean parodies, see Kröller, 'Postmodernism, Colony, Nation: The Melvillean Texts of Bowering and Beaulieu'; and Knutson, 'Bowering and Melville on Benjamin's Wharf.'

35 See Vancouver, *A Voyage*, 2:482; and *Menzies' Journal of Vancouver's Voyage*, 3.

36 See also Berry, 'A Deckchair of Words,' 316; and Kamboureli, 'A Window onto George Bowering's Fiction of Unrest.' The sailor George Delsing also appears on pages 129 and 225. In Bowering's *Mirror on the Floor* (Toronto: McClelland and Stewart 1967), George Delsing, an exseaman, is a friend and confidante of the protagonist, Bob Small.

37 John Livingston Lowes, *The Road to Xanadu* (Boston: Houghton Mifflin 1955), 75; Tiffin, 'Post-Colonial Literatures and Counter-Discourse,' 22. For explorations of Coleridgean intertexts, see also Visser, 'Historicity in Historical Fiction'; and Lobb, 'Imagining History.' Lowes quotes James Cook: *'During a calm ... some parts of the sea seemed covered with a kind of slime*; and some small sea animals were *swimming about ... that had a white, or shining appearance* ... When they began to swim about, which they did, with equal ease, upon their back, sides, or belly, they emitted the brightest colours of the most precious gems ... Sometimes they ... assum[ed] various tints of *blue* ... But ... the colour was, chiefly, a beautiful, pale *green*, tinged with a *burnished gloss*; and, in the dark, it had a faint appearance of *glowing fire*. They proved to be ... probably, an animal which has a share in producing ... *that lucid appearance, often observed near ships at sea, in the night'* (Lowes, 42–3). Archibald Menzies also refers to Cook's writings when he mentions 'a most beautiful species of *Oniscus*' which 'emitted various colours of the brightest hue' (*Menzies' Journal*, 2).

38 Terry Goldie, 'Signs of the Themes: The Value of a Politically Grounded Semiotics,' in Moss, ed., *Future Indicative: Literary Theory and Canadian Literature*, 86

39 Robin Fisher, *Contact and Conflict: Indian-European Relations in British Columbia, 1774–1890* (Vancouver: University of British Columbia Press 1977), xi; Bruce G. Trigger, *Natives and Newcomers: Canada's 'Heroic Age' Reconsidered* (Kingston and Montreal: McGill-Queen's University Press 1985), 4; Goldie, *Fear and Temptation*, 28

40 This letter is reprinted in Vancouver, *A Voyage*, 4:1587–90.

41 Hopwood, 'Explorers by Sea,' 61; Vancouver, *A Voyage*, 2:584. On the missing chapter in *Burning Water*, see also Lobb, 'Imagining History,' 125.

42 Vancouver, *A Voyage*, 3:795; Lamb, Introduction, *A Voyage*, 123

43 Kröller, 'Postmodernism, Colony, Nation,' 57

44 Lobb, 'Imagining History,' 126, n. 17. On the two boats called *Discovery*,

see Lamb, Introduction, *A Voyage*, 22.

45 T.D. MacLulich, 'Canadian Exploration as Literature,' *Canadian Literature* 81 (1979), 76. Lobb ('Imagining History,' 115) calls *Burning Water* '[a tragedy] of unfulfilled ambition.' One might argue that – in connection with Hayden White's original typology rather than with MacLulich's 'Canadianization' of it – the ending is satirical. Whatever interpretation one prefers, the generic change is and remains a parodic one.

46 Visser, 'Historicity in Historical Fiction,' 107

47 Twigg, 'For Batter or Verse,' 10

48 Hans Vilmar Geppert, *Der 'andere' historische Roman: Theorie und Strukturen einer diskontinuierlichen Gattung* (Tübingen: Niemeyer 1976), 34

49 MacLulich, *Between Europe and America*, 253; Ken Norris, Introduction, *Essays on Canadian Writing* 38 (1989), 1; Goldie, *Fear and Temptation*, 139; Scott, 'A Bum Rap for Poor George Vancouver,' 9

Chapter 5 Atwood: Parodies from a Feminist Point of View

1 Huxley, *Brave New World*, 36; Orwell, *Nineteen Eighty-Four*, 35

2 Howells, *Private and Fictional Words*, 55, 2; Irvine, *Sub/version*, 11. See also Davey, *Reading Canadian Reading*: 'What remains most available to someone who would write as woman are parodies and subversions of official discourse, ungrammatical and non-generic fracturings of it, or the muse's silence to which women have usually been relegated' (81).

3 Waugh, *Feminine Fictions*, 3, 6, 9; Hutcheon, *The Canadian Postmodern*, 138. For an analysis of *Bodily Harm* as an instance of consciousness-raising, see Hansen, 'Fiction and (Post) Feminism in Atwood's *Bodily Harm*.'

4 Rigney, *Margaret Atwood*, 127; Margaret Atwood, 'What's So Funny? Notes on Canadian Humour,' in *Second Words: Selected Critical Prose* (Toronto: Anansi 1982), 181

5 Hansen, 'Fiction and (Post) Feminism in Atwood's *Bodily Harm*,' 5; Davey, 'Translating Translating Apollinaire,' 41; Howells, *Private and Fictional Words*, 29

6 Barbara Godard, 'Telling It Over Again: Atwood's Art of Parody,' *Canadian Poetry* 21 (1987), 1–2

7 Howells, *Private and Fictional Words*, 54. See Catherine Sheldrick Ross, 'Calling Back the Ghost of the Old-Time Heroine: Duncan, Montgomery, Atwood, Laurence, and Munro,' *Studies in Canadian Literature* 4, no. 1 (1979), 43–58, as one of the interpretations of *Lady Oracle* as parody, and of parody as a technique generally employed by Canadian women writers.

8 Rigney, *Margaret Atwood*, 104; Howells, *Private and Fictional Words*, 29

9 Ezra Pound, *The Spirit of Romance* (1910; London: Peter Owen 1970), 8

10 Atwood, *Bodily Harm*, 128. Further references to this work appear in the text.

11 See Stanley S. Atherton, 'Tropical Traumas: Images of the Caribbean in

Recent Canadian Fiction,' *Canadian Literature* 95 (1982), 8–14.

12 Davey, *Margaret Atwood: A Feminist Poetics*, 57, 63

13 Davey, *Margaret Atwood*, 67; Atwood in Jan Garden Castro, 'An Interview with Margaret Atwood, 20 April 1983,' in VanSpanckeren and Castro, eds., *Margaret Atwood: Vision and Forms*, 221; Hansen, 'Fiction and (Post) Feminism,' 6; Smith, 'Margaret Atwood and the City,' 253; Wilson, 'Turning Life into Popular Art,' 138; Davey, *Margaret Atwood*, 72. For comments on Rennie's increasing political awareness, see also Rubenstein, 'Pandora's Box and Female Survival: Margaret Atwood's *Bodily Harm*,' 128. It is interesting to see that in the other 'epiphanic' novel in this study the epiphany is equally associated with active involvement in community life: David Canaan in Buckler's *The Mountain and the Valley* at one stage dreams of becoming the scribe of his rural tribe. In both cases, the realization of the epiphanic insight, its development into something socially more than symbolic, is doubtful at best.

14 Hansen, 'Fiction and (Post) Feminism,' 9. For other examples of the indicated pattern, see also the beginning of the second section of part 4: 'If I could do it over again I'd do it a different way, says Lora' (168); and the beginning of the second section of part 5: 'I ran into Paul in Miami, says Lora' (212).

15 Irvine, *Sub/version*, 42; Wilson, 'Turning Life into Popular Art,' 136. See also *Bodily Harm*, 142: 'When pictures begin moving and threaten to become real, Rennie imposes the frames of television, video, and movie screens ...'

16 Rubenstein, 'Pandora's Box,' 132

17 Ildikó de Papp Carrington, 'Another Symbolic Descent,' rev. of *Bodily Harm, Essays on Canadian Writing* 26 (1983), 58

18 Dorothy Jones, ' "Waiting for the Rescue": A Discussion of Margaret Atwood's *Bodily Harm*,' *Kunapipi* 6, no. 3 (1984), 92

19 Smith, 'Margaret Atwood and the City,' 253

20 Roberta Rubenstein, 'Nature and Nurture in Dystopia: *The Handmaid's Tale*,' in VanSpanckeren and Castro, eds., *Margaret Atwood: Vision and Forms*, 101. For the novel's intertextual relationship to the utopian or dystopian traditions, see, for example, Arno Heller, 'Die literarische Dystopie in Amerika mit einer exemplarischen Erörterung von Margaret Atwoods *The Handmaid's Tale*,' in *Utopian Thought in American Literature: Untersuchungen zur literarischen Utopie und Dystopie in den USA*, ed. Arno Heller, Walter Hölbling, and Waldemar Zacharasiewicz (Tübingen: Narr 1988) 185–204; or Barbara Korte, 'Textuelle Interdependenzen in Margaret Atwoods Roman *The Handmaid's Tale*,' *Zeitschrift der Gesellschaft für Kanada-Studien* 10, no. 1 (1990), 15–25. See also Chris Ferns's argument in 'The Value/s of Dystopia' that 'in this context, it becomes all the more interesting to examine a dystopian fiction not only written by a woman, but featuring a woman as its central character – and to see whether, and how far, this changes the terms of the dystopian equation'

(376).

21 For Atwood's personal connections with New England, and the reasons behind the dedication of the book to her 'mentor' Perry Miller and her witch ancestor Mary Webster, see, for example, John Godard, 'Lady Oracle,' *Books in Canada* 14, no. 8 (November 1985), 6–10; and Reingard M. Nischik, 'Back to the Future: Margaret Atwood's Anti-Utopian Vision in *The Handmaid's Tale*,' *Englisch-amerikanische Studien* 9 (1987), 139–48.

22 Cowart, *History and the Contemporary Novel*, 105; 'Gilead,' in *The Interpreter's Dictionary of the Bible*, ed. George Arthur Buttrick, 4 vols. (New York: Abingdon Press 1962)

23 See Atwood, *The Handmaid's Tale*, 240. Further references to this work appear in the text. See also the questioning of the reliability of family albums in Findley's *The Wars* (chapter 3).

24 Davey, 'Translating Translating Apollinaire,' 44–5; Lacombe, 'The Writing on the Wall: Amputated Speech in Margaret Atwood's *The Handmaid's Tale*,' 5

25 I have to admit, though, that some of Woolf's chauvinist males also come close to citing the Bible in order to support their own point of view.

26 Hutcheon, *The Canadian Postmodern*, 8

27 Zamiatin, *We*, 14, 217

28 Huxley, *Brave New World*, 25

29 Ibid., 38–9, 176

30 Huxley, *Brave New World Revisited* (1958; Harper & Row / Perennial 1965), 5; Foreword to *Brave New World*, 9; Orwell, *Nineteen Eighty-Four*, 34

31 Orwell, *Nineteen Eighty-Four*, 15

32 Turner, 'Atwood's Playing Puritans in *The Handmaid's Tale*,' 86

33 Hutcheon, *The Canadian Postmodern*, 8

34 Styron quoted after Douglas Barzelay and Robert Sussman, 'William Styron on *The Confessions of Nat Turner*: A Yale Lit Interview,' in *Conversations with William Styron*, ed. James L.W. West III (Jackson: University Press of Mississippi 1985), 96; Robert Canzoneri and Page Stegner, 'An Interview with William Styron,' in ibid., 78; C. Vann Woodward and R.W.B. Lewis, 'The Confessions of William Styron,' in ibid., 88; Canzoneri and Stegner, 'An Interview,' 78

35 Cowart, *History and the Contemporary Novel*, 118

36 Lacombe, 'The Writing on the Wall,' 9

37 Sharon Wilson has pointed out the importance of these kinds of parodic fairy-tale echoes in Atwood's novels, in 'Bluebeard's Forbidden Room: Gender Images in Margaret Atwood's Visual and Literary Art,' *American Review of Canadian Studies* 16, no. 4 (1986), 385–97.

38 Cf. Turner, 'Atwood's Playing Puritans,' 90

39 See W.J. Keith's claim in 'Apocalyptic Imaginations: Notes on Atwood's *The Handmaid's Tale* and Findley's *Not Wanted on the Voyage*,' *Essays on Canadian Writing* 35 (1987), 124, that ' "what was then Canada" (322–23)

Canadian Writing 35 (1987), 124, that ' "what was then Canada" (322–23)
is soon to be taken over by the Inuit (presumably because of a decline in the white birth rate).' As far as the restriction of women to oral communication is concerned, see Mario Klarer, 'The Gender of Orality and Literacy in Margaret Atwood's *The Handmaid's Tale*,' *Arbeiten aus Anglistik und Amerikanistik* 15, no. 2 (1990), 151–70.

40 Lacombe, 'The Writing on the Wall,' 4. See also W.F. Garrett-Petts, 'Reading, Writing, and the Postmodern Condition: Interpreting Margaret Atwood's *The Handmaid's Tale*,' *Open Letter* 7, no. 1 (1988), 82.

41 Davidson, 'Future Tense: Making History in *The Handmaid's Tale*,' 115

42 Davey, 'Translating Translating Apollinaire,' 45. For an emphasis on the feminist focus of *The Handmaid's Tale*, see also Amin Malak, 'Margaret Atwood's *The Handmaid's Tale* and the Dystopian Tradition,' *Canadian Literature* 112 (1987), 9–16.

43 Hutcheon, *The Canadian Postmodern*, 138

44 Ibid., 144

45 Ferns, 'The Value/s of Dystopia,' 382

46 Davidson, 'Future Tense,' 120

47 Chinmoy Banerjee acknowledges 'the parodic nature of this framing discourse' but comes to a completely different conclusion concerning the 'sophisticated enjoyment of parodic exercise,' in which criticism 'is dissolved through parodic frames and is ultimately irrelevant' ('Alice in Disneyland: Criticism as Commodity in *The Handmaid's Tale*,' *Essays on Canadian Writing* 41 [1990], 89, 90).

Chapter 6 Concluding Remarks

1 Susanna Moodie, *Roughing It in the Bush*, NCL ed. (Toronto: McClelland and Stewart 1970), v

2 *Alibi* (1983; Toronto: General Publishing 1984), 210

3 See, for example, Walter L. Knorr, 'Doctorow and Kleist: "Kohlhaas" in *Ragtime*,' *Modern Fiction Studies* 22 (1976), 224–7; Maria Diedrich, 'E.L. Doctorow's Coalhouse Walker, Jr.: Fact in Fiction,' in *E.L. Doctorow: A Democracy of Perception*, ed. Herwig Friedl and Dieter Schulz (Essen: Blaue Eule 1988), 113–23.

4 See, for example, Julian Symons's opinion in 'Deep Down,' *London Review of Books* 12, no. 12 (1990), 20–1: 'The incongruities are similar in kind to performances of Shakespeare that make Troilus a yuppie investment broker or offer a version of *Othello* in Victorian dress. It would be wrong to think them symbolic, or otherwise meaningful. Ransmayr, like some Shakespearean producers, is just having fun.'

Selected Bibliography

Abastado, Claude. 'Situation de la parodie.' *Cahiers du vingtième siècle* 6 (1976), 9–37

Allen, Peter. *The Crown and the Swastika: Hitler, Hess and the Duke of Windsor.* London: Robert Hale 1983

Atwood, Margaret. *Bodily Harm.* 1981; Toronto: McClelland and Stewart–Bantam 1982

– *The Handmaid's Tale.* Toronto: McClelland and Stewart 1985

Bakhtin, Mikhail. *The Dialogic Imagination: Four Essays.* Ed. Michael Holquist. Trans. Caryl Emerson and Michael Holquist. Austin: University of Texas Press 1981

– *Problems of Dostoevsky's Poetics.* Ed. and trans. Caryl Emerson. Minneapolis: University of Minnesota Press 1984

– *Rabelais and His World.* Trans. Hélène Iswolsky. Bloomington: Indiana University Press 1984

Balakian, Anna, and James J. Wilhelm, eds. *Proceedings of the Tenth Congress of the International Comparative Literature Association / Actes du Dixième Congrès de l'Association Internationale de Littérature Comparée: New York 1982.* 3 vols. New York: Garland 1985

Beasley, David R. *The Canadian Don Quixote: The Life and Works of Major John Richardson, Canada's First Novelist.* Erin, Ont.: The Porcupine's Quill 1977

Beja, Morris. *Epiphany in the Modern Novel.* London: Peter Owen 1971

Benson, Eugene. ' "Whispers of Chaos": *Famous Last Words.' World Literature Written in English* 21, no. 1 (1982), 599–606

Berger, Carl. *The Writing of Canadian History: Aspects of English-Canadian Historical Writing since 1900.* 2d ed. Toronto: University of Toronto Press 1986

Berry, Reginald. 'A Deckchair of Words: Post-colonialism, Post-modernism, and the Novel of Self-projection in Canada and New Zealand.' *Landfall* 159 [40, no. 3] (1986), 310–23

Berryman, Jo Brantley. *Circe's Craft: Ezra Pound's 'Hugh Selwyn Mauberley.'* Ann Arbor: UMI Research Press 1983

Bogaards, Winnifred M. 'Sir Walter Scott's Influence on Nineteenth Century Canadian Historians and Historical Novelists.' In *Scott and His Influence: The Papers of the Aberdeen Scott Conference, 1982*. Ed. J.H. Alexander and David Hewitt. Aberdeen: Association for Scottish Literary Studies 1983, 443–54

Bowering, George. *Burning Water*. 1980; New Press Canadian Classics. Toronto: General Publishing 1983

– *George, Vancouver: A Discovery Poem*. Toronto: Weed / Flower Press 1970

– *A Short Sad Book*. Vancouver: Talonbooks 1977

Buckler, Ernest. *The Mountain and the Valley*. 1952; Toronto: McClelland and Stewart 1970

Carpenter, Humphrey. *A Serious Character: The Life of Ezra Pound*. London: Faber and Faber 1988

Cowart, David. *History and the Contemporary Novel*. Carbondale: Southern Illinois University Press 1989

Davey, Frank. *Margaret Atwood: A Feminist Poetics*. Vancouver: Talonbooks 1984

– *Reading Canadian Reading*. Winnipeg: Turnstone 1988

– 'Translating Translating Apollinaire: The Problematizing of Discourse in Some Recent Canadian Texts.' In *Cross-Cultural Studies*. Ed. Mirko Jurak. Ljubljana: English Department, Edvard Kardelj University 1988, 41–6

Davidson, Arnold E. 'Future Tense: Making History in *The Handmaid's Tale*.' In *Margaret Atwood: Vision and Forms*. Ed. Kathryn VanSpanckeren and Jan Garden Castro. Carbondale: Southern Illinois University Press 1988, 113–21

Deguy, Michel. 'Limitation ou illimitation de l'imitation: Remarques sur la parodie.' In *Le Singe à la porte: Vers une théorie de la parodie*. Ed. Groupar. New York: Lang 1984, 1–11

Donaldson, Frances. *Edward VIII*. London: Weidenfeld and Nicolson 1974

Duffy, Dennis. 'Let Us Compare Histories: Meaning and Mythology in Findley's *Famous Last Words*.' *Essays on Canadian Writing* 30 (1984–5), 187–205

– *Sounding the Iceberg: An Essay on Canadian Historical Novels*. Toronto: ECW Press 1986

Eliot, T.S. 'Ulysses, Order, and Myth.' *Selected Prose of T.S. Eliot*. Ed. Frank Kermode. New York: Harcourt Brace Jovanovich / Farrar, Straus and Giroux 1975, 175–8

Espey, John. *Ezra Pound's 'Mauberley': A Study in Composition*. 1955; Berkeley: University of California Press 1974

Ferns, Chris. 'The Value/s of Dystopia: *The Handmaid's Tale* and the Anti-Utopian Tradition.' *Dalhousie Review* 69, no. 3 (1989), 373–82

Findley, Timothy. *Famous Last Words*. 1981; Harmondsworth: Penguin 1982

– *The Wars*. 1977; Markham, Ont.: Penguin 1978

– 'The Wars' MS. Findley Papers, vol. 17. National Archives, Ottawa

Fleishman, Avrom. *The English Historical Novel: Walter Scott to Virginia Woolf*. Baltimore: Johns Hopkins Press 1971

Foley, Barbara. 'From *U.S.A.* to *Ragtime*: Notes on the Forms of Historical Consciousness in Modern Fiction.' *American Literature* 50 (1978–9), 85–105

– *Telling the Truth: The Theory and Practice of Documentary Fiction*. Ithaca: Cornell University Press 1986

Foucault, Michel. *L'Archéologie du savoir*. Paris: Gallimard 1969

Frye, Northrop. 'New Directions from Old.' In *Fables of Identity: Studies in Poetic Mythology*. New York: Harcourt Brace Jovanovich 1963, 52–66

Fussell, Paul. *The Great War and Modern Memory*. New York: Oxford University Press 1975

Genette, Gérard. *Palimpsestes: La littérature au second degré*. Paris: Seuil 1982

Goldie, Terry. *Fear and Temptation: The Image of the Indigene in Canadian, Australian, and New Zealand Literatures*. Kingston and Montreal: McGill-Queen's University Press 1989

– 'Timothy Findley: Interview.' *Kunapipi* 6, no. 1 (1984), 56–67

Grove, Frederick Philip. *Consider Her Ways*. 1947; Toronto: McClelland and Stewart 1977

– 'Man: His Habits, Social Organization and Outlook.' Grove Manuscripts, box 5, folder 4. Special Collections Division, University of Manitoba Archives

– 'Retroaction/Of the Interpretation of History.' In 'An Edition of Selected Unpublished Essays and Lectures by Frederick Philip Grove Bearing on His Theory of Art.' Ed. Henry Makow. PHD diss., University of Toronto, 1982, 128–54

Hansen, Elaine Tuttle. 'Fiction and (Post) Feminism in Atwood's *Bodily Harm*.' *Novel* 19, no. 1 (1985), 5–21

Higham, Charles. *The Duchess of Windsor: The Secret Life*. New York: McGraw-Hill 1988

Hopwood, Victor G. 'Explorers by Sea: The West Coast.' In *Literary History of Canada*. 3 vols. Gen. ed. Carl F. Klinck. 2nd ed. Toronto: University of Toronto Press 1976, 1:54–65

Howells, Coral Ann. ' "History as she is never writ": *The Wars* and *Famous Last Words*.' *Kunapipi* 6, no. 1 (1984), 49–56

– *Private and Fictional Words: Canadian Novelists of the 1970s and 1980s*. London: Methuen 1987

Hulcoop, John F. 'The Will to Be.' Rev. of *Famous Last Words*. *Canadian Literature* 94 (1982), 117–22

Hutcheon, Linda. 'Canadian Historiographic Metafiction.' *Essays on Canadian Writing* 30 (1984–5), 228–38

– *The Canadian Postmodern: A Study of Contemporary English-Canadian Fiction*. Toronto: Oxford University Press 1988

– 'Parody without Ridicule: Observations on Modern Literary Parody.' *Canadian Review of Comparative Literature* 5, no. 2 (1978), 201–11

– *A Poetics of Postmodernism: History, Theory, Fiction*. New York: Routledge 1988

- 'The Postmodern Problematizing of History.' *English Studies in Canada* 14, no. 4 (1988), 365–82
- *A Theory of Parody: The Teachings of Twentieth-Century Art Forms.* New York: Methuen 1985

Huxley, Aldous. *Brave New World.* 1932; St Albans: Triad/Panther 1977

Irvine, Lorna. *Sub/version: Canadian Fictions by Women.* Toronto: ECW Press 1986

Jurak, Mirko, ed. *Cross-Cultural Studies: American, Canadian and European Literatures, 1945–1985.* Ljubljana: English Department, Edvard Kardelj University 1988

Kamboureli, Smaro. '*Burning Water*: Two Stories / One Novel: Narrative as Exploration.' *Island* 10 (1981), 89–94
- 'A Window onto George Bowering's Fiction of Unrest.' In *Present Tense.* Ed. John Moss. The Canadian Novel 4. Toronto: NC Press 1985, 206–31

Karrer, Wolfgang. *Parodie, Travestie, Pastiche.* Munich: Fink 1977

Kiremidjian, David. *A Study of Modern Parody: James Joyce's 'Ulysses' – Thomas Mann's 'Doctor Faustus.'* New York: Garland 1985

Kroetsch, Robert. *The Lovely Treachery of Words: Essays Selected and New.* Toronto: Oxford University Press 1989

Kröller, Eva-Marie. 'Postmodernism, Colony, Nation: The Melvillean Texts of Bowering and Beaulieu.' *Revue de l'Université d'Ottawa / University of Ottawa Quarterly* 54 (1984), 53–61

LaCapra, Dominick. *History and Criticism.* Ithaca: Cornell University Press 1985
- *History, Politics, and the Novel.* Ithaca: Cornell University Press 1987

Lacombe, Michèle. 'The Writing on the Wall: Amputated Speech in Margaret Atwood's *The Handmaid's Tale.*' *Wascana Review* 21, no. 2 (1986), 3–20

Lamb, W. Kaye. Introduction. *A Voyage of Discovery to the North Pacific Ocean and round the World 1791–1795.* By George Vancouver. 4 vols. London: Hakluyt Society 1984, 1:1–256

Lobb, Edward. 'Imagining History: The Romantic Background of George Bowering's *Burning Water.*' *Studies in Canadian Literature* 12, no. 1 (1987), 112–28

Logan, J.D. 'Re-Views of the Literary History of Canada: Essay II – Canadian Fictionists and Other Creative Prose Writers.' *Canadian Magazine* 48 (1916–17), 125–32

Lukács, Georg. *The Historical Novel.* Trans. Hannah Mitchell and Stanley Mitchell. London: Merlin Press 1962

McGregor, Gaile. *The Wacousta Syndrome: Explorations in the Canadian Langscape.* Toronto: University of Toronto Press 1985

MacLulich, T.D. *Between Europe and America: The Canadian Tradition in Fiction.* Toronto: ECW Press 1988

Marquis, Thomas Guthrie. 'English-Canadian Literature' (1913). In '*Our Intellectual Strength and Weakness,*' by John George Bourinot; 'English-Cana-

dian Literature,' by Thomas Guthrie Marquis: 'French-Canadian Literature,' by Camille Roy. Ed. Clara Thomas. Toronto: University of Toronto Press 1973, 493–589

Marshall, Tom. 'Re-visioning: Comedy and History in the Canadian Novel.' *Queen's Quarterly* 93, no. 1 (1986), 52–65

Martin, Arthur Shadwell. *On Parody.* 1896; New York: Folcroft Library Editions 1973

Melmoth, John. 'The Off-the-Wall Writing on the Wall.' Rev. of *Famous Last Words. Times Literary Supplement,* 24 April 1987, 435

Menzies, Archibald. *Menzies' Journal of Vancouver's Voyage: April to October, 1792.* Ed. C.F. Newcombe. Archives of British Columbia Memoir no. 5. Victoria, BC: William H. Cullin 1923

Morson, Gary Saul. 'Parody, History, and Metaparody.' In *Rethinking Bakhtin: Extensions and Challenges.* Ed. Gary Saul Morson and Caryl Emerson. Evanston: Northwestern University Press 1989, 63–86

Moss, John, ed. *Future Indicative: Literary Theory and Canadian Literature.* Ottawa: University of Ottawa Press 1987

Norris, Ken. 'The Efficacy of the Sentence as the Basis of Reality: An Interview with George Bowering.' *Essays on Canadian Writing* 38 (1989), 7–29

O'Donnell, Patrick, and Robert Con Davis, eds. *Intertextuality and Contemporary American Fiction.* Baltimore: Johns Hopkins University Press 1989

Orwell, George. *Nineteen Eighty-Four.* 1949; Harmondsworth: Penguin 1974

Pound, Ezra. *Hugh Selwyn Mauberley.* In *Selected Poems.* Ed. T.S. Eliot. 1928; London: Faber and Faber 1948, 171–87

Proust, Marcel. *A la recherche du temps perdu.* Ed. Pierre Clarac and André Ferré. Bibliothèque de la Pléiade. 3 vols. Paris: Gallimard 1954

– *Remembrance of Things Past.* Trans. C.K. Scott Moncrieff and Frederick A. Blossom. New York: Random House 1934

Richardson, John. *Wacousta; or, The Prophecy: A Tale of the Canadas.* Ed. Douglas Cronk. Centre for Editing Early Canadian Texts Series 4. Ottawa: Carleton University Press 1987

Ricoeur, Paul. *Temps et récit.* 3 vols. Paris: Seuil 1983–5

Ricou, Laurie. 'Never Cry Wolfe: Benjamin West's *The Death of Wolfe* in *Prochain Episode* and *The Diviners.' Essays on Canadian Writing* 20 (1980–1), 171–85

Rigney, Barbara Hill. *Margaret Atwood.* Houndmills, Basingstoke, Hampshire: Macmillan Education 1987

Rose, Margaret A. *Parody//Meta-Fiction: An Analysis of Parody as a Critical Mirror to the Writing and Reception of Fiction.* London: Croom Helm 1979

Rosenthal, M.L., and Sally M. Gall. *The Modern Poetic Sequence: The Genius of Modern Poetry.* New York: Oxford University Press 1983

Ross, Catherine Sheldrick, ed. *Recovering Canada's First Novelist: Proceedings from the John Richardson Conference.* Erin, Ont.: Porcupine's Quill 1984

Rotermund, Erwin. *Die Parodie in der modernen deutschen Lyrik.* Munich: Eidos Verlag 1963

Rubenstein, Roberta. 'Pandora's Box and Female Survival: Margaret At-
wood's *Bodily Harm.*' *Revue d'études canadiennes / Journal of Canadian
Studies* 20, no. 1 (1985), 120–35
Schermbrucker, Bill, et al. '14 Plums.' *The Capilano Review* 15 (1979),
86–107
Scobie, Stephen. 'Eye-Deep in Hell: Ezra Pound, Timothy Findley, and
Hugh Selwyn Mauberley.' *Essays on Canadian Writing* 30 (1984–5), 206–27
Scott, Chris. 'A Bum Rap for Poor George Vancouver.' Rev. of *Burning
Water. Books in Canada*, November 1980, 9
Shields, E.F. 'Mauberley's Lies: Fact and Fiction in Timothy Findley's *Fa-
mous Last Words.*' *Revue d'études canadiennes / Journal of Canadian Studies*
22, no. 4 (1987–8), 44–59
– ' "The Perfect Voice": Mauberley as Narrator in Timothy Findley's *Famous
Last Words.*' *Canadian Literature* 119 (1988), 84–98
Smith, Rowland. 'Margaret Atwood and the City: Style and Substance in
Bodily Harm and *Bluebeard's Egg.*' *World Literature Written in English* 25,
no. 2 (1985), 252–64
Spettigue, Douglas. Editor's Introduction. *Consider Her Ways.* By Frederick
Philip Grove. Toronto: McClelland and Stewart 1977, vi–xvi
Swift, Jonathan. *Gulliver's Travels.* Ed. Robert A. Greenberg. 2d ed. New
York: Norton 1970
Thomson, Clive R. 'Parody/Genre/Ideology.' In *Le Singe à la porte: Vers une
théorie de la parodie.* Ed. Groupar. New York: Lang 1984, 95–103
Tiffin, Helen. 'Commonwealth Literature: Comparison and Judgement.' In
The History and Historiography of Commonwealth Literature. Ed. Dieter Rie-
menschneider. Tübingen: Narr 1983, 19–35
– 'Post-Colonial Literatures and Counter-Discourse.' *Kunapipi* 9, no. 3
(1987), 17–34
Todorov, Tzvetan. *Mikhail Bakhtin: The Dialogical Principle.* Trans. Wlad
Godzich. Minneapolis: University of Minnesota Press 1984
Turner, Alden R. 'Atwood's Playing Puritans in *The Handmaid's Tale.*' In
Cross-Cultural Studies. Ed. Mirko Jurak. Ljubljana: English Department,
Edvard Kardelj University 1988, 85–91
Twigg, Alan. 'For Batter or Verse.' *Books in Canada*, 16, no. 8 (November
1987), 7–10
Vancouver, George. *A Voyage of Discovery to the North Pacific Ocean and
round the World 1791–1795.* Ed. W. Kaye Lamb. 4 vols. London: Hakluyt
Society 1984
VanSpanckeren, Kathryn, and Jan Garden Castro, eds. *Margaret Atwood:
Vision and Forms.* Carbondale: Southern Illinois University Press 1988
Vauthier, Simone. 'The Dubious Battle of Story-Telling: Narrative Strategies
in Timothy Findley's *The Wars.*' *Gaining Ground: European Critics on Cana-
dian Literature.* Ed. Robert Kroetsch and Reingard M. Nischik. Edmonton:
NeWest Press 1985, 11–39
Verweyen, Theodor, and Gunther Witting. *Die Parodie in der neueren*

deutschen Literatur: Eine systematische Einführung. Darmstadt: Wissenschaftliche Buchgesellschaft 1979

Visser, Carla. 'Historicity in Historical Fiction: *Burning Water* and *The Temptations of Big Bear.' Studies in Canadian Literature* 12, no. 1 (1987), 90–111

Wall, Anthony. 'Vers une notion de la colle parodique.' *Etudes littéraires* 19, no. 1 (1986), 21–36

Waller, Margaret. 'An Interview with Julia Kristeva.' In *Intertextuality and Contemporary American Fiction.* Ed. Patrick O'Donnell and Robert Con Davis. Baltimore: Johns Hopkins University Press 1989, 280–93

Waugh, Patricia, *Feminine Fictions: Revisiting the Postmodern.* London: Routledge 1989

White, Hayden. *The Content of the Form: Narrative Discourse and Historical Representation.* Baltimore: Johns Hopkins University Press 1987

– 'The Historical Text as Literary Artifact.' In *The Writing of History: Literary Form and Historical Understanding.* Ed. Robert H. Canary and Henry Kozicki. Madison: University of Wisconsin Press 1978, 41–62

– *Tropics of Discourse: Essays in Cultural Criticism.* Baltimore: Johns Hopkins University Press 1978

Williams, David. *Confessional Fictions: A Portrait of the Artist in the Canadian Novel.* Toronto: University of Toronto Press 1991

Wilson, Sharon R. 'Turning Life into Popular Art: *Bodily Harm's* Life-Tourist.' *Studies in Canadian Literature* 10, nos. 1–2 (1985), 136–45

Windsor, Duchess of (Wallis Simpson). *The Heart Has Its Reasons: The Memoirs of the Duchess of Windsor.* 1956; London: Sphere Books 1980

Windsor, Duke of (Edward VIII). *A King's Story: The Memoirs of the Duke of Windsor.* New York: Putnam's 1951

Witemeyer, Hugh. *The Poetry of Ezra Pound: Forms and Renewal, 1908–1920.* Berkeley: University of California Press 1969

York, Lorraine. *The Other Side of Dailiness: Photography in the Works of Alice Munro, Timothy Findley, Michael Ondaatje, and Margaret Laurence.* Toronto: ECW Press 1988

Zamiatin, Eugene. *We.* Trans. Gregory Zilboorg. 1924; New York: Dutton 1959

Index

THEORY/CULTURE SERIES